ON FURTHER REFLECTION

60 YEARS OF WRITING
JONATHAN MILLER

The Overlook Press
New York, NY

This edition first in published hardcover in the United States in 2015 by
The Overlook Press, Peter Mayer Publishers, Inc.

141 Wooster Street
New York, NY 10012
www.overlookpress.com

For bulk and special sales, please contact sales@overlookny.com,
or write us at the address above.

First published in Great Britain in 2014 by Skyscraper Publications Ltd

Library of Congress Cataloging-in-Publication Data
Miller, Jonathan, 1934-
[Works. Selections]
On further reflection : 60 years of writing / Jonathan Miller.
pages cm
Includes index.
ISBN 978-1-4683-1164-8
1. Miller, Jonathan, 1934- 2. Theatrical producers and
directors--Great Britain--Biography. I. Title.
PR6063.I3737A6 2015
828'.91409--dc23
                              2015026709

Manufactured in the United States of America

ISBN 978-1-4683-1164-8

2 4 6 8 10 9 7 5 3 1

On Further Reflection

On Further Reflection

by

Jonathan Miller

CONTENTS

Introduction

Some people know a little about a lot of different things; others know a lot about a few things. Jonathan Miller seems to know an awful lot about an awful lot of things. I owe it to him that I first read and came to love Proust. One day over a drink in a wine bar, astonished to discover that I had never tackled *Remembrance of Things Past,* he pretty well *ordered* me to, and I have never regretted it. When we made the television series *The Body in Question* together, our discussions were punctuated by insights into how the body works – not unexpected in that context – but also into the significance of small coral brooches in the paintings of Madonnas by North Italian artists of the renaissance, or the profile of Mussolini visible in the newel posts of one of his palaces.

I have been surprised at the way Jonathan Miller and his work are recognised by the generation that grew up between 1960 and 1980, but not by anyone much younger, even though hardly a year has gone by without a Jonathan Miller production somewhere in some art form. As his writings show, his ideas and observations can be appreciated by anyone, because his deep and sometimes breathtaking erudition is usually worn lightly and always tempered with humour, a constant element in his work since the wildly successful revue, *Beyond the Fringe,* which set him off on an unexpected career path. And often the starting point for an ideas-rich piece of writing is some everyday event that could happen to anyone. An incident with a pair of broken spectacles leads to a meditation on words, and the difference between 'copying' and 'reproducing'. The behaviour of a cat outside Miller's house introduces an essay on reflection. The different uses of the word 'in' help to convey Miller's ideas on why novels can't easily be turned into films. A Robert Frost poem is the trigger for a long and fascinating essay on how photography and cinematography tackled the task of representing movement.

The choice of pieces in this book is Jonathan Miller's. They represent what he is most proud of in over sixty years of writing. There is something in it for all interests, and the juxtaposition of short pieces with long ones; paintings with neurology; mesmerism with Dickens; or zoology with epistemology often leads the reader in directions he or she might not have expected.

Karl Sabbagh

Three cartoons from a series drawn for Granta in 1956

From England to America

I don't think I wrote a word until I left Cambridge in 1956, although I drew occasional cartoons for *Granta*. But while I was engaged in clinical medicine, at University College Hospital in Gower Street, my brother-in-law, Karl Miller, whom I got to know while I was at Cambridge, had become literary editor of the *Spectator*. He was housed in an office a few doors down from UCH and he invited me to write an occasional short article, including an account of time spent at a Rudolph Steiner school, to which I gave a false name in the piece.

Schooldays: Led Astray

The Friar House was a progressive school set in large grounds with a gnarled orchard in which a moth-eaten donkey grazed. The building was a converted farmhouse spread about in barns and outhouses which had been turned into huge, draughty classrooms.

'We like to think of education as a sort of leading-out,' cooed the headmistress at the first interview, and before long I was equipped for the business in a spinach-coloured jumper with a high polo neck. My leading-out only lasted six months but it took six years to lead me back again to a condition where I could take a useful place in society. I believe that the conventional subjects did feature somewhere in the curriculum, but I have only the haziest recollection of them. I seem to recall that they were telescoped in some strange way in order to make room for the more crucial aspects of the leading-out process. Mathematics and languages were, for example, conveniently elided when we learnt the multiplication tables in French.

The morning got off to a good start with prayers, but these were nothing like any prayers I had come across before and nothing like them ever turned up again. In the midst of the restrained Anglican assemblies of later schools I often found myself longing for the wilder practices of the Friar House. The headmistress would stand before us with one hand placed delicately on the piano lid. After a formal cough she would lead us off into a sort of Jungian chant to which I never somehow managed to learn the words. There were a lot of hand movements, however. I remember these clearly. Both fists were placed together, side by side over the heart. Then, as the chant grew to a crescendo (something about 'the spirit of the sun within us glows'), the arms reached up and out in an expansive double arc of spiritual ecstasy. This was always the signal for a lot of facetious horseplay; the idea being to fell both neighbours with one's outstretched arms. The mistress never seemed put out by this scuffling climax. Perhaps she interpreted it as some sort of transport. Even if she had been ruffled she would never have struck us, as there was a strict embargo on violence of any sort. What discipline there was, was conveyed in a curious system which consisted of ascribing different coloured auras to the various pupils on the basis of their conduct in the previous week. My aura was brown at the end of every week, though there were people who basked in a pink one. I never discovered a way of life which succeeded in getting the wavelength of my aura switched.

After prayers we would settle down to the morning's work, much of which was taken up with garbled Oriental mythology. 'How Manu led his peoples out of Atlantis' was always a popular theme. After the lesson the boys and girls would troop off through the autumn mist to the art room, which occupied one of the barns on the other side of the orchard. Here, with the Manu myth still fresh in our minds, we would interpret our ideas of the story on paper. Wet paper. It had to be wet paper, for dry paper gave hard lines and the art mistress explained that there were no hard lines in nature. 'Moisten your papers,' she would cry flutily, and the class would set about the ritual douche. Once this was done it was not only impossible to get a hard outline, it was impossible to confine the paint to any outline at all, the colours running together into a maddening archetypal blur. The more blurred and iridescent our designs the more it pleased the mistress, who told us that this expressed the confluence of the great subconscious. The method was a great leveller, however, since the bad draughtsman could comfortably hide his incompetence in the aqueous confusion.

Subject-matter suffered the same sea-change, so, that 'Manu leading his peoples out of Atlantis' was hard to distinguish from 'Elijah ascending to heaven in a fiery chariot.' One boy even managed to pass off a detailed representation of 'What he would like to do to Betty Grable' as 'Prince Gautama teaching the Word.' Exasperated by the blur, a group of us formed a 'hard outline' break-away group and surreptitiously transferred our feelings about Manu on to dry paper. 'Someone has been painting on dry paper,' cried the art mistress when we handed in our suspiciously distinct pieces at the end of the class. I was downgraded aura-wise for some weeks after this. Many years later I came across a book about painting by Rudolf Steiner. In the colour plates I recognised the familiar hopeless struggle with drenched paper.

Eurhythmics took the place of PT and in these seemingly endless classes we would act out the story of Manu in sinuous movements with which Manu could not possibly have led his peoples anywhere; except perhaps to a police station. Once a term the doctor would visit the school and prescribe eurhythmic exercises for any complaints the parents mentioned. My mother was once unwise enough to let drop that I got a sweat on me at night. The doctor immediately prescribed eurhythmic exercises which differed only marginally from the Manu routine. In the course of these exercises I found myself wondering whether Manu ever sweated at night, and if perhaps that was the reason why he got out of Atlantis.

I also took weaving, though I never completed a single useful garment. During my six months I was continuously engaged upon a long strip of Aztec design which could, I suppose, have been used for ritual strangling. The recorder featured prominently in the leading-out programme and during these lessons we would gather in front of the teacher, copying her finger movements as she took us through 'Lillibullero.' I can still hear the banshee howls of this performance. We never learnt musical notation as we did everything by copying the teacher's movements. I could not master this method. I have never been able to tell my right hand from my left and since, by facing us, her right hand became equivalent to my left, I became hopelessly confused and produced a hideous mirror-image of the tune.

After six months of this life I had been seduced into a womby confusion of thought and action which boded ill for my academic future. When my father discovered that my knowledge of mathematics was confined to an inaccurate version of the French multiplication tables he removed me to a conventional cap-and-blazer establishment. Here, apart from an impressive showing on all questions bearing upon Manu, I shaped up as a high-grade moron incapable of understanding even schoolboy conundrums. On my first morning, during prayers, my neighbour nudged me and whispered aggressively, 'Charles the First walked and talked half an hour after his head was cut off. What's wrong with that?' I stared at him in dumb misery, quite unable to fathom the basic meaning of his question. He smiled sarcastically and as the congregation launched out into a hymn I consoled myself by designing in my mind's eye an enormous painting of the posthumous performance—on wet, wet paper.

Spectator, 11 May, 1961, p. 12

A year after I qualified as a doctor, with the intention of taking up neuropsychology, I was unexpectedly diverted into showbiz, having yielded to an invitation to collaborate with Peter Cook, Alan Bennett and Dudley Moore in writing and performing in a late night review which was entitled *Beyond the Fringe*, visualized as it was by the management as an official competitor to the disconcertingly successful Fringe. In the naïve belief that it would be nothing more than a brief interlude, I took time out, never suspecting that the success of the show would lead me into a lifelong occupation in the theatre. We were hailed as the theatrical exponents of satire.

While we shared the authorship, which was largely based on collaborative improvisation, as far as I can remember I was responsible for creating this pastiche of Shakespeare's historical drama.

Beyond the Fringe

So That's The Way You Like It

This is played with great vigour at tremendous speed in the modern Shakespeare style. The performers wear various period hats to suit their characters. Enter Peter.

Peter: Sustain we now description of a time
           When petty lust and overweening tyranny
           Offend the ruck of state.
           Thus fly we now, as oft with Phoebus did
           Fair Asterope, unto proud Flanders Court.
           Where is the warlike Warwick
           Like to the mole that sat on Hector's brow
           Fair set for England, and for war!

Enter Jonathan and Alan.

Jonathan: And so we bid you welcome to our Court
           Fair cousin Albany and you our sweetest Essex.
           Take this my hand, and you fair Essex this
           And with this bond we'll cry anon
           And shout Jack Cock o'London to the foe.
           Approach your ears and kindly bend your conscience to my piece.
           Our ruddy scouts to me this hefty news have brought:
           The naughty English, expecting now some pregnance in our plan,
           Have with some haughty purpose bent
           Aeolis unto the service of their sail.

So even now while we to the wanton lute
do strut
Is brutish Bolingbroke bent fair upon
Some fickle circumstance.

Alan and Peter: Some fickle circumstance.

Jonathan: Get thee to Gloucester, Essex. Do thee to
Wessex, Exeter.
Fair Albany to Somerset must eke his route
And Scroop do you to Westmoreland, where
shall bold York
Enrouted now for Lancaster with forces of
our Uncle Rutland
Enjoin his standard with sweet Norfolk's host.
Fair Sussex, get thee to Warwick's bourne,
And there, with frowning purpose, tell our plan
To Bedford's tilted ear, that he shall press
With most insensate speed
And join his warlike effort to bold Dorset's side.
I most royally shall now to bed
To sleep off all the nonsense I've just said.

All go and re-enter as rude mechanicals.

Jonathan: Is it botched up then, Master Puke?

Alan: Ay, marry and is, good Master Snot.

Dudley: 'Tis said our Master, the Duke, hath contrived
some naughtiness against his son, the King.

Peter: Ay, and it doth confound our merrymaking.

Jonathan: What say you, good Master Puke? I am
for Lancaster, and that's to say for good
shoe leather.

Peter:	Come speak, good Master Puke, or hath the leather blocked up thy tongue?
Dudley:	Why then go trippingly upon thy laces, good Grit.
Peter:	Art leather laces thy undoing?
Dudley:	They shall undo many a fair boot this day.
All:	Come, let's to our rural revel and with our song enchant our King.

All go off.   Re-enter Alan and Dudley.

Dudley (sings):	Oh Death his face my shroud hath hid And Lethe drowned my poor love's soul So flee we now to Pluto's realm And in his arms shall I grow old.
Alan:	Wise words in mouth of fools do oft themselves belie. Good fool – shall Essex prosper?
Dudley:	Aye, prosper.
Alan:	Say you, prosper, fool?
Dudley:	Aye, prosper.
Alan:	Marry then, methinks we'll prosper. And saying prosper do we say to cut the knot which crafty nature hath within our bowels lockéd up. But soft, who comes here?

Enter Peter

Peter:	Oh good my Lord, unstop your ear and yet Prepare to yield the optic tear to my experience. Such news I bring as only can crack ope The casket of thy soul. Not six miles hence

There grows an oak whose knotty thews

Engendered in the bosky wood doth raise itself

Most impudent towards the solstice sun.

So saying did there die and dying so did say.
(Goes off)

Alan: God! this was most gravely underta'en

And underta'en hath Essex gravely answered it.

Why then we'll muster and to the field of
battle go

And unto them our English sinews show.

*Goes off. Smoke. Peter and Jon enter
with swords.*

Jonathan: Why then was this encounter nobly entertained

And so by steel shall this our contest now be
buckled up.

Come sir, let's to it.

Peter: Let's to it.

Good steel, thou shall thyself in himself
thyself embowel.

Jonathan: Come sir.

They fight.

Ah, ha, a hit?

Peter: No, sir, no hit, a miss! Come, sir, art foppish i'
the mouth

Jonathan: Art more fop i' the mouth than fop i' the steel.

They fight again. Peter 'hits' Jon.

Jonathan: Oh god, fair cousin, thou hast done me wrong.

Jonathan goes into protracted death throes, weaving on and off stage.

Now is steel 'twixt gut and bladder interposed.

Finally dies.

Peter: Oh saucy Worcester, dost thou lie so still?

Enter Alan.

Alan: Now hath mortality her tithe collected
And sovereign Albany to the worms his corse committed.
Yet weep we not; this fustian life is short
Let's on to Pontefract to sanctify our court.

After performing in London for a year, the four of us were invited to take the show to Broadway. Still believing that I would be continuing with my medical degree I persuaded the Broadway producers to let me visit New York to investigate the possibility of further medical training while performing *Beyond the Fringe* in the evenings. This visit sparked the first of several pieces about the excitement of being in the United States in the early sixties

Been to America

The plane leapt enthusiastically down the runway. After a few buoyant surges we left the rain, pierced the cloud and began to cruise in the sunlit emptiness that lies backstage of the weather. Six hours later we arrived at the same moment that we left: a clock trick which is an important part of the mystery of going to America. It gives the feeling of arrival without travel, journey without transit. It is as if visiting America was a process brought about by waiting around in the air six miles above England, a process rather like Wells's Time Machine, which moved backwards and forwards in time without ever leaving the inventor's study. In this case one seems to change position without ever moving in space. The physical detail of the American scene, especially around the airport, strengthens the feeling that one has not so much travelled as undergone a dream transformation. As I left Idlewild for Manhattan, sealed in a silent limousine with tinted windows, the scenery seemed disturbingly familiar. Disturbing, because at the same time it was also indefinably alien. The road signs were in English but the names were meaningless, and the type in which they were set had a worrying novelty. We hissed along the freeway that could have been in Hendon but somehow wasn't. There were huge blocks of brick flats, *circa* 1948, the colour of horsemeat in the drizzling murk. As in a dream landscape no one seems to be walking. All around our vehicle other cars advanced and retreated, fell back and overtook, bearing in them the intent profiles of anonymous drivers. The mist had wiped out the Manhattan skyline, and I was still left with no evidence to convince me that I was in America. I was, instead, in some drably strange, glumly enchanted annex of England. This strangeness of America – a feeling that stayed with me until I left – is as powerful and unsettling as a *déjà vu*.

Nearly everyone appears to hold America in special regard. It may be admiration; it may be scorn or even bilious envy. Distant, inaccessible and rare, it hangs like a mirage, like Fournier's Secret Realm, or Alice's garden. Arriving on my first visit, I remembered that Kafka had actually written a whole novel about the country without having ever visited it. In 20 years or so, I also had built and lived in my own imaginary America. There were many layers to this construction. It started with an image of vulgar abundance stimulated by those mythic servicemen who dole out gum and candy from their marsupial pouches and haversacks. Then there was that impression of unattainable hygiene, of *Time*-faces, scrubbed and creased, each little wrinkle rimed with soap. Films gave Technicolor finished this picture, in which Disney manikins moved brilliantly about in a dazzling utopian landscape. The image has darkened and grown more devious since then, of course. America, my private America, has been a country of intellectual ferment organised by enlightened, wise, laconic Jews. At other times I have fallen in with some of the less appealing fantasies of the Left and seen it as a hodgepodge of hedonism, violence, corruption or just timid conformity. My America is a very elaborate palimpsest of ideas, a compendium of practically every hopeful or depressing social notion one could conceive. When I was working in an English hospital, the joint degree of BTA was conferred by his colleagues on any doctor who had Been To America. The joke may be fairly cynical but there are overtones of awe.

Our car plunged into the Mid-Town Tunnel and surfaced somewhere in the Forties. Coloured cabs dwindled down the long, dank vistas of the avenues. It was a Sunday evening and there seemed to be very few people about. When we stopped at the lights a negro drunk staggered, as if pushed, up to our window, peered absently in, mouthed something and swam off into the rain. The buildings seemed depressingly small. Occasionally a Portland-stone cliff shot up into the darkness, its electric sign bleeding out into the foggy heights. Everything seemed strangely *old*. It was a 19th-century modernism, like a futurist city in Wells or Verne, crushed in Byzantine terra-cotta.

I checked in at the Algonquin and was shown up to my room where I sat, on the edge of the bed, staring at the clanking radiator. Next door my neighbour hawked and gargled as he prepared for bed or something. I might have been anywhere. I was like the two old ladies locked in the lavatory – nobody knew I was there. I passed a restless night, drying out slowly in the even central heat. (Why not peripheral heat? I thought in my delirium.) The next morning I got out early and mingled with the Monday crowd on Fifth Avenue. A frieze of identical Brooks Brothers men wound jerkily passed me, like a spool of UPA cartoon. Wherever I went, around Madison Avenue and Park, little flotillas of these men would suddenly ticker past. I wandered lonely as a cloud, wandered into Woolworths and pushed a dime into a phone.

"Where the hell are you?" said a chipmunk voice.

"In Woolworths on Fifth Avenue."

"You must be crazy," the phone chirped and gave me its address.

I no longer felt transparent.

I had come over partly to see and hear some of the nightclub satirists who had attracted so much attention by hearsay in England. I went first to the Upstairs at the Downstairs, a plush little midtown boîte run by Julius Monk, a Southerner with the carriage and manners of Clifton Webb.

"It's nothing like as good as it used to be," my escort hissed as the lights dimmed.

Upstage, behind a curtain of scarlet robes two pianists smiled and nodded at the audience as they tinkled out the overture. For the next hour a small cast worked confidently through their routine.

"No. Not what they used to be," sighed my escort and gave me a glance that pitied me for having missed the boat.

There had certainly been nothing very mordant in what I had seen. Still this was only the first go.

"We'll go tomorrow and see Nipsey Russell", said my friend and gave me a look which promised all.

I spent the next morning at the UN. There were no sessions in action that day so I joined a conducted tour instead. The hostess was a slim girl in a blue uniform. Everything she said had a note of cool reverence and her text was studded with curious little phrases that tripped off her tongue as if she had learned them in some UN catechism.

We paused from time to time before a number of rather daunting Finnish tapestries, the gifts of various arctically neutral countries. She was quick to decipher the UN creed woven into the fabric.

"Here you see the ear of corn representing prosperity. The figure giving birth represents the rebirth of hope and peace. The dark figure in the foreground with the iron girder through his chest represent the horrors of war and all that that entails."

Her voice echoed down the marble nave.

That evening I rode with friends uptown to Harlem. The idea was to visit the Apollo Theatre, a shabby vaudeville where, on Wednesday nights, negro amateurs would parade the various talents. We would, everyone agreed, have a ball. When we arrived the theatre was closed for Christmas and we huddled in the darkened foyer stamping and blowing into our hands. It was *very* cold. "What about Nipsey Russell?" Someone said.

Nipsey Russell is something of a cult with the New York literati. Knots of giggling initiates often make their way to the Baby Grand in Harlem to hear this negro comedian, who refuses to be winkled out of the grimy little niterie in which he made his reputation. Here he comperes a variety show of staggering mediocrity, taunting and teasing the various performers as they trot on to do their tawdry bit. Between the strippers and the singers he tells rambling blue stories which frequently plunge into breathtaking obscenity. All put over with a seductive porcelain smile. Nipsey himself is a delicate, lithe little fellow. He moves lasciviously and eyes his female audience with sarcastic innuendo. He uses an intriguingly complex turn of phrase. Incredible polysyllables fall from his smiling lips and a deep irony seems to lurk in this mad scholasticism, the aping of white pedantry with which he mocks his audience.

I missed the Premise by an oversight. On my last night however I battled down town through a snowstorm to see the Second City, who had set up house in the Village after a flop on Broadway. These are a group of Chicago students and graduates interested in improvised theatre and in social and political satire. Elaine May and Mike Nichols graduated from this group to a successful Broadway season in which they delighted audiences with their caustic psychological vignettes ("We were just your ordinary middle-class family... You know, there was proximity but no *relating*"). Shelley Berman also passed through the Second City. All of these performers have a distinctive theatrical gift, a forceful dramatic presentation which, in a way, makes them much more viable in the long run than a 'talk' man like Mort Sahl, who will often lose the attention of his audience by sheer unrelieved garrulousness. This present group does not have the professional edge and attack of Nichols and May, nor on the other hand the slightly more commercial abrasiveness of Shelley Berman. They do maintain, though, an extremely high standard of intelligent and imaginative comedy. The group seems to draw most of its spirit from a shambling Ustinovian figure with the unlikely name of Severn Darden. This flabby man with a thin, red beard and a wide mouth set with peg teeth moves through the pieces like a professorial gnome. He injects a weird note of Dada into everything he touches. In one sketch, for example, where he plays a mathematician lending his magic dice to a gambler, he whispers into his cupped hands before he shoots the craps: "number 7 or it will be ze hot iron for you". Another sketch, brilliantly poignant in execution, has a neurotic feverishly feeding nickels into a psychoanalysing machine.

There is precious little political satire, as such, although in a piece which is by no means their best, they improvise, somewhat dutifully I felt, a press conference with Kennedy and Krushchev. They devote a whole section to improvised sketches. These are built around words and phrases shouted up from the audience, who seem to participate without any of the haughty embarrassment that takes an English audience on such occasions. This section of the show confirmed my suspicions about improvisation – one of the aspects of modern American satire which have gained a magical reputation in England. In fact the improvised sketches had long patches of tedious fumbling. It is clearly a good way of writing sketches and this is one of the ways in which the best permanent set pieces of the show originate. But the finished, rehearsed sketches were *always* much better.

That evening the snow came down even more heavily. I began to think that I would not leave the next day, or indeed ever. I wandered some more, calling on the all-night joke shop on 42nd Street, where I bought a plaque of plastic vomit ("45 cents – sprinkle water for realism"). At midday, though, the plane scrunched along the icy runway, and in a few minutes we had left the whirling snow, pierced the clouds and were flying in the meaningless sunlight that lies in the back of the weather.

New Statesman, 19 January, 1962

January in New York

A walk with Alfred Kazin to the south end of Manhattan and then to Brooklyn. He'd taken off his galoshes by the time I answered his ring at the door and they were lying at his feet like snake casts. We took a cab and roared down the bumpy cobbles of the Westside Highway. A cold Sunday mist, unheated by weekday activity, hung over the silent docks. Past the Cunard sheds, past the Dutch and French lines. A large Israeli liner with blue stars on its funnel – there's something incongruous about a Jewish boat.

Below 14th Street. The green and brick-red timber façades of the Erie and Pennsylvania Railroad sheds. Crudely classical stage proscenia with elegant lettering in faded gold printed across the pediments. Print everywhere – fading in plastery palimpsests on huge side walls of buildings. Hoardings held up by big skeletal scaffolds. Printed roadway signs: arrows and indications.

The taxi took a dip off the highway, down into the long, foggy vaults of the dockside. We got out in the misty, icy silence of Sunday in the city. From somewhere out in the bay came the bronchitic groans of fog-bound shipping. Long, high ravines sheered off on each side; shadowy and darkly silent.

Aztec Deco banks – sooty porticoes – the industrial Palladian of the old Germania building with the date 1865 chiselled, augustly severe and shadowed with grime.

Across the Brooklyn Bridge with Kazin now slightly out of breath with exertion or possibly excitement at the approach of Brooklyn, still invisible. A timber promenade runs down the centre of the bridge, raised above the traffic which howls by on each side. It's like entering a huge cat's cradle of steel as the suspension cables swing up in vertiginous crescents fore and aft. In the middle of the bridge you lose sight of land altogether and you seem to be aboard the *Pequod* with steel shrouds strung from the granite masts.

To the north I can just make out the Manhattan Bridge lightly printed on the blotting-paper of the fog.

Nowhere in Particular, Mitchell Beazley, 1999

By train, New York to Chicago

An empty winter landscape.

Even the cities are deserted, with scuds of snow blowing down passages behind factories. Flags at half-mast across the whole landscape.

Warehouses, printed chimneys, timber shacks. Piles of rusty oil drums.

Lopez body-shop. Broil-a-foil. Radio antennae thin as hemlock against the snow. *Cook 's Industrial Lubricants. Linden NJ. Sterling extruder.*

Factory ventilators – fan vents – rusty galvanised iron hoods with jointed pipes. White clapboard estates among the upright pewter machinery of the winter trees. An ice-bound copse, cold girders set at angles to the old cast-iron trunks. Twisted, frost-busted wreckage of the neighbourhood dump.

In the fields and on the edges of the woods, streams lie like open blades half-sheathed in scabbards of aluminium ice.

Darkly silent herds of freight trucks with roofs like the horizontal spines of stockaded cattle. *Appliance distributors.*

Whitened fields. The snow raked thin and
scraped to the furrows. Harsh tubular stalks
of corn, black and broken in a silhouetted
hypotenuse. Frame house farms present their
wintry constructions – isosceles, trapezoids and
parallelograms in turn as they rotate about the
advancing train.

Scrawled in white paint on a tiny rural
railway tunnel:

JO MORADISI LIKES IKE.

There is a young army recruit in the
compartment. He is much too small for his huge
uniform and his blunt ferret's head pokes from
the top of it as if it were coming out of a stiff
piece of inherited furniture.

The train keeps slowing down. They say there
is a large freight wreck up the line. By the time
darkness comes down, the train stops every few
minutes as we approach the wreck. We begin to
see bituminous flares set up along the track. The
train draws slowly by the overturned freight cars
like a herd of cattle dead of foot-and-mouth.
Gangs of black railway workers like Masai
hunters dismembering their prey.

It was while I was performing in *Beyond the Fringe*
in New York that I was asked to stand in during the
vacation of the *New Yorker* television critic. My first
piece happened to coincide with the assassination of
President John F. Kennedy.

Views of a Death

On November 22, when John Fitzgerald Kennedy was shot in the back of the head, he experienced, in the agonising incommunicado of sudden death, the most public private moment of his life. The objective image of the moment was seen by a thousand people who lined the route, and a few hours later, when the negatives and prints had been washed and dried, millions more had seen it on television, or at least they had seen a grainy hieroglyph representing it, but what they saw only suggested, and could never communicate, the excruciating pith of the victim's own obliterating experience. Never was the rift between privacy and publicity so wide, and perhaps part of the shock of the event resulted from the paradox of this division. The publicity was total, and what it did was to conceal, in the very instant that it exposed, the inexorable solitude of dying.

The President's death forced television into a brief maturity. Death gagged the vulgar infant, and stifled its greedy squalling for a few days. As unvarnished metaphysical austerity flowed –undisturbed, for once–through the channels, the medium itself seemed to take on grandeur. Some of the active contributions made by the television people during this period were intelligent and restrained and technically brilliant, and some were simply drab and dutiful. There were few conspicuous lapses in taste, and there were few signs of creative inspiration. The reporting, for the most part, was direct, humane, ungaudy. There was far less false eloquence than one might have expected. Mainly, there was an unprecedented majesty about the whole affair, a harsh *mésure* that came with the endless, almost inadvertent accumulation of funereal imagery. The pure accidents of repetition and duplication proved valuable. A tic was turned to splendid advantage, allowing the instrument, as the hours wore on, to illustrate every twist and conundrum of mortality. Moreover, the repetition offered a new form of mourning and provided a crash program in grief. Unaided, the mind has a deliberate tempo in this matter, for mourning is some sort of spiritual labour, a lengthy moral exertion in which the outlets to the will are blocked as the feelings are slowly and painfully withdrawn from their familiar attachments.

In the normal way of things, this ritual works to a natural andante. It is gracefully hesitant and has its own proper period. Television set a new pace. The whole process was concentrated and speeded up. The assassination, the cortege, the funeral, and the eulogies recurred in what seemed an infinite series of statements and recapitulations. Every channel was taken up with the dire scene, and even the ordinarily distracting atmospherics of television helped to create a dark new aesthetic. For instance, when a local station borrowed a transmission from one of the networks, the original picture and the reproduction, although they were essentially identical, reinforced each other's psychic effect by means of their electronically determined differences. The borrowed picture was of a blurred, Pointillist version of the original, so that as one switched from channel to channel the fact of the president's death was brutally confirmed by the electronic variations on the one, inescapable theme. It was as if, in the space of a few hours, there had been accumulated all those pictorial versions of a tragic event which usually gather in albums over the years, and which, through the myriad tiny differences within the common pattern, approach some comprehensible embodiment of the long-ago fatal incident. But the mystery of such an event can never really be embodied; it can only be approximately reconstructed, or circumscribed, by drawing innumerable pictorial tangents to the mysterious curve of the occasion. Like a computer flickering through a problem that would take a mathematician years, television did a lightning calculation and completed the spiritual algebra of grief in less than four days. As a result the whole matter seems to have been formulated and disposed of by the time the commercials came yapping back on Tuesday.

There were other metaphysical vignettes during that dark weekend. The display of time's arrow for example, and of the grinding, irreversible determinism in human affairs. Most touching of all, perhaps, one of those unbearable playbacks of the events leading up to, but never quite reaching, the moment of the assassination: those happy, slightly lurching newsreel shots of the Kennedys arriving at the airport, the breakfast speech at Fort Worth – all now just innocent hindsight on the approaches of death. It all seems so orderly – possibly still reversible – giving way only at the last instant to the photographic topsy-turvy of tragedy

There was also that microscopic dissection of Oswald's murder, played over and over, reduced by the slow motion camera to the actual molecules of the murderer's own onward-moving process, each molecule of incident mysteriously linked to the next as they clicked, one by one, toward the detonation. And then, just as with the President's last moment, everything flies apart – a sublime dehiscence – at the moment of death itself. Images blur; the eyes of the camera roll upward and the cement ceiling of the Dallas police station streaks past; the brim of a Stetson cuts in close to the screen; there is a dilating eye, and then blackness. An hour later, on another network, the clip is screened again: the same orderly staccato, the same upward roll of the eyes, the ceiling streaking by, the Stetson, staring eyes, blackness. And again and again, as if the camera were searching out but never quite reaching the marrow of the instant. It has been said that this was the first televised murder but there was more to it than that, for in being so inquisitive, television may have become an accomplice in the crime – they actually have joggled events in the direction they took. Perception may have contributed to the act and introduced the slippery risks of Heisenberg into the Dallas police garage. One can almost feel the lens urging Ruby out of the crowd. In fact, in the pictures, it looked as if he came out of the camera itself. In a word, television has become too effective. It gets in on too much. Like some nimble amoeba, it can poke its sensitive tendrils into the world's minutest crannies, put a vast audience in touch with the world's faintest twitch. The trouble is not so much that there will be no privacy any more as that there will be no inaccessibility. The imagination will be totally usurped.

The funeral itself, the lying in state, the catafalque, provided some forceful images of death that had vanished from modern life – for, whatever else has happened, death has been bowdlerized out of the modern text. Yet suddenly, for three days, the domestic screen was almost continuously occupied with the fearful oblong simplicity of the casket. One saw, too, the dreadful heaviness of the dead as the eight enlisted men crouched and staggered under the load. One felt that not all the weight was in the bronze but that at the moment of dying some negative quantity, like phlogiston, goes out of the body, leaving it in a state of hideous density, the better to drag on the straining hawsers that lower the coffin into the grave.

New Yorker, 28 December, 1963, p. 63

By the time I knew we were going to New York to do *Beyond the Fringe* I was already acquainted with the recordings of the Canadian comedian Mort Sahl and I was convinced that there was something special about American humour. Around this time I first came across

Lenny Bruce who had been invited to appear at Peter Cook's Establishment Club in Soho. We were astounded and entranced by his foul mouthed monologues. I next saw him at a downtown Theatre in New York about 10 days after President Kennedy's assassination. No one there could imagine how he was going to handle this and were surprised that the event had not been cancelled. With a single gesture he put at us our ease. He drew his finger across his throat saying "Vaughan Meader". He was referring to a television comedian famous for imitating Kennedy in a best selling record album called *The First Family.* We got it, and the evening was a hysterical success as we allowed ourselves to relax.

Back in London we witnessed his descent into a paranoid battle against charges of obscenity and drug addiction which had been brought against him. After he died Robert Silvers asked me to write about him for the *New York Review of Books* and I was able to look back at the complex feelings Bruce had aroused in me

On Lenny Bruce (1926–1966)

It is hard to write fairly about Lenny Bruce now that he's dead. At least it is difficult to be just, in the way that he, in his more realistic moments, might have preferred. For Bruce became an issue in the last years of his life. He became the focus of controversy between opposing vested interests, neither of which really gave a damn for the man himself. The complementary roles of mascot and victim proved inevitably fatal, and through a strange mixture of simple-minded vanity and courageous generosity he lived up too thoroughly to a public personality partly supplied by his sponsors and tormentors. In the end it led quite inexorably to an ordeal which both sides, with different types of satisfaction, saw coming a long way off. The villains of the piece were all those thick-necked hypocritical authorities who hounded him down, in state after state, until he was finally too poor, too weak, and too confused to survive. All along he was up against a brutal, prejudiced society which somehow seemed unable to afford the easy conversational freedom that Bruce offered to his audiences. But we, his sponsors, his eager fluting publicists, must also bear some of the responsibility for the way things turned out. Bruce was in many ways a willing sucker for the sort of martyrdom upon which affluent, free-thinking liberals vicariously thrive. His dreadful ordeal through the courts, destitution, and ultimate death, provided a nice, flourishing proof of the liberals' conviction that the world is cruel, repressed, and indifferent. But Bruce was too ready to sacrifice *himself* on behalf of this demonstration. He was too accommodating, and those of us who supported him in print were sometimes too excited, or else too selfish, to notice that Bruce's uneducated simplicity often led him to yield without criticism to the flattery of over-elaborate interpretation. Underneath all that hipster cool, it is to be remembered that Bruce was rather an innocent bloke, badly read, and so keen to be accepted and admired by educated people that he was sometimes deceived by the over-complicated program which certain missionary intellectuals read into his act. It's possible that he suffered very badly from being taken up quite like this. As intellectual support for his act grew, he began to take seriously all that stuff about being the prophet of a new morality and would replace a lot of his regular material with sententious sermons. He would quote from Doctor Albert Ellis, M.D., recite dubious pharmacological justifications for "pot," and generally became quite boring.

He was so generously open to intellectual flattery, so pleased to discover that he had authoritative support, that he sometimes failed to realize how much he was being used as a dispensable stalking horse for middle-class liberal dares. Strangely enough, by stepping up the dirt in the service of this mission he was to some extent being exploited by a mirror image of the very prejudice which finally hounded him to his death. I can still, with some shame, recall my own euphoric horror at hearing him come out with four-letter words in front of a solid middle class audience at The Establishment in London. It seems contemptible now, the way in which we used him to do our dubious dirty work of evangelical sexual shock therapy. For the marvellous thing about Bruce was not the way in which he deliberately introduced obscenity into his act, though as time went on, with encouragement from us, he did do more and more of this, but the way in which he never held back obscenity if it was relevant to his subject. He spoke to his audience just as most of us speak to each other in private, without feeling that he had any need to button his lip when dealing with pelvic affairs. But we got too zealously worked up on behalf of this particular aspect of his act, and egged him on to fresh excesses of sexual radicalism. Left to himself, I sometimes doubt whether he would have pressed on this point quite so much. But as it is, he rose a bit too eagerly to the bait of our shady approval, and found himself assuming more and more the role of persecuted prophet of a slightly phony gospel. For as Christopher Lasch has pointed out, "by insisting that sex was the highest form of love, the highest form of human discourse, the modern prophets of sex did not so much undermine the prudery against which they appeared to be in rebellion...as invert it."

It would be foolish, simply in the light of his painful death, to exonerate Bruce himself altogether from the comparative absurdity of this position. Intellectually underprivileged in several important respects, he was in every other way fully aware and even proud of his participation in the campaign for utopian sexual enlightenment. He did feel, I'm quite sure, that if only prudery would relax we could screw our way to peace and prosperity for all. That in some hypothetical millennium, bigotry and suffering would not be heard for the swishing of the pricks. Perhaps it's significant that it was *Playboy* magazine which serialized his autobiography. Commercially this publication also embodies the half-formed belief that sexual knots alone contort the body politic. Heffner's interminable editorial philosophy often reads like a transcript of one of Bruce's more didactic bits, and the rest of the magazine, too, reverberates with the idea that by being honestly sybaritic human beings will simply forget to be nasty and collapse instead into a voluptuous communion, peacefully 'noshing' on Plumrose Playmates, their savagery soothed by first-class hi-fi. It is sad that Bruce should have allowed himself to be hanged until he was dead from the yard-arm of this particular ship of fools. But he was encouraged to do so by people who were prepared to push a much more sophisticated version of the same argument. I doubt if Lionel Trilling's essay on "Freud and the Crisis of Our Culture" ever got to Bruce's immediate attention, but the general idea was familiar to intellectuals with whom Bruce came in contact. They believed, sincerely, though I think mistakenly, that the biological core of human nature, inaccessible to the repressive threats of culture, offered a life-saver for the individual who found himself drowning in modern life. Without fully wishing to understand the complex institutional history of this proposal, certain intellectuals leaped at its utopian possibilities and then found Bruce a conveniently self-sacrificing public spokesman on behalf of the doctrine.

But that's enough carping. I make it sound as if Bruce was no more than a gullible ass who went down in the name of something completely ludicrous, although even if that were the case there would be a certain pathetic honor in his death. But even if the cause, as fought, was riddled with absurdity, so, of course, were the brutal idiots who considered it important enough to oppose it to the death. Anyway, there was much more to Bruce than that. So that his life and death *are* significant and serious attention must be paid.

Bruce was a great stage artist, a soloist of unbelievable virtuosity. The thousands of people who filled two houses of an old movie theater in Greenwich Village in December 1963 are a witness of that. So were the audiences that came back night after night during his month in London. The people who followed him were charmed by the free conversational directness of the man. He liked his audiences and took great pains to feel his way towards the individual temperament of each one. And if he felt comfortable with a group there was no end to the effort he would make to entertain and delight them. It's not really true that he thrived on hostility, though he sometimes managed to put on a show of hard, glittering verve when the animals were in—people who talked loudly throughout his act, sounding "like tape played backwards." But generally an unfriendly audience made him stiff and defiant, and then he would sometimes become brutally dirty, just for the hell of it. He also had amazing resources of descriptive finesse with which he would reward friendly attention. He had an uncannily accurate ear and a novelist's eye for the sort of crucial visual detail which could suddenly delight spectators with a shock of recognition. Midgets with blue suits and brown boots, hands only visible on the steering wheel of a car, speeding along the Santa Anna freeway; or holidaymakers sunning themselves on a sward of green paper grass laid out in front of their trailer. He could reproduce the whole screenplay of old movies or daytime radio serials, twisting them here and there with touches of nutty invention—the Lone Ranger as a 'fag'. And mad Catholic fantasies too—Christ at St. Patrick's Cathedral:

"Don't look now, but you'll never guess who's in tonight."

"Which one, which one?"

"The one that's glowing, dummy."

"Police! You've got to get me out of here. I'm up to my ass in wheel chairs and crutches."

Or a theatrical agent on the line to Pope John—"Sure we can get you the Sullivan show. But wear the big ring, Johnny. No. No one'll guess you're Jewish."

He did not actually create all this stuff on the stage as he went along. Anyone who saw him regularly began to realize that he had a vast repertoire of "bits" and that the improvisation consisted in the unexpected way he would weave it all together, sometimes only alluding to sketches which he might have played in full the night before.

This would often madden people who only managed to see him once or twice. But it was an indication of the affectionate trust he had in his audience. Without any arrogance, he expected people to come again and again, to join him in creating the rambling, show-biz-saturated saga of American life. He was not a conventional nightclub comic who could be guaranteed to deliver a self-contained package of laughing matter for a casual door trade. But like an old-time story teller he was always filling out familiar routines with unexpected additions of vivid new detail. It was impossible to judge him fairly on a single showing. It's a shame that we'll never have a chance of arriving at a just summary. Because apart from a few rather meager and slightly inaudible records, his creation dies with him. Unlike his conventional colleagues, most of whom held him in contempt, he was quite unfitted for mechanical reproduction, since his art and his personality were indistinguishable.

He came to London during the summer of 1961 and I met him for the first time about ten days before he was due to open. He was upstairs in the office of The Establishment, seated on the edge of a desk, bent over an electrical gadget which he was trying to fix with a bread knife. He had obviously been engaged in this for some time because a secretary was twiddling her thumbs at another desk, plainly rather at a loss. He was dressed in a black uniform with a high Nehru collar, open to show an orange T shirt. On his feet he had what looked like high-heeled white cricket boots. The secretary introduced me tentatively, and Bruce looked up, sweating from the exertion of his obscure task. "Hiya Jonathan. Hey, yah." He breathed with vague unfocused enthusiasm. And then he caught sight of a motorcycle helmet I was holding. "Hey man, what do you ride?" "A motor scooter," I said apologetically. After which it took nearly ten days to regain his interest and confidence. But then he never really displayed anything one could call direct personal interest. It was just a restless, incoherent curiosity which he would try to satisfy by quizzing more or less anyone with whom he came in contact. And he was always off at odd tangents—worrying about some gadget, or else running on about a doctor he had heard of who could get him prescriptions. Then there was endless trouble about his hotel accommodation. Largely because of girls, but also because hotel proprietors were badly jangled by his eccentric diurnal routines. Not that he was a night person, or anything straight-forwardly hippy like that. He followed no discernible rhythm whatever in his sleeping and waking. He might sleep for twenty-four hours, and then race around for another forty-eight, walking the streets of Soho, taking down notes about clothes in shop windows, or stopping passers-by to ask them about their jobs. Sometimes he would cat-nap in the office while the secretaries clattered on all round him. And as the opening drew nearer he became more and more noncommittal about what he was actually going to do on the stage; though he would spend hours panting and squawking over a grubby screed to which he kept adding and then crossing out. Or out of the blue he would dictate some dubious paragraph to one of the bewildered girls in the office who had by this time developed a distracted affection for the man. Then he held a press conference and baffled all the reporters, who had expected to find a ferocious slavering junkie, by mildly asking them so many questions about themselves that they never seemed able to get one in edgeways about him. He was always intrigued by their cameras and anyone unlucky enough to be sporting an unusual model had to suffer endless catechism while Bruce turned the machine over lovingly in his hands, breathing and crooning with a naive, savage wonder. Bruce had plenty of "character" but seemed to possess nothing that one could properly call a personality. There were so many epicycles of interest and activity that it was impossible to make out the central point around which they all moved. Perhaps there wasn't any. I often thought of him like Peter Pan, resolutely fickle and somehow in flight from his and everyone else's maturity. He was comparatively young when he died and yet it was hard to imagine him being any older. His special talent arose from a sort of daft, alienated infantilism which ruled out the possibility of his ever enjoying senior citizenship. Perhaps in some obscure vision of expediency he sought the ordeal which brought about his own annihilation. The horrible thing is that in willing his own execution Bruce actually found society only too willing to oblige him with cruel and extravagant fulfillment.

New York Review of Books, 6 October, 1966

A Gower Street Scandal

Soon after my return to London my somewhat simple-minded intention to go back to clinical research was thwarted by the unexpected invitation to edit and present BBC Television's arts series *Monitor*. After doing this for a year I was given the opportunity to direct two films for the BBC – *The Drinking Party* and *The Death of Socrates*, both based on Plato's dialogues. And after this I was allowed to make a film of *Alice in Wonderland*.

After these distractions I made another attempt to return to medicine and took up a research fellowship in the Department of the History of Medicine at University College. There I embarked on what I hoped would be a book on the history of animal magnetism, the idea underlying mesmerism and hypnotism. This work led to two long articles based on my research, of which *A Gower Street Scandal* was the second, published in the *Journal of the Royal College of Physicians*.

The story of mesmerism is often regarded as a colourful but regrettable episode in the otherwise steady development of scientific medicine. In many popular accounts it is treated as yet another example of quackery preying on gullibility. But this attitude reflects an unhelpfully Whiggish view of intellectual history, and it is much more fruitful to try and analyse the context within which such ideas had their natural place.

Mesmerism, or animal magnetism as it was often called, struck root in England in 1785, shortly after its founder had been humiliated by the findings of a Royal Commission hastily convened in France to examine the claims of this melodramatic medical novelty.

Franz Anton Mesmer was born in Germany in 1734, and after studying medicine in Vienna he published a doctoral thesis on the influence of the celestial bodies on human disease. According to him the universe was filled with an imponderable fluid through which the tidal influence of the sun, moon and planets exerted its effect upon the physiological fluids of the human physique.

Mesmer, however, did not invent the idea of a universal fluid, but took his inspiration from an idea which had already been formulated by Isaac Newton. In his *General Scholium* to the Third Book of the *Principia*, Newton postulated the existence of an aether which mediated the transmission of light, gravity and magnetism. In his *Queries* to the more popular *Optics* he elaborated this idea and suggested that the same fluid was perhaps responsible for transmitting impulses within the nervous system. This idea was eclipsed in the years immediately following Newton's death, but was reinstated in the middle of the eighteenth century, partly as a result of new discoveries in the study of static electricity. Mesmer's theory therefore fitted comfortably into the context of European scientific ideas. According to him it was possible to manipulate human physiology by making 'passes' with the hand. This manoeuvre set up tidal disturbances in the physiological fluids of the patient, and, by redistributing the pressures under the influence of so-called animal 'magnetism', health would be restored without the intervention of either drugs or surgery.

After a painful conflict with the Viennese medical establishment Mesmer fled to France where he inaugurated a stunningly successful 'magnetic' salon and soon grew rich from the payments of a prosperous clientele. The controversy which this created eventually led to the establishment of an investigating commission headed by Benjamin Franklin, and by 1785 the results of Mesmer's treatment were dismissed as the effects of imagination.

But this unfavourable judgement did not prevent the new doctrine from spreading to the UK, and during the last years of the eighteenth century there was a flourishing if controversial movement, which attracted the same sort of clientele. As in Paris, many of the visitors belonged to the aristocracy, but the membership also included people whose interest in the subject was redemptive rather than remedial, Swedenborgians and Rosicrucians who recognised a mystical millennial promise in the trances induced by the mesmeric 'passes'.

The movement soon fell into disrepute as a result of being identified with revolutionary themes, and with the advent of the Napoleonic war it was politically risky to be associated with it. For the next 30 years, therefore, it is almost impossible to find any mention of the subject. The topic re-emerged in 1829 with the publication of a series of articles written in the London Medical and Physical Journal by an Irish chemist named Richard Chenevix. During his long stay on the continent Chenevix had encountered the magnetic activities of the Abbé Faria, and in the effort to introduce these practices to the British medical establishment he invited a number of doctors to witness a set of demonstrations conducted at St Thomas's Hospital. The group included a number of eminent scientists – Benjamin Brodie, Samuel Prout and Michael Faraday. They were, it seems, unimpressed by the demonstration and the subject might have been extinguished forever had it not been for the activities of one peculiar man.

The distinguished scientists who agreed to act as impartial witnesses of Chenevix's demonstration in 1829 would have been dismayed to learn that one of their number was destined to undergo a catastrophic conversion to animal magnetism, and that by 1850 the name of John Elliotson would take pride of place in the annals of British mesmerism.

And yet the memorandum which he submitted as an appendix to Chenevix's article gives no indication of the self-destructive enthusiasm which was to blight the career of one of the most successful members of the Victorian medical establishment. Admittedly Elliotson kept fuller and more detailed notes than any of his colleagues, and it is tempting to infer that he already had an exorbitant interest in the subject. But the non-committal reticence of his records seems oddly inconsistent with his fanatical reaction to a comparable demonstration which he attended seven years later.

In 1836, when already established as Professor of Medicine at the newly founded University College in London, he attended a mesmeric séance conducted by a visiting French magnetist, and although the trance phenomena elicited on this occasion were more or less indistinguishable from the ones which he had seen in 1829, Elliotson reacted with ungovernable enthusiasm, and for the next 30 years he was to become mesmerism's most controversial patron. Between 1836 and 1839 he was the centre of a great public scandal, and the events following his conversion were so peculiar and so exorbitant that it led one of his contemporaries to describe them as the most astonishing and bewildering chapter in the history of medicine.

Compared with some of his more obscure colleagues in the mesmeric movement, Elliotson left a wealth of biographical material which makes it possible to reconstruct a vivid portrait from which it soon becomes apparent that it was only a matter of time before he assumed the role of martyred heretic, and that the impartiality he displayed in 1829 was an unrepresentative interlude in a life that had always been devoted to emblematically unorthodox causes.

Although it was complicated by a streak of easily offended vanity and a fatal tendency to seek and nurse ornamental grudges, Elliotson's personality corresponds very closely to the one which is developed in the tragically idealistic figure of Dorothea in *Middlemarch*. Like George Eliot's heroine, Elliotson was driven by a need for some 'illimitable satisfaction', and finding 'no epic life wherein there was a constant unfolding of far resonant action', he improvised unfoldings of his own, and consistently made rash and ill-advised alliances upon which he was able to raise epic constructions. In fact by 1849, with his martyrdom confirmed by the contempt of his colleagues and the loss of his professorship, Elliotson had developed the implications of mesmerism so that they extended well beyond the frontier of medicine as such, claiming that animal magnetism was 'a mighty engine for man's regeneration, vast in its power, and unlimited in its application, rivalling in morals the effect of steam in mechanics.' Predictably, this millennial hope came to nothing. The vast power of mesmerism proved to be inapplicable on such an ambitious scale, and by the time Elliotson died in 1868, with his judgement clouded by outdated and irrelevant enthusiasms, he had even lost touch with the genuinely practical possibilities of mesmerism which had since been developed under the more modest heading of medical hypnotism. Elliotson proved to be the founder of nothing, and by the end of his life, when he was already forgotten by his opponents and merely pitied by his friends, it was apparent that his intelligence and good will had been 'dispersed among hindrances instead of continuing in some long-recognisable deed'. As his tragic biography unfolds, it is possible to see that the male, but not altogether masculine, figure of John Elliotson contains Dorothea and Casaubon rolled into one.

Elliotson's affiliation with unorthodox scientific causes began at an early stage in his career, and when the doctrines of phrenology first made their appearance in the British Isles he expressed a growing interest which culminated in the decision to found a London society devoted to promulgating the ideas of Gall and Spurzheim. His presidency was punctuated by a series of unattractive quarrels, and in the year that he attended Chenevix's demonstration he angrily terminated a long correspondence with the leader of the Edinburgh phrenological movement, George Combe. It is not possible to identify the exact reasons for the disagreement, but the trouble seems to have arisen over Combe's failure to publicly condemn a scurrilous pamphlet in which the author appears to have made slighting references to Elliotson's phrenological competence. Combe had clearly grown impatient of Elliotson's volatile vanity, and in an effort to pacify his awkward disciple he stressed that the disruptive article was only worthy of contempt. With a candour that proved intolerably wounding he accurately identified one of Elliotson's principal flaws:

'Your late letter strongly impressed me with the conviction that your organ of love of approbation and some others are in a state of morbid excitement. Matters of very little moment appear to affect you as if they involved your whole existence, present and to come: and this pamphlet of Stones is another example of the same melancholy fact.'

Although Elliotson had obligingly supplied him with the cast of his own skull some years earlier, Combe needed no phrenological skill to reach the conclusions just quoted. In a correspondence lasting for nearly seven years Elliotson repeatedly betrayed 'the melancholy fact' that his love of approbation was always in a state of morbid excitement, and that small professional slights were invariably blown up into inexcusable personal offences. When Combe committed the fatal blunder of issuing a well-intended rebuke, Elliotson reacted with characteristic pique. Proclaiming 'the injustice, cold selfish coarseness, the sophistry and disingenuousness of Mr. Combe's preceding letter', he haughtily concluded his communication with 'that gentleman' and never wrote to him again.

Fortunately, Combe preserved the correspondence, and from this it is possible to reconstruct a fascinating, if somewhat distressing picture which foreshadows Elliotson's peculiar behaviour when confronted for the second time with the startling results of mesmerism. At a previously undocumented stage of his career it is possible to recognise tendencies which later became much more florid. The apparently uncritical readiness to sponsor ideas which some of his more cautious, though not necessarily less intelligent, colleagues found questionable; the eagerness to ally himself with causes which would automatically distinguish the recruit as someone interestingly 'different'; and above all the regrettable tendency to identify stupid enemies outside the movement and envious rivals within.

Elliotson had begun writing to Combe in 1822, shortly after the Edinburgh lawyer had helped to found the first Phrenological Society in Great Britain. Combe himself had undergone a characteristically abrupt conversion to phrenology in or about 1815 when Spurzheim visited the Scottish capital to deliver an emergency defence of the topic after it had been wittily attacked in the *Edinburgh Review*. Elliotson's quixotic spirits had evidently been stirred by the controversy, and although he confessed himself to be an untutored phrenologist, he wrote to Combe insisting that 'Of the validity of the science I have long been more than satisfied'. On 11th April 1822 he was ardently soliciting advice from Combe, and since he was obviously determined to found a Phrenological Society of his own, he urged Combe to pay an evangelical visit to London.

"If you could come over and help us, great would be the harvest. We have an abundance and are destitute of spirit to gather it in. I really think a visit from you this spring or summer would be an inestimable benefit.

You would infuse an ardour into us, make us good phrenologists as well as ardent ones, and perhaps establish a Phrenological Society in London by which the science would be gloriously cultivated."

Elliotson encouraged Combe to follow the example of the Bible Society whose organisers despatch charismatic leaders to encourage the formation of auxiliary groups. By expressing himself in this way, and by couching his invitation in biblical language, Elliotson conveys the essentially sectarian character of the enterprise, and as the letters follow one another it becomes more and more apparent that he had adopted phrenology as little less than a secular church. This attitude became even more explicit when he emerged as the self-appointed bishop of mesmerism. But until he could appropriate a cult of his own, he was happy to recognise

Combe's Pauline role, and to repeat his increasingly urgent requests for a pastoral visit.

Undeterred by Combe's failure to come south, Elliotson went ahead with his plans for establishing a London society, and on 10th March 1823 he wrote to Combe proudly announcing the inaugural meeting. Among the founding members there was a man whose participation might have had some relevance to Elliotson's later interest in animal magnetism.

Like his father John Tulk, who was one of the first subscribers to the Theosophical Society in 1783, Charles Augustus Tulk, MP, was an active Swedenborgian, and, according to Elliotson, took advantage of their shared interest in phrenology to expound the doctrines of the New Jerusalem. Although he was a self-confessed enemy of traditional Christianity, Elliotson undertook a concentrated course of Swedenborgian reading and admitted to Combe that he found the visionary works 'really elegant, deeply learned and most ingenious'. His reaction was so favourable that Tulk declared him to be 'in a state of recipiency and under the influence of the general influx'. Whether he was truly under its influence or not, it is not unreasonable to suppose that his familiarity with the concept of the 'influx' made him unusually receptive to the analogous doctrines of animal magnetism.

Meanwhile Elliotson shouldered the clerical burdens of the new society and kept Combe closely informed about the fortnightly meetings. He emphasised that suggestions and advice would be welcome and that 'an account of all that is done by the Edinburgh Society would be very instructive'. By March 1823 he was pleased to report that the new science was 'gaining proselytes [sic] daily', and in May he triumphantly reported that the newly formed society had been privileged to act as host to 'the founder of our science'. Quite understandably, the arrival of Franz Gall caused great excitement among the phrenological brethren, and Elliotson breathlessly claimed that the founder looked like 'the finest old philosopher that ever existed. I would match Plato or Socrates with him'.

The occasion was crowned by the ritual ceremony of taking a plaster cast of Gall's distinctive cranium.

Less than a month later there was a characteristic note of criticism in Elliotson's account. The distinguished visitor had apparently spent too much time lecturing to other groups, and Elliotson took exception to his 'incessantly saying something against Spurzheim', and huffily declared that he had now lost all interest in him.

Elliotson's break with Gall was the first of many disagreements which divided the members as they fought with one another over matters of precedence and priority. Elliotson soon reported an ugly fracas with Deville, the craftsman who had undertaken the commemorative cast of Gall's Socratic cranium. Deville had proved himself to be indispensable to the society by making and supplying the plaster casts which constituted the essential study material. At each of the fortnightly meetings the members would examine the contours of some representative skull – that of a statesman, a philosopher or a newly executed murderer – and by correlating its distinctive bumps with the personality and behaviour of its owner they sought confirmation of the phrenological doctrine.

According to Elliotson the 'cockney plasterer' had an exaggerated sense of his own phrenological importance.

'He is an illiterated vulgar being and because he is not considered a founder of our Society, and made one of the council, he has abused us all. ... I am convinced he is rather insane. Inflated by being made too much of by us, and by preaching phrenology to crowds who go to his shop to view his casts.'

Elliotson recognised however that he was caught in a cleft stick. Deville 'had been of the greatest importance to phrenology and to our Society, which yet cannot exist without him, for we have no funds, no busts, and all the world go to him to be cast', but at the same time Elliotson obviously found his ignorance and commercial vulgarity intolerable. 'I am really ashamed of my connection with him: yet what can I do?'

It is ironic that Elliotson should have been so irritated by Deville's flair for personal publicity, for in condemning him for exploiting phrenology in order to attract fashionable sensation-seekers, Elliotson was expressing criticisms indistinguishable from those levelled at his own behaviour during the mesmeric scandals of 1838.

Elliotson's snobbish disdain for the uneducated soon brought him into conflict with one of his other colleagues in the Phrenological Society. This time the dispute became so heated that it threatened the very existence of phrenology in London.

On this occasion Combe was the unsuspecting cause of the row. In January, 1824, the Edinburgh phrenologist had apparently agreed to make his long-awaited visit to London, and Elliotson was dismayed to learn that one of his own colleagues, a Dr. Willis, was determined to set himself up as a competitor, coolly insisting that he, Willis, knew just as much phrenology as Mr. Combe. Elliotson was furious, recognising that Willis' lectures would distract attention from Combe's, and thereby confuse a public which was largely hostile to the new science. In any case, Elliotson refused to acknowledge Willis' claim to be 'the first phrenological teacher in London', insisting that he would be seen as a clever, but 'half-educated raw Scottish laddie'. Disclaiming that he had any ambitions of his own, Elliotson pointed out that while he was prepared to take on the drudgery of the society, Willis was interested in the brilliant reputation which he might win.

By April the relationship between Elliotson and Willis had reached a crisis, and although Combe's visit had not materialised, the rivalry had reached a point where Elliotson felt it necessary to resign not merely as secretary, but as member of the Phrenological Society. In a long, wounded letter to Combe, Elliotson betrayed his pompous vanity and at the same time he conveys a vivid impression of the competitive and schismatic tendencies so characteristic of the nineteenth century pseudo-scientific sects.

These events culminated in the resignation of Elliotson and at least 20 other members who immediately formed a splinter group and in the effort to distinguish themselves from the rump which was now headed by Willis they constituted themselves under a new and somewhat combative title as 'The London Phrenological Society: Established March 31st 1824'. In the society Elliotson finally ruled supreme, predicting that the old one would wither away since it was headed by someone whose illiteracy would soon bring it into disrepute. In the same letter Elliotson exulted at the Greek and Latin howlers which were repeatedly committed by Willis, and he announced that phrenology needed educated spokesmen, and that it would otherwise deteriorate into a commercial sideshow.

The snobbery which Elliotson expressed with such unembarrassed vigour is a recurrent theme in the history of both phrenology and mesmerism, and it reflects an important class distinction between the two types of men who were drawn to the new sciences. Someone like Elliotson who came from a prosperous background and enjoyed all the privileges of a good university education identified lofty philosophical principles and believed that these could only be fully developed and upheld by those whose training had been 'sufficiently profound and elegant', and 'enlarged by every advantage of education'.

For men of this sort both phrenology and mesmerism contained not only metaphysical truths of the most resounding and far-reaching importance, but philanthropic possibilities whose realisation depended on the supervision of people whose commercial interests were subordinate to the love of man. Such patrician enthusiasts were dismayed that some of their fellow recruits were considerably less literate and quite noticeably less elegant, and that for many of these phrenology and mesmerism provided a source of education as opposed to being subjects upon which the results of education could be brought to bear. For obvious reasons highly qualified professional men such as Elliotson were irritated by those who seemed to exploit the new sciences for self-improvement and even downright commercial gain, and although Elliotson was a prominent member of various organisations which promoted the spread of useful knowledge among the less fortunate members of Victorian society, he was rattled to find himself competing with men who had previously accepted his educational charity.

While the Phrenological Society was undergoing its internal upheavals, Elliotson also had to endure the ridicule and hostility of less credulous outsiders, especially scientists.

> 'I dined yesterday with a violent anti-phrenologist –
> Dr. Prout – one of the council of the Royal Society,
> eminent for physiological chemistry & well known
> to your brother. ... He is a sincere lover of truth:
> even labouring after it, and a most bashful, good
> – quiet man – but he almost threatens to write a

parallel between Astrology & Phrenology, calls you a madman, says that all his friends (who are savants of the Royal Society) laugh at the science – As to the similar reception of Harvey's discovery, he turned his nose up in the air on my mentioning it …'

Although Elliotson managed to feign a contemptuous indifference to such comments, he was worried by the thought that his affiliation with phrenology would jeopardise his chances of being accepted as a "serious" member of the scientific establishment. And since he had not yet developed his suicidal disregard of professional opinion, his loyalties sometimes wobbled. In 1824 he wrote a curiously revealing postscript to Combe in which he confided that his Fellowship of the Royal Society was just coming up for consideration, and that he would be grateful to have his phrenological affiliations played down, 'lest I be stigmatized and black-balled'. In the light of this touchingly tactless request it is tempting to conclude that the prudence of his mesmeric testimonial in 1829 was dictated by a tender concern for his forthcoming appointment to the post of Lumleian Lecturer at the Royal College of Physicians, and his not too distant candidacy for the chair of medicine at University College.

Such a request was unnecessary as well as tactless. Elliotson's association with phrenology was a well-known fact, as his own account of the conversation with Prout shows. And although it is easy to exaggerate the intellectual standard of the Royal Society, the fact that Elliotson won his election implies that his orthodox qualifications were enough to withstand the stigma of being associated with an unorthodox science.

In the unreformed era of the Royal Society, election to a Fellowship did not depend on a body of published research. Armchair speculations were often regarded as acceptable offerings, as long as they were consistent with what was perceived as 'normal' science – although of course the concept of science, normal or otherwise, had not yet been explicitly articulated. In this respect Elliotson had made his mark at a comparatively early stage in his career. In 1810, shortly after he graduated from the University of Edinburgh, he published a graceful translation of Blumenbach's *Institutions of Physiology*. In 1816 he issued a second edition to which he added many reflective notes of his own, and by the time the third edition followed in 1820 he had earned a reputation as an interesting 'philosophical' mind. Since he also had an appointment as assistant physician to a London teaching hospital his meditations carried the authority of someone who had practical experience. But with or without his famous Blumenbach, Elliotson's formal credentials were enough to outweigh the criticism aroused by his phrenological activities. He had an MD earned by thesis, and his Cambridge degree entitled him to full membership of the Royal College of Physicians. In 1822 he became a Fellow of the Royal College and thereby earned the coveted right to undertake the private practice of physic. And with the added advantage of 'a good independence', Elliotson felt himself 'in that happy and proud situation so desirable for every man of real mind and feeling, that he is not driven to practice as a trader, but is enabled to select his connexion, and to go through his professional duties with the liberality and conduct of the gentleman, trusting to his own talents, his industry, and attention without any mean solicitation for his ultimate success'.

Ironically, the wealth which bought Elliotson the right to 'select his connexion' was inherited from the profit of medical trade, for Elliotson was the eldest son of a successful druggist and no expense was spared to guarantee a prosperous and respectable future. He was privately educated, and in 1805 at the unusually early age of fourteen he entered the University of Edinburgh as a medical student. For the next five years he conscientiously attended all the necessary courses in Physic, Surgery and Materia Medica.

As a medical student Elliotson was obliged to take the Arts course, which means that he would have attended lectures in Moral Philosophy and Metaphysics. Now, apart from its undisputed claims to be the most important medical university in the British Isles, Edinburgh was understandably regarded as the home of speculative philosophy, and although the Scottish Enlightenment was on the wane by the time Elliotson was a student, the tradition which had been established by men such as Hume, Fergusson, Brown and Adam Smith was still very much alive.

When Elliotson took the Arts course in 1808 the chair of'Moral Philosophy was occupied by Dugald Stewart, and although it is not possible to identify any particular idea which Elliotson owed to him, the number of references which are made to Stewart in the footnotes to the later editions of Blumenbach imply that the Scottish philosopher played an important part in stimulating Elliotson's lifelong interest in the philosophy of mind. This suspicion is perhaps confirmed by the fact that when Elliotson went to Cambridge, he continued to take out Stewart's works from the library of Jesus College.

In view of his early interest in phrenology and his later enthusiasm for animal magnetism it would be interesting to know what Elliotson thought about the relationship between mind and brain. Unfortunately, it is not easy to decide. In the 1820s the religious implications of this question meant that there was considerable risk in publishing anything but the most orthodox opinions on the subject, and that anyone who dared to identify mind with the material organisation of the brain was likely to be accused of atheism. Since the political authorities regarded atheism as something inseparably associated with revolutionary radicalism, anyone with professional ambitions tended to blur their public statements on the topic.

In Elliotson's case, the situation was complicated by the fact that his graduation from Cambridge happened to coincide with a dangerously controversial episode in the history of biology. For someone who stood on the threshold of what seemed like a promising professional career, the decision to publish editorial notes on the subject of life and mind would have been shaken, or at least influenced by the news that prominent men had endangered their public reputations by sponsoring what was then known as Materialism. For someone as thoughtful as Elliotson the philosophical problems were unavoidable, for, as Temkin wrote: 'Physiology is confronted with philosophical issues on two sides. At one end, so to speak, it touches on the relationship between matter and life, while at the opposite end, it meets the problem of body and mind.'

To put it as simply as possible, opinion divided in the following way. For the so-called Vitalist, life was the expression of some immaterial principle – some spiritual agency whose presence in, and operation upon otherwise inert matter conferred the characteristic properties of warmth, assimilation, irritability, sensitivity and growth.

When it was cloistered in the more elaborate forms of nervous system this principle endowed the creature with thought, will and moral purpose. The claim that this principle could outlive the organism was reassuring for those who insisted upon the immortality of the soul.

For the Materialist, on the other hand. life and mind were emergent properties of what they called organised matter. As far as they were concerned the distinctive characteristics of living things were the inevitable outcome of their physical structure. When atoms arranged themselves in certain critical patterns, that is to say when things were organised in a particularly complex and idiosyncratic way, the stage was automatically set for liveliness and even for thought itself.

For obvious reasons the doctrine of Materialism was recognised as a dangerous threat to religious orthodoxy. For if life and mind were indistinguishable from material organisation, they would presumably perish with the disorganisation of the material body. Such a conclusion obviously threatened the foundations of traditional morality, which relied on the threat that the immortal soul would have to answer for the sins of its mortal owner. In any case, if personality was the expression of one's inherited brain-work, the notion of culpability vanished into thin air. It is hardly surprising that when the English surgeon William Lawrence expressed these sentiments in his notorious 'Lectures on Physiology, Zoology and the Natural History of Man' he was accused of encouraging 'faction in politics and infidelity in religion'. In 1819, when these lectures were published, such encouragement was regarded as an intolerable threat to political security, so much so that when Lawrence tried to secure a copyright and thereby prevent a pirated edition of his lectures, Lord Chancellor Eldon refused to uphold the injunction on the grounds 'that the law does not give protection to those who contradict the scriptures'.

It is hard to believe that Elliotson was unimpressed by such considerations, but since he left no record of his private opinions on the subject it is impossible to evaluate the claim that his sentiments 'on materiality and immateriality' are accurately represented in his note to Blumenbach's chapter on health and human nature.

He starts by making the somewhat evasive comment that 'the essential nature of life is an impenetrable mystery and no more a subject for philosophical enquiry than the essential nature of attraction or of matter'. He goes on to dissociate himself from the idea that life can be explained by the 'unfounded hypothesis' of a vital fluid; by which he was presumably referring to Abernethy's widely discussed version of John Hunter's theory which claimed that life is literally galvanised into existence by the operation of electricity – often identified as an imponderable fluid. 'By attributing life ... to subtle and mobile fluids, we not only do not advance a single step, for we still have to explain what these fluids are and how they obtain their powers ... but we make the additional mysteries of their being united with ordinary matter, and so united that life appears a power possessed by it.' But when it comes to saying what life is, Elliotson begins to equivocate. At one moment he seems to be sponsoring straightforward materialism, by arguing that life is 'the property of organised systems, producing various effects by various kinds of organisation ...' He then slips in a footnote which says that 'Organisation cannot be the cause, but in truth organisation is the effect of life, although when produced it becomes the instrument of life', at which point Elliotson introduces a phrase that indicates the extent to which the current controversy had influenced his thought. He refers to 'the erroneousness of the French doctrine to which Mr. Lawrence is a proselyte ... that life is the result of organisation.' And in the effort to convince his readers that this is not what he believes, he repeats his claim that far from being the result of organisation life is 'a power to which organisation is an instrument'.

Elliotson uses a comparable argument in his discussion of the mind. He points out that 'the mind is a power of the living brain' and leaves others at liberty 'to fancy a hypothesis of this power being a subtle, immaterial, immortal substance...' He goes on to argue that the power of mind

is inseparably associated with the material organisation of
the brain so that 'when the brain ceases to live the power
necessarily ceases'.

Elliotson recognised that this idea had unfavourable
implications for the prospects of a future life, at which point
he insisted 'that the promises of revelation are the proper and
only foundation of our hopes of immortality' and that since
the Holy Scriptures guaranteed the resurrection of the body
there was nothing to fear from the mortality of the brain;
since the Almighty had originally endowed matter with the
gifts of life and mind, he was free to restore them at any
time he chose. Elliotson was thus able to conclude his note
with the claim that 'if I have written a syllable that can be
proved contrary to Scripture or to the Articles of the Church
of England, I acknowledge it false and declare it unsaid'.

The social circumstances under which Elliotson
published the third edition of his Blumenbach may have
had some influence on his decision to emphasise the truth
of revelation, although it would be rash to conclude
that he cynically introduced the doctrine of resurrection
just to protect himself against accusations of subversive
materialism. This passage from a letter to Combe is perhaps
a more reliable indicator of' his attitude to Christianity.

> 'How any man of good sense who has reached
> thirty years of age can believe in miracles and
> prophecies, especially such ridiculous ones as are
> many in the bible, how he can so vilify the Almighty
> as to believe in future and eternal rewards and
> punishments and an atonement by the sufferings
> of God himself or any other being ... exceeds my
> comprehension. The Christian doctrines appear
> to me the grossest libel that was ever published
> upon the deity.'

Taken in conjunction with some of the books he read at Cambridge, especially Voltaire, Gibbon and Lucretius, this quotation seems to imply that his loyalty to Holy Scripture was somewhat partial, and that his materialism was much stronger than he cared to admit. Nevertheless, it would be a mistake to interpret literally any of these statements. Since Elliotson was such a volatile and unstable personality it would be safer to conclude that he was someone in at least two states of mind. His readiness to undertake the laborious course of Swedenborgian reading shows that he had unsatisfied spiritual yearnings, and although his phrenological interest was presumably an expression of his more materialistic persuasion, the fact that his abrupt conversion to mesmerism coincided with the death of his mother suggests that this doctrine may have supplied a long-felt spiritual want.

In the meantime Elliotson's career continued to prosper, which meant presumably that his carefully worded notes to the third edition of Blumenbach had successfully allayed any suspicions which he might have aroused among the medical authorities. After graduating from Cambridge in 1816, he walked the wards of Guy's Hospital, and three years later his reputation as a conscientious and observant student had earned him the post of assistant physician at St Thomas's Hospital. In 1821 he applied for the post as full Physician, at which point he encountered stiff opposition. The sketchy records make it almost impossible to identify the issues. Elliotson's combative personality may have had something to do with it, but the main stumbling block seems to have been a technical one. Elliotson had apparently expressed the wish to lecture in Forensic Medicine, and since there were constitutional objections to such a scheme, Elliotson overcame the problem by addressing students at a private medical school in the vicinity. This aroused the hostility of his surgical colleagues, and, as a result, his application for the post of Physician was unsuccessful on several occasions. Eventually his own reputation carried the day, and with the added support of his father, whose post at a local dispensary made him a force to reckon with, Elliotson was finally appointed.

This appointment marks the beginning of the most successful and happy period in Elliotson's life. With his phrenological and literary activities squeezed into a few spare evenings, Elliotson began to flourish as a clinical physician. His subsequent interests have obscured his obviously remarkable abilities as a bedside observer. He had unrivalled clinical sensitivity and a sharp eye for the signs and symptoms of physical illness. He was one of the earliest physicians in England to take an interest in Laennec's newly invented stethoscope, and his readiness to recognise the association between the sounds of the heart in life and the morbid findings at autopsy bore fruit in the remarkable observations which he put together when invited to give the Lumleian Lectures in 1829.

At the same time his restless and quixotic tendencies were still in evidence, and he frequently alarmed his colleagues by rashly administering enormous doses of heavy metal salts. In spite of his many quirks, Elliotson entered his fortieth year with the reputation of a great medical teacher. His lectures were over-subscribed, and his private practice had added substantially to his already considerable wealth. When the new University of London was established in 1826 he was the undisputed candidate for the chair of Medicine.

Apart from his continued association with phrenology there was no indication of the crisis that was soon to overtake him. In 1836, however, Elliotson encountered yet another demonstration of animal magnetism. From the abruptness of his conversion one can only assume that his imagination had been subliminally primed by the phenomena which he had witnessed seven years earlier.

Instead of the guarded comments which he submitted as an appendix to Chenevix's article, he immediately undertook magnetic treatment of his patients in the wards at University College Hospital. Fortunately, Elliotson's casebooks have been preserved, so that it is possible to trace the growth of his mesmeric conversion. One by one patients are switched from conventional therapy to that of magnetic sleep, induced by passes made by the hand in front of the subject's face. The most dramatic example is the case of two sisters, Elizabeth and Jane Okey, who were admitted to the wards for the treatment of fits. With Dupotet's assistance the girls were put into a magnetic trance, and in the first instance at least, appeared to undergo remission of their symptoms. The improvement was short-lived not because the treatment was ineffectual, but because it was to the advantage of both practitioner and patient to maintain a self-repeating cycle of complaint and treatment. This does not mean that there was any conspiracy or collusion between Elliotson and the Okeys. Unconsciously, however, patient and practitioner satisfied complementary needs by their association in the magnetic relationship, and to sustain this mutual dependence, the notion of cure gradually gave way to one of interminable treatment.

As with Charcot's famous patients at the Salpêtrière, the hysterical sisters flourished under the special attention which their behaviour in trance excited. As the custodian of a dramatic medical phenomenon, it would not have been in Elliotson's interests to cure and then discharge his colourful patients. Inevitably, therefore, the Okeys became conditioned to show the signs which provoked Elliotson's approving curiosity, until, by means of an unspoken pact, patient and physician were locked inseparably together. The next stage was equally predictable in terms of what we now know about patient-doctor relationships. While in the trance, the sisters began to acquire some of the transcendental abilities associated with clairvoyant mesmerism. According to the reports, they were able to visualise their own innards, and as the trance deepened, their clairvoyance extended to the interiors of other patients. Before long Elliotson was steering them around the wards where they claimed to be able to diagnose the state of other patients' organs. In this respect, the course of events closely follows the career pattern of the Shaman, in which, as Professor Ioan Lewis has shown, a phase of involuntary possession, during which the subject is treated as a sufferer, is followed by a phase of repeated voluntary possession, at which point the subject graduates in the eyes of those around to the status of a Shaman capable of supernatural vision or insight.

It is interesting to note that the Okey sisters were not altogether unfamiliar with visionary experiences. In his memoir of Professor Elliotson, the then Assistant Editor of *The Lancet* pointed out that the girls had previously been members of Edward Irving's Catholic Apostolic Church in Regent Square. The services of this sect were characterised by ecstatic interventions from the congregation, interventions in which the witness spoke in strange tongues – so-called glossolalia. It is evident that the sisters were susceptible to hysterical fits of one sort or another, and unconsciously acquired the ability to enact them within a social context which assigned special importance to such behaviour. Naturally, the behaviour was subtly modulated in order to conform to the ideological requirements of the two sets of situation: in Regent Square they were Pentecostal prophets, whereas in Gower Street they became mesmeric Shamans. Thus, as Professor Lewis points out, 'the link between affliction and its cure as the royal road to the assumption of shamanistic vocation is plain enough'. In the case of the Okey girls the course of events bears out his further thesis that such occurrences are frequently associated with socially unfortunate females, for whom the gradual assumption of prophetic power represents a fire-escape from a situation of intolerable social alienation.

By the spring of 1838 Elliotson was completely intoxicated by the situation, and the wards were in an uproar. He had become his own evangelist and was soon holding huge publicly attended séances in the lecture theatre of the hospital. Fashionable London came in droves and he now set out to prove that the Okeys were endowed with the ability to pick out mesmerically-magnetised coins and to see through walls.

By this time the hospital authorities had become so outraged that they appealed to the Council of the Royal College of Physicians, which insisted that Elliotson break off the practice of animal magnetism and discharge the Okeys. Elliotson refused to obey, and resigned. During the last few months of the controversy he was ruthlessly mocked and criticised in the editorial columns of the recently-founded *Lancet*. Oddly enough, the author responsible for these attacks was a close personal friend of Elliotson, Thomas Wakley, a pioneer in medical journalism and a hard-headed radical who was obviously nauseated by the confused mysticism which he had detected beneath Elliotson's apparent materialism. The point is that Elliotson was claiming the discovery of a new physical principle. Unlike his Neoplatonist friend Townshend, for whom the mesmeric phenomena bore witness to the existence of a transcendental reality beyond that of the physical senses, Elliotson insisted that animal magnetism merely extended the frontiers of physical reality to include a principle which operated according to the laws of Newton. Like his successor the chemist William Crookes, who was photographed arm-in-arm with a buxom ghost, Elliotson was claiming the existence of a previously unacknowledged force in nature. Wakley, however, was not impressed, and after a humiliating experiment which Wakley insisted on conducting at his own house, he showed to his own – and I think one must admit to our – satisfaction that the Okeys' powers could all be accounted for in terms of the traditional five senses.

After his resignation from University College Hospital, Elliotson continued a prosperous practice and remained respected throughout the profession. His honesty had never been called into question. It is apparent from Thackeray's portrait of him in Pendennis that he struck those who knew him as a man of considerable intellectual stature, and his intellectual stature was matched by his warmth and compassion.

Throughout the 1840s he edited and largely wrote a periodical called *The Zoist*, subtitled 'A journal of Phreno-Mesmerism' and devoted to cerebral physiology and mesmerism. In Elliotson's opinion, the study of the brain had stood still for at least 15 years, largely as a result of the obstinate refusal of the medical establishment to acknowledge the new science of mesmerism.

Other scientists agreed that the study of the brain had come to a standstill. In 1831 Sir David Brewster insisted that 'while new sciences have been created and every other branch of knowledge has made the most extensive acquisitions, the philosophy of mind has remained almost stationary. It has made no advances, and the whole of this field, where observation and experiment might so fitly and profitably be employed, lies at this moment an unmentionable waste'. According to Elliotson, the situation could only be repaired by paying serious attention to the phenomena of mesmerism. He forecast that the fruits of such research 'may transcend in value and utility all that man has yet dared to hope for from science'. The pages of *The Zoist* are filled with accounts of animal magnetism used to effect dramatic cures and as an effective anaesthetic.

Given that Elliotson's assumptions are false or even meaningless, it is important to see what he made of them. He was convinced that the universal fluid existed, and that through its agency the brain could be brought to a state of unprecedented activity. If this heightened activity could somehow be perpetuated beyond the period of the trance, it might be possible to use cerebral physiology as a means for improving the moral and intellectual capacities of the human race. The millennial vistas were unlimited. In spite of editorial avowals, he was not really interested in descriptive physiology as such. What fascinated him was the possibility of engineering the improvement of society on the largest possible scale, not through political upheaval or by any of the radical manoeuvres which so alarmed the anxious liberals of the 1840s, but by improving the intellectual and moral faculties of the whole population. Before he became associated with mesmerism, Elliotson had been associated with Brougham's Society for the Diffusion of Useful Knowledge, with the foundation of Mechanics' Institutes, and with all those movements whereby it was hoped that social misery would be alleviated through the peaceful cultivation of the mind. In the light of these interests, the possibilities of mesmerism would obviously have been very intriguing. In place of the slow spread of useful and improving knowledge, improvements could now be pumped into society at high speed.

According to him, cerebral physiology indicated that certain people were predestined to exhibit socially unacceptable behaviour. They were victims of their own brains. Elliotson, confirmed phrenologist and President of the

London Phrenological Society, thought that it was possible to predict such tendencies by inspecting a man's skull. By combining the diagnostic finesse of phrenology with the cerebral influence of mesmerism, Elliotson supposed that criminal behaviour might be nipped in the bud. Once the location of the constructive instincts had been defined, these could be encouraged to the point where their heightened activity would outweigh any tendencies towards theft or murder. Prisons would be replaced by clinics run on phreno-mesmeric lines.

From now on Elliotson continued to practise medicine without the benefit of a hospital appointment. Although his reputation had suffered within the profession he continued to enjoy a prosperous practice and his colourful social life included eminent friends such as Dickens, Harriet Martineau and Macready. He founded a flourishing Mesmeric Clinic in Weymouth Street, and the board of this establishment included many eminent men.

In 1856 *The Zoist* ceased publication, and by all accounts Elliotson began a steady and somewhat humiliating descent into a senile and querulous old age. He was soon incapable of looking after himself and was taken into the house of one of his old students from University College. His quarrels now extended to his family, and the last few years of his life were marked by ungracious disputes with his spinster sisters. When he died in 1868 he was more or less forgotten, and the study of mesmerism had already been taken over and rationalised by scientists such as William Benjamin Carpenter and Thomas Laycock.

One by one the unmarried offspring of the Southwark druggist died, leaving neither human nor intellectual descendants. When the last surviving sister died in 1885 she left a codicil to her will which seems to express the wish to bring the Elliotson story to a quick and uninvestigated conclusion. She requested that her body should be buried with the rest of the family in the vault at Kensal Green. The door of the mausoleum was to be locked and the key thrown in through the grille.

The Samuel Gee Lecture, 1982, J. Roy. Coll. Physicians Lond., 1983,
17: 181-91

The Body in Question

An invitation in 1976 to choose some aspect of medicine as the basis for a television series that I would write and present was too good to resist. It allowed me to develop my thoughts on the history of ideas about the human body and present them to a general audience. This became *The Body in Question.*

Natural Shocks

Of all the objects in the world, the human body has a peculiar status: it is not only possessed by the person who has it, it also possesses and constitutes him. Our body is quite different from all the other things we claim as our own. We can lose money, books and even houses and still remain recognisably ourselves, but it is hard to give any intelligible sense to the idea of a disembodied person. Although we speak of our bodies as premises that we live in, it is a special form of tenancy: our body is where we can always be contacted, but our continued presence in it is more than a radical form of being a stick-in-the-mud.

Our body is not, in short, something we have, it is a large part of what we actually are: it is by and through our bodies that we recognise our existence in the world, and it is only by being able to move in and act upon the world that we can distinguish it from ourselves. Without a body, it would be difficult to claim sensations and experiences as our own. Who or what would be having them, and where would they be happening? Without a body, it would be hard to make sense of the notions of effort and failure and, since the concept of powers and their limits is built into the definition of personality, the absence of a physique through which these could readily be realised or frustrated would make it almost impossible to speak about the existence of a recognisable person.

The body is the medium of experience and the instrument of action. Through its actions we shape and organise our experiences and distinguish our perceptions of the outside world from the sensations that arise within the body itself.

Material objects make themselves apparent by the fact that we can walk around them, get different views of them and eventually arrive at the conclusion that they exist independently of our own experience of them.

We can, however, also perceive our body as if it were one object among others. We can gaze at it, touch it, grope many of its contours, as if it were another of the many items in the world's furniture. Each of us, then, has two images of the bodily self: one which is immediately felt as the source of sensation and the spring of action, and one which we see and sometimes touch. In growing up, in emerging from the 'blooming, buzzing chaos' of infancy, these two images blend with each other so that the body which we see becomes the visible manifestation of the one which we immediately feel.

Nevertheless, a moment's introspection will show how different these two images actually are.

When you close your eyes and try to think of your own shape, what you imagine (or, rather, what you feel) is quite unlike what you see when you open your eyes and look in the mirror. The image you feel is much vaguer than the one you see. And if you lie still, it is quite hard to imagine yourself as having any particular size or shape. Once you move, once you feel the weight of your limbs and the natural resistance of the objects around you, the felt image of yourself starts to become clearer, almost as if it were called into being by the sensations you create by your own actions.

The image you create for yourself has rather strange proportions: certain parts feel much larger than they look. If you poke your tongue into a hole in one of your teeth, the hole feels enormous; you are often startled by how small it looks when you inspect it in the mirror. The 'felt' self is rather like the so-called anamorphic pictures with which artists entertained themselves in the Renaissance. The most famous example is the strange object hovering like a flying saucer in the foreground of Holbein's *The Ambassadors*: it is actually a splayed-out skull, which becomes immediately recognisable as such when viewed from the right angle. During the seventeenth century artists became very skilled at creating these transformations, which, if you place a cylindrical surface on the canvas, are at once restored to their normal proportions. So it is with the felt self and the visible self.

But although the felt image may not have the shape you see in the mirror, it is much more important. It is the image through which and *in which* you recognise your physical existence in the world. In spite of its strange proportions, it is all one piece, and since it has a consistent right and left and top and bottom, it allows you to locate new sensations as and when they occur. It also allows you to find your nose in the dark, scratch itches and point to a pain.

The Ambassadors by Hans Holbein the Younger

If the felt image is impaired for any reason – if it is halved or lost, as it often is after certain strokes which wipe out recognition of one entire side – these tasks become almost impossible. What is more, it becomes hard to make sense of one's own visual appearance. If one half of the felt image is wiped out or injured, the patient ceases to recognise the affected part of his body. He finds it hard to locate sensations on that side and although he feels the examiner's touch he locates it as being on the undamaged side. He also loses his ability to make voluntary movements on the affected side even if the limb is not actually paralysed. If you throw him a pair of gloves and ask him to put them on he will glove one hand and leave the other bare. And yet he had to use the left hand in order to glove the right. The fact that he could see the ungloved hand doesn't seem to help him, and there is no reason why it should: he can no longer reconcile what he sees with what he feels. That ungloved object lying on the left may look like a hand but since there is no felt image corresponding to it why should he claim the unowned object as his?

Naturally he is puzzled by the fact that this orphan limb is attached to him but the loss of the felt image overwhelms that objection and he may resort to elaborate fictions in order to explain the anomaly, actions which are even more pronounced if the limb is also paralysed. He may claim, for example, that the nurses have stuck someone else's arm on while he wasn't looking; he may be outraged by the presence of a foreign limb in his bed and ask to have it removed; he may insist that it belongs to the doctor or that prankish medical students have introduced it from the dissecting room. One patient insisted that his twin brother was attached to his back. When one half of the body image is eclipsed in this way, the patient frequently has difficulty in acknowledging or making sense of the corresponding half of the outside world. He finds it difficult, for instance, to draw symmetrical objects such as daisies or clock faces, and tends to crowd all the petals or numerals on to one side. Such a patient may be able to tell the time between noon and six but be quite unable to read the hours between six and midnight. It is hard for him to find his way around the hospital, since he can appreciate turnings in only one direction and seems quite oblivious of the other. It is as if the world itself had suffered a partial eclipse.

An intact body image is an essential prerequisite for a full understanding of the shape of the world, which is not altogether surprising. The most inescapable experience we have is the sensation of our bodily self, and it is only in the course of growing up and acquiring skilled movements that we learn to tell the difference between the part of the world that is us and the part that is outside us And just as the shrinking Roman Empire left Latin relics in the place names of modern England – Manchester, Chester and Chichester – we leave linguistic remnants of our infant fantasy and label the world as if it were a huge body: hills have feet and brows, clocks have faces and hands, chairs have arms and legs, the sky frowns and the bosom of the ocean heaves.

Very occasionally, a patient appears to lose not just half but the whole image of his felt self, and it is then impossible for him to identify any sensations as his own. Mrs. Gradgrind's death in *Hard Times* is a wonderful example of this:

"Have you a pain, mother?"

"There's a pain somewhere in the room, but I cannot be certain that I have got it."

Before you can recognise that a sensation is yours – before you can claim it and regard it as something that has happened to you rather than to the world at large – there has to be a felt self where it can be housed. Sensations happen in a rather strange part of the world, so strange that, strictly speaking, they don't happen in the world as such – at least, not in the way that explosions happen –but in an isolated annexe called the self, and if that annexe is missing or halved the sensations float around in a sort of elsewhere. If you have a ring on your finger and your hand is resting on the table, it makes perfectly good sense to say that the ring is resting on the table too. But if you have a pain in your hand and your hand is resting on the table, it sounds very odd to say that the pain is on the table as well. Pains don't happen in hands or heads or anywhere physical; they happen in the *images* of heads or hands, and if these images are missing the sensations are homeless. The reason we talk so glibly of having pains in our heads or in our hands is because under normal circumstances the subjective image of these parts coincides with their physical existence.

This situation can be reversed: the patient can lose a limb, and retain the image of it. Patients who lose legs and arms as a result of surgery or accident often report the feeling of a 'phantom' limb. They know that the physical limb has vanished, and when they look they can see that it is no longer there. Nevertheless, they feel an image of it, and they may even have phantom pains in it. The phantom limb may seem to move – it may curl its toes, grip things, or feel its phantom nails sticking into its phantom palm. As time goes on, the phantom dwindles, but it does so in very peculiar ways. The arm part may go, leaving a maddening piece of hand waggling invisibly from the edge of the real shoulders; the hand may enlarge itself to engulf the rest of the limb.

These phantom limbs are a painful ordeal, and surgeons are often frustrated in their attempts to abolish them. It used to be thought that the sensation arose from the irritated ends of the wounded nerves, and surgeons used to cauterise these, generally to no avail. In fact, you can pursue the phantom to its source in the depths of the central nervous system, and still it persists. It is as if the brain has rehearsed the image of the limb so well that it insists on preserving the impression of something that is no longer there.

If the felt image of the physical self is in the nature of a fiction, an imaginary space which is usually occupied by the body of which it is supposed to be an imitation, where is this image housed? Where is the fiction created? If a surgeon opens the skull of a conscious patient and lightly stimulates the surface of the middle part of the parietal lobe, asking the patient to report what he feels, the patient will not mention or complain about sensations at the site of the stimulus. Instead, he will report strange tinglings in various parts of his limbs. As the needle is moved about, these sensations will alter their positions accordingly. By laboriously testing point after point, you find that the body is mapped on to the surface of the brain. It is the nervous activity of this map that creates the three-dimensional phantom we have of ourselves.

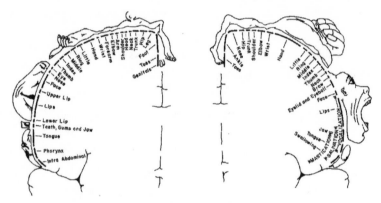

Location on the surface of the brain of sensations felt in various parts of the body

The brain map is not drawn to scale. Certain parts of the body are represented over a much wider area of brain than others, and not necessarily in proportion to their size. The face, especially the mouth, is allocated much more room than the leg; the hand, and especially the thumb, seem to have more than their fair share of space. It is like an electoral map as opposed to a geographical one. Because of their functional importance, the hand and the mouth have more sense organs per square inch than the leg or the trunk, and, since all of the parts of the body are clamouring for attention, they have many more Members representing them in their Parliament, that is to say, in the brain. This is what accounts for the strange anamorphic appearance of the felt image. The image that we see in the mirror reproduces the anatomical proportions of the body, whereas the image that we feel reproduces its Parliamentary proportions.

The electoral map is not a *picture* of the body, it is a neurological *projection* of it; that is, it is not painted on the surface of the brain, but called into existence through the nervous connections it has with the part it represents

We feel pain in the appropriate part of our felt image because there is a line of nervous connections between the sense organs in the skin and muscles and the Parliamentary representative in the brain which answers for each. If you trace the nerve fibres leading from the skin you find that they join up forming larger and larger cables as you go from the hand towards the shoulder. These cables enter the spinal cord in an orderly series of entrances. They then turn upwards and, as they make their way towards the brain they form great bundles which grow still more as they are joined by new ones entering at each level. Within these bundles the nerve fibres preserve an anatomical pattern: nerves from the leg are grouped near the centre with nerves from the arm neck and face joining them on the outside. At the top of what is called the brain stem, the sensory fibres are all collected and squeezed together, rather like the separate beams of light passing through a projector lens. After going through a section of the brain called the internal capsule, they spread out again and project themselves on to the surface of the brain. Certain important parts of the body – the heart, the liver, the kidneys – are conspicuous by their absence from the brain map. Although the map is three-dimensional, it appears to be hollow, with nothing inside: it is as if a large part of the working population had no Parliamentary representation. This is why we have no felt image of the heart or the liver. The conscious relationship we have to our internal organs is rather like the one which brain-damaged patients have to their limbs: we may *know* that we have a heart, we have been *told* that we have a liver but there is no felt image corresponding to them. Of course, patients with heart disease feel pain, and, as anyone who has had a kidney stone knows, you can get pains from the kidney, but we don't feel the pain in the heart or in the kidney because there is no felt image in which to have such sensations. All such pains are referred: they are felt by proxy in a part for which there is already a felt image, and for each organ the proxy is always the same. The pain of coronary heart disease, for example, is felt across the front of the chest, in the shoulders, arms and often in the neck and jaw. It is not felt where the heart is – slightly over to the left. The reason that other internal organs consistently choose the same Parliamentary proxy lies in the embryological origin of the organ in question and the fundamental architecture of the vertebrate body. Man and his vertebrate ancestors descended from a common stock and shared a basic plan.

If you look at the earthworm, you can see that it is pleated at regular intervals from head to tail. This is not a surface ornament. When you open the worm, you find that the animal is arranged in a longitudinal series of segments, in each of which certain organs are repeated with monotonous regularity. In each segment, for instance, there is a pair of kidney tubes and a paired nerve supply branching off right and left. This structure is laid out at an early stage in foetal development, and the pattern is repeated in all creatures which have descended from this line of ancestors.

In fish, the chevrons of muscle correspond to the serial segments of the earthworm, and if you open the spinal cord you can see that the segmental pattern is repeated in the orderly sequence of nerves. In the higher vertebrates, this arrangement has been extensively remodelled, and it is often hard to detect signs of it without making a very careful dissection. Segments coalesce and the component parts are often reshuffled to adapt the body to the life of the individual creature. For example, the wing of a bird and the forelimb of a horse are both derived from the same embryonic segments.

The nervous system, however, often preserves the ancestral pattern. Nerves exit from the spinal cord in an orderly ladder and, although these cables run together, divide and re-join, it is still possible to map their segmental distribution among the skin and muscles. During the First World War clinical neurologists compiled an atlas of segmental territories by studying gunshot wounds in the spinal cord. By charting the losses of sensation which followed known injuries to certain nerve roots, they were able to draw up a territorial diagram which, they discovered, preserved the old segmental pattern of simpler vertebrates.

In man, the nerve segments which together form the neck and the arms are also the ones where the heart appears. The result is that the nerves bringing sensations from the heart are in the same segments as the nerves which bring sensation from the neck and arm. This relationship is preserved despite the fact that in the course of foetal development the heart migrates to a position which is quite remote from its original site. It sinks down through the neck into the thorax and comes to rest on the diaphragm, whose muscles are also derived from the neck segments. But the heart maintains its ancient Parliamentary representation, despite its position in the body: the neck, arm, and upper chest continue to feel the pain for it. The same form of representation applies to all those parts which one would loosely call the 'innards'. The spleen, like the heart, develops from the same segments which give rise to the neck and upper arm, so that when someone injures this organ in a football accident he frequently feels the pain at the tip of the left shoulder. An ulcer on the back of the tongue may refer its pain to its old segmental partner in the ear. As a kidney stone travels down the ureter it refers its sensations one after another to its old segmental sites: the pain characteristically pursues a long spiral course from the loin, round the side, and down to the top of the penis.

The experience of illness can be divided into two relatively distinct types. *Symptoms* on the one hand, and *signs* on the other. A symptom is a personal experience which presents itself to the individual without having to be observed – pains, nausea, muscular weakness etc. Signs on the other hand are publicly noticeable peculiarities such as pallor, jaundice, blueness, rashes, spots, eruptions; all changes in size, shape and weight – general wasting, local swelling, enlargements and shrinkages. These are in a sense the publicly observable features of illness: they are potentially noticeable to everyone, although some of these signs are only detectable to observant experts

It is this conspicuousness that sets them apart from feelings or sensations which can be known only by the person who has them. Pain is a private experience, so is nausea, so are hunger and thirst. There are though public *signs* of these states – groans, frowns, writhings, and so forth – but the actual pain and nausea and hunger and thirst are locked up in the unfortunate sufferer. The person with jaundice has only to exhibit it, someone with a pain has to announce it. Furthermore, having pain and knowing you have it are one and the same thing. If someone insisted he had a pain he couldn't feel, we would say that he had not learnt to speak English properly.

Sensations or feelings are also distinguished by the fact that there is no intelligible answer to the question 'What do you recognise them *with*?' You recognise swellings or rashes with your eyes, but you don't recognise pain *with* anything.

It is obvious that a sense organ must be involved at some point in the proceedings. Why aren't we aware of this?

The answer is that the sense organs involved are very small and inconspicuous. The nerve endings which register these sensations are embroidered like millions of seed-pearls throughout the fabric of our body. With the help of a microscope you can find them in the skin, in the muscles and ligaments, in the walls of the blood vessels and in the membranes that line the abdominal cavity. If you link up their nerve fibres to an electronic recording device, you will see that they are constantly registering changes in their immediate environment, but they are much too small to be seen with the naked eye, and in any case, they are tucked away in inaccessible places.

There are however three visible sense organs – ones that we can see by looking in a mirror. But although we are acquainted with their appearance the extent to which we understand the way in which they afford us the experience of vision, hearing and smell is still remarkably limited. Take eyesight for example. How is it that when we open our eyes in the morning we are immediately acquainted with a three dimensional vista beyond us. In other words although we see with our eyes, that is not where we see the world, and what we still don't quite understand is the way in which we exercise visual attention – what is it that determines that at one moment we can fail to see one aspect of what we are looking at and without changing our gaze see something which we failed to notice a moment before?

The fact that a sense organ is visible is much less important than the fact that we can control its performance, choosing and influencing the sensations we obtain. What makes us appreciate the visual function of our own eyes is not the fact that we can see that they are on either side of our nose, but that we can choose what we see through them: we can shade our eyes and reduce the glare; we can screw them up and blur what we see; we can close them and extinguish sight altogether; we can swivel our gaze this way and that, enlarging and exploring the visual field and most significantly of all we can attend to different aspects of what we already have in view. Our ears are much less manoeuvrable than our eyes, but we can still muffle and sharpen our hearing at will; we can locate noises by rearranging the attitude of our head and as with vision we can switch our auditory attention from one thing to another.

Of all our external senses, touch is the one in which action plays the most important part. Although the nerve endings are invisible, the fact that they are mounted on a mobile surface means that we can choose how and when they will be stimulated. We can squeeze them into action by gripping, stroking and poking; instead of having to wait for the world to touch us, we can reach out and obtain sensations when we choose. If we were completely immobilised – if all our touch sensations were imposed on us, and we were unable to take any action either to obtain or avoid them – the experience would be almost exactly like that of internal pain.

Although it would be difficult to give an intelligible answer to the question 'What do we feel pain with?', it would be even harder to make sense of someone who claimed to have a pain but was unable to say where it was. As we have seen, sensations are sometimes referred away from the place where the mischief is, but they are always located somewhere: they have a distinct and characteristic site, even if it is misleading.

Naturally, some pains – those we call 'pricks', 'stabs' and 'shoots', for instance – are more sharply located than others. Those we call 'aches' tend to have a woolly, voluminous feeling without any sharp outline. But even the vaguest pain can be pointed to, although you may have to use your whole hand rather than the tip of your finger. In fact, a lot can be learnt about a pain from the way in which the patient points to it. Apart from saying something about where it is, the movement of the hand is often a tell-tale sign of its quality: if someone has angina, he often presses the front of his chest with a clenched list; the whole fist shows that the pain is widespread; the fact that the hand is clenched tells us the pain has a gripping quality. The pain from peptic ulcer is often closely localised, and the patient usually tells you so by delicately pointing to it with the tip of his index finger. When a stone lodges in the outlet to the kidney, the pain, as we have seen, tends to radiate in a long oblique line from the loin to the groin. Even if the patient doesn't describe this movement in words, he will sometimes do so by holding his side with the thumb at the back and the fingers pointing down at the front. If a pain is more or less superficial – what would normally be called soreness – the patient may lightly brush the surface of the skin with the outstretched tips of all five fingers. This sometimes happens in the early stages of shingles. The skilled physician can learn a lot from the pantomime of complaint.

Although it is hard to imagine an unlocated pain, there are strong sensations or feelings which are not recognisably associated with a particular part of the body. It is very hard to say where you feel nausea, for example. If you ask people, they often simply say that it is what they feel when they know they are going to be sick. But what about people who have never been sick? What do they feel?

The problem of location becomes even more puzzling with experiences like hunger or thirst. Thirsty people usually complain about a dry mouth, but if that were all there was to it, the feeling of thirst would be wiped out at the first mouthful of water, and it isn't, as a very elegant experiment has proved. If the gullet of a dog is taken out through its neck and the dog is made thirsty, it will continue to gulp water incessantly for twenty-four hours. It never relieves its thirst. The same difficulty applies to hunger: although there are abdominal pangs associated with extreme hunger, the sensation of craving for food has no definite location. We now know that thirst and hunger are due to changes in the chemistry of the blood and that these are registered by sense organs in the brain. However, one doesn't feel hunger either in the blood or the brain – one simply feels it, and that is that.

Up to this point I have dealt with two of the major categories of pathological experience: findings and feelings. Now we come to the third and last category, that of experiences which can be conveniently grouped under the single heading 'failings', that is, errors of *performance*. Some of these are experienced as if they were feelings, but do not fit quite comfortably into that group: numbness, for instance, blurred vision, and hardness of hearing. Most people would call numbness a sensation, but unlike pain it is not really a sensation in its own right: it is the feeling you get when the normal feeling of touch is not working properly. If you think of the body as a map, pain is like a stain on the surface of the map, and numbness a drop of bleach. In the case of pain you are adding a feature to the map; in the case of numbness you are removing the possibility of it happening. This also applies to blurring of vision, which you can have only by trying to see normally. It is a comparative sensation – just as deafness is. For that reason, numbness, blurring of vision and hardness of hearing should be regarded as failures of performance, more closely related to symptoms like paralysis and tremor than they are to sensations like pain or itch. Although paralysis is an observable sign, the patient experiences it as an unexpected failure of part of what he regards as his normal repertoire of powers.

All errors of performance – failures of sense organs on the one hand, and straightforward failures of mechanical power on the other – are comparatively simple. But human performance can fail in much more elaborate ways, on both the sensory and the executive side. Patients with serious forms of brain injury often show dramatic errors in their sensory performance, in spite of the fact that their eyes, ears and hands are intact. If a patient has received an injury to that part of the brain which classifies, judges and criticises the information provided by the eyes, he will fail to recognise an object which is presented to him in a visual form, although he promptly identifies it when it is placed in his hand. With another type of injury, the patient is quite unable to make sense of the familiar object placed in his hand, but accurately names it as soon as he opens his eyes. Such failures of recognition form a large class of illnesses which go under the general name of agnosia – failures to make sense of what the senses provide. A comparable failure, known as apraxia, occurs when the link between the understanding of the request and the action that fulfils it has been broken. Patients whose muscles are in perfect working order – who automatically groom and dress themselves – fail to obey simple orders although they appreciate what they have been asked to do and have the muscular wherewithal to do it.

Language can also fail as a result of disease, and the character of the failure depends on whether it breaks down at the level where it is uttered, or at the point where the utterance is conceived. A local paralysis of the vocal chords may render someone completely silent, but his mastery of language remains unimpaired: he can still convey his thought by means of writing and make graceful and eloquent use of sign language.

The same is true of disturbances of articulation: speech may be slurred, staccato or, as in certain cases of multiple sclerosis, may acquire a strange syllabic rhythm – so-called 'scanning' speech – but the patient's linguistic competence remains intact. However, if the damage occurs at a higher level, as it does in strokes, the patient may suffer from one of the various forms of *aphasia,* the inability to express himself linguistically. The neuromuscular apparatus of the voice and tongue may be intact, but he cannot put his thoughts into words. By examining the brains of such patients at post-mortems, neurologists discovered that this happens when people suffer a haemorrhage on the left side of the brain which shows that the linguistic centres are localised in one particular part of the brain.

Memory, too, may fail as the result of brain damage. Acute head injuries, for instance, can rob the patient of any memory of the events immediately leading up to the accident. A crash victim may recall everything up to the point where he opened his garage door in the morning, but be quite unable to remember what happened next. Or the defect may be much more diffuse. Slowly developing brain damage, due to arteriosclerosis or chronic alcoholism, can cause a widespread impairment, and the patient may find it impossible to retain the simplest facts: engagements, dates, names and ideas; he may not know where he is or even who he is. In some cases he may try to cover this up by inventing florid and plausible details – a combination of amnesia and confabulation which is known as the Korsakov Syndrome. Although some neurologists insist that the confabulation is just another aspect of the patient's mental confusion, there are others who claim that it illustrates a natural tendency of the brain to complete or fill in unaccountable gaps in experience.

Failures of performance are not confined to neurological diseases. A person's performance can falter in a large number of alternative ways. Under normal circumstances, for instance, one expects to be able to empty one's bladder as soon as it is felt to be full. The evacuation starts promptly, continues fluently and finishes conclusively – and one doesn't expect it to leak in between. However, when the outlet from the bladder is partially obstructed, as it sometimes is by an enlarged prostate, a patient's ordinary performance begins to fail: he may have difficulty in starting, the stream is feeble and hesitating, and he is unable to finish off, so that he continues to dribble. A normal function has become inefficient, and it is this inefficiency which makes him complain. Conversely, the failure may be one of containment rather than evacuation. A normal bladder can retain its contents even when the pressure is high, but if the muscular outlet is weakened, as it sometimes is after a mismanaged or strenuous childbirth, the patient may suffer from stress incontinence. Coughing, sneezing or laughing will overcome the normal efficiency of the intact sphincter, and the patient will wet herself.

The trio of findings, feelings and failings covers most of the ways in which disease can make itself known, but there are certain episodes which don't fit comfortably into any of these three categories. One would hardly, for instance, call vomiting a 'finding'; and, although it is preceded by a feeling and accompanied by some unpleasant sensations while it is going on, it is quite clearly an incident in its own right. On the other hand, one wouldn't want to call it a failure of performance either, since it is not something which one could do better. It is a performance, a physiological competence which accompanies illness and represents the body's attempt to overcome it. We should be in trouble if we couldn't vomit. The same principle applies to coughing and diarrhoea, which, like vomiting, are attempts on the part of the body to rid itself of irritants, infections or poisons.

Sudden haemorrhage is different. It may present itself as a finding, it can result in a feeling, but one can't really regard it as a failure of performance. Perhaps one should simply regard it as an eruption – something which bursts upon the scene, creating anxiety and terror.

One of the most peculiar experiences is convulsion. Although such episodes usually originate in the nervous system, they are not failures of performance: they may *interrupt* performances and in a sense even be performances. Nervous tremors or tics vitiate the movements which they accompany, whereas convulsions interrupt the flow of life by compelling the patient to do things he would prefer not to: perhaps we should call them 'compulsions', or 'brief tyrannies'.

These, then, are the experiences which make up the concept of illness: the 'natural shocks that flesh is heir to'. The attention that is given to them, however, and the actions to which they give rise depend on the person to whom they are happening. A large, unsightly lump may pass unnoticed by one person, while a small swelling can cause great alarm in someone else; a pain which is played down by one person can cause another to cry out; a vain man with a well-lit mirror will often recognise the first tinge of jaundice, whilst a more complacent person might have to turn bright yellow before he became aware of a colour change. Some people are simply more stoical. People who have been trained to look out for abnormal signs – such as medical students – tend to be hypochondriacal. Fear also plays an important part both in alerting and in blinding people to the possibility of illness: someone who is over-anxious about his health tends either to recognise signs and symptoms which his neighbour would overlook altogether, or to avoid examining himself for fear of finding out the worst.

The patient's command of language is also influential in the experience of illness. Patients with a small vocabulary may be at a loss to describe their feelings, even to themselves – and when someone hasn't got a name for something, it is much easier for him to neglect or forget it. But even when the patient is comparatively articulate, the doctor can never be sure just how he is using words. It is particularly hard when it comes to feelings – aches, pains and itches – where the witness has no way of sharing the experience. One of the ways in which we try to overcome this problem is by mentioning the type of accident or injury which might produce a pain of that sort. We talk about stabbing pains or scorching pains or heartburn, or we say that a pain is like being squeezed in a vice.

But there are drawbacks to using language in this way. How many people have actually been stabbed? It is all very well to try to imagine what it might be like, but if neither of us has ever been stabbed, I may imagine something completely different from you. In fact, it is surprising that there is as much agreement as there is: when people talk about stabbing pains they are usually referring to sensations which come and go with great speed and violence. Presumably the patient has abstracted from his *idea* of stabbing an image of violent penetration which he uses in a metaphorical way to refer to his own pain. Oddly enough, people who have actually been stabbed rarely talk about the pain in this way. And vice versa: the events which cause a so-called stabbing pain are not actually stabs. Similarly, when someone talks about a bursting headache you don't necessarily expect to find something bursting inside his skull. In fact, when a blood vessel does burst inside the head, patients usually describe the pain as a blow rather than an explosion: 'I felt as if I'd been struck on the back of the head by a bat,' they often say.

So the quality of the pain is not always a reliable picture of what is happening inside, just as the place where the patient feels the pain is not necessarily the seat of the mischief. In fact, compared to our knowledge of the external world, we have a very limited acquaintance with our own physique. Close as it is, we know much less about it than about anything else. In the normal course of events all we can feel is the vague mass of our head, trunk and limbs. As the day goes on, we forget about the clothes on our back, and when we do become conscious of our own surface it is usually because it has been assaulted by unexpected sensations. And the feelings we get are almost invariably ascribed to the outside events which are responsible: for instance, if you pick up a pencil, what you feel is an object of a certain weight, size and shape – you are not aware of the dimples in the tip of your finger. Exertion or effort can strengthen the feelings of joint and muscle, but no one is aware of the individual muscles involved in clenching one's fist.

This state of affairs is not just a regrettable accident, however: we cannot expect any improvement. Our nervous system is designed to emphasise what's going on in the outside world; our intelligence faces outwards, and our survival depends on the way in which we appreciate the threats and opportunities of the world beyond. It is as if our bodies formed a political state in which the Prime Minister or President takes over the portfolio of the Foreign Secretary, leaving the conduct of Domestic Affairs to a Home Secretary who works independently, supervising all the necessary changes and adjustments without having to refer to the highest office.

The inside of the body – blood vessels, heart, intestine, lungs and bladder – is literally studded with instruments capable of registering changes in pressure, temperature and chemical composition. But none of these meters has any dials: they are not meant to be read by human consciousness, but are linked up with the reflex systems which obey automatically. Although you can sometimes, when the variations are extreme, become aware of the adjustments going on inside, most of the time you are quite unconscious of the hectic activity. When you start to exercise, your heart automatically speeds up in order to supply the working muscles with the blood they need. But you don't make the decision to speed up your heart. You simply choose to run, and the reflex arrangements automatically take care of the rest. And when you stop running, you don't have to remember to switch off your heart: as the sensory messages stop arriving from the muscles, the heart begins to slow down automatically; one of the first signs that something is wrong with the circulation is that it takes the heart longer than normal to slow down after exercise.

This principle applies most of all to systems which have a closed cycle: the circulation of the blood, for instance, which follows an unbroken sequence without coming into immediate contact with the outside world; the blood vessels are constantly adjusting themselves, redistributing blood from the skin, the muscles and so forth. When you need to lose heat, the radiators of the skin flush with warm blood, whereas when you need to conserve heat, the blood vessels contract and the skin whitens and cools. You can sometimes feel the results of all this, but you are not actually conscious of the act of contraction or expansion. You can't blush at will.

Certain cycles, however, open directly into the outside world, and in these cases we are made aware of the sensations in order to introduce voluntary control of what happens. Take the urinary system. The kidneys manufacture urine from the blood, following biochemical instructions which never enter our consciousness. If the body is short of water for some reason, the urine is automatically reduced in volume and becomes more concentrated. If it is short of salt, the kidneys reabsorb as much as they can. The blood is continually being monitored or tasted by sense organs linked up to systems which do everything they can to maintain the *status quo*. All this is quite automatic: the urine sweeps into the bladder through the ureter, and, although there are muscles to help it on its way, we are quite unaware of their action. In animals which live in the sea, the urine can flow straight out into the environment without the animal having to pay any attention.

Such carelessness isn't possible on dry land: an unsupervised flow of urine would soon ulcerate the skin, and before long, infections would backtrack into the ureter. Land animals have therefore developed a muscular reservoir for holding the urine until it can be thrown clear in one go. In lower animals, this act is more or less automatic, but in animals like cats and dogs the sensations of a full bladder arouse enough of their attention to cause them quite complicated behaviour, and in species which live in communities, like ours, the part played by consciousness is even more important. What happens is this: the urine accumulates unnoticed until the pressure begins to stretch small sense organs embedded in the wall of the bladder; in an untrained infant, these impulses bring about an automatic reflex; in an adult, the sensations rise into consciousness, and etiquette takes care of the rest. In patients suffering from a broken back, the messages between bladder and brain are interrupted, and their urine accumulates until it reaches a critical pressure, at which point the bladder opens automatically, regardless of where the patient happens to be, The same principle of dual control applies to the intestine, except that this system is open to negotiation at two ends. Although it is automatic throughout its huge length, it still has to be filled and emptied at the right moment, and at both points this involves a conscious transaction with the world. The feelings of hunger and taste allow us to negotiate for the right meal, whereas the sensation of a full rectum reminds us when to visit the lavatory. Between these two archways of conscious sensation lies the vast unconscious Amazon of the intestine. All its movements are quite automatic. (Which is just as well – imagine what it would be like if you had to supervise the passage of food through its whole length.) Fortunately, the muscles of the intestine move of their own accord, and the peristaltic waves follow one another in an orderly fashion.

But we have to pay a price for this labour-saving efficiency. When anything goes wrong, neither the quality nor the location of the sensation tells us what is happening. A kidney stone, for instance, produces an agonising pain, but unless you have had it before and know that this is the sort of pain you get with a stone, you are almost bound to be mystified by it. In one way or another, this applies to all our innards – heart, lungs, intestines. In emergencies, the sensations and feelings may be extremely vivid and can in fact monopolise our attention altogether, but the feelings we get are almost entirely uninformative. Designed to work without conscious instruction, these interior systems are at a loss for words when they try to speak up for themselves. And, to make it worse, the vocabulary of internal sensation is so small that several illnesses have to share the same feelings. Breathlessness may be the result of anaemia, pneumonia or heart failure. A bad internal haemorrhage with concealed loss of blood produces symptoms almost indistinguishable from a sudden fall in blood sugar. Nausea may arise from food poisoning, kidney failure, appendicitis, brain tumour or migraine.

Although our experience of our body is so vague and muddy, our mind does everything it can to intensify the images with which it is supplied – like the computers which sharpen the pictures sent from distant planets. In the absence of any immediate knowledge of our own insides, most of us have improvised an imaginary picture in the hope of explaining the occasional feelings which escape into consciousness. Our mind, it seems, prefers a picture of some sort to having to live through the chaos of sensations that would otherwise seem absurd.

To some extent, this applies to all our experience. One way or another, our senses introduce us to a world, and not just to a kaleidoscope of sensations. The visual world, for example, is not just a patchwork of tints although that is all there is on our retina. A blotch of green on a rural horizon is usually seen as a tree. It may turn out to be something else – a painted barn or a group of camouflaged soldiers – and until the issue is settled one way or another we alternate between these interpretations. But we never stick half-way and see what is actually on our retina. In the very act of entering consciousness, sensations are somehow made up into scenery and we experience them as objects in a world. But this doesn't happen automatically. The mind has to make a guess about the identity of what it sees, hears or feels, and the odds are determined by all sorts of hints and hot tips. There is a well-known painting by Salvador Dali, called *Slave Market with the Disappearing Bust of Voltaire,* which shows this process very neatly.

What appears to be a group of Dutch courtiers jumps into sharp relief as a bust of Voltaire, particularly if the idea of the bust is planted. By a strong effort of the will – whatever that means – the spectator may be able to wipe out the face and restore the courtiers. But it is hard to hold your vision mid-way and see the picture just as it strikes your retina. This principle also applies to our conception of our own internal world although here the patterns are much less coherent and picturesque. We talk about feeling liverish or having heartburn or chills on the kidney, but all these visceral images have to be invented, and our only source of information for the inventions is what we have been told. We reconstruct our insides from pictures in advertisements for patent medicines, from half-remembered school science, from pieces of offal on butchers' slabs and all sorts of medical folklore.

These promptings may account for the otherwise inexplicable fact that the French seem to have far more trouble with their liver than the English do. It is hard to believe that this organ is so much more threatened in France than it is in England even allowing for what we have been told about their drinking habits. It seems more reasonable to assume that the French interpret their symptoms in the light of a national fantasy about the liver and unconsciously reshape their sensations in terms of this phantom organ. The English, on the other hand, are obsessed with their bowels. When an Englishman complains about constipation, you never know whether he is talking about his regularity, his lassitude, his headaches, or his depression. Once an organ gains a hold on the collective imagination, its influence is almost invariably exaggerated, and a wide range of symptoms are explained in terms of it.

The experience of friends and neighbours also plays a large part in the editing of sensations. If someone we know has heart trouble, it is only too easy to reshape our own sensations until they come to resemble his. Most of us have scattered pains in and around the chest at some time or another, and, unless we are abnormally sensitive, we disregard them. But if one of our friends or relatives is known to have something wrong with his heart, these otherwise scattered sensations grow together and easily assume the shape and permanence of the rumoured pain.

Almost invariably it is the sufferer who shapes the experience of illness into an intelligible situation. At some level or other suffering gives way to a personal diagnosis. In the end the victim becomes a patient because he guesses that something is wrong or odd about him and that he is the unwilling victim of this process.

From the instant when someone first recognises his symptoms to the moment when he eventually complains about them, there is always an interval, longer or shorter as the case may be, when he argues with himself about whether it is worth making his complaint known to an expert. Naturally, it varies from symptom to symptom: someone who recognises that he is steadily losing weight measures this by a different standard from the one he would apply to a headache; the thoughts aroused by a painless swelling on the cheek are not the same as the intense irritation caused by an itching rash on the hand; when someone eventually decides to complain about increasing breathlessness he has rated himself on a different scale from the one he would use if he had blood in his water.

There are four independent scales which can be applied to a symptom to decide whether or not it demands attention. First, there is the symptom's intrinsic nastiness. Pain is intrinsically nasty, and most people would agree that nausea is, as well. The straightforward feeling of having either of these symptoms is quite enough to make you wish you hadn't.

In contrast to these, there are symptoms whose nastiness has to be inferred. The painless appearance of blood in the urine is not obviously unpleasant as a thing in itself. It is unsettling not because it causes discomfort, but because it carries alarming implications. The same principle applies to a painless, invisible lump in the breast.

Symptoms are also complained about because they reduce efficiency or restrict freedom of action. A patient who becomes steadily more breathless when he exerts himself eventually complains because he is frustrated by the way in which this cuts down his movements. It is not the feeling of breathlessness as such, but the results of it which lead him to complain. This also applies to tremor or muscular weakness of one kind or another: unless they come on rapidly enough to cause immediate suffering or alarm, they excite complaint because of the frustration they cause.

Finally, there is the question of embarrassment or shame. Patients may complain about a symptom simply because they regard it as unseemly. A painless blemish on the mouth can bring a patient to the clinic much sooner than a large, painful lesion on the shin. This applies to any publicly noticeable anomaly – a squint, drooping eyelid, harelip, rash, loud intestinal noises, hoarseness – which seems to threaten the patient's self-esteem and which might be regarded as a stigma.

Obviously, a symptom can appear on more than one scale – perhaps on all four. The pain associated with cystitis – infection of the bladder – is extremely unpleasant in its own right, so it scores quite high on the intrinsic nastiness scale. On the other hand, it poses no threat to life, so that although it may excruciate the patient it doesn't actually alarm her. However, patients who suffer from severe cystitis know only too well how much it limits their freedom of action: long journeys are almost inconceivable, and while the illness lasts the unfortunate patient tends to hover within easy reach of a lavatory. So it gets a high score on the incapacity scale, and since it alters the patient's behaviour in what she regards as a noticeable way, it also gets a substantial score in terms of stigma and shame.

Angina is a pain that is unquestionably nasty, and since most people have learnt to associate it with the heart they are often alarmed by it as well. But greater perhaps than the discomfort and alarm is the sheer frustration of being brought to a standstill after walking less than 100 yards. It may be exasperation that eventually drives the patient to a doctor.

Breathlessness is an even more interesting example. It is more or less unpleasant in itself and if the patient associates the symptom with his heart or his lungs he may also be alarmed by it. But, as with angina, the sense of incapacity may weigh most heavily, and if the patient prides himself on being able-bodied he may experience an intolerable sense of shame when his friends or colleagues leave him panting on a short stroll. However, if it comes on very rapidly or very severely, the scale changes. Someone who is awakened at night by an attack of paroxysmal breathlessness finds the feeling almost insufferable in itself so that it now hits the very top of the intrinsic nastiness scale. Since most people would interpret it as a serious threat to life, it notches up a heavy score in terms of sheer alarm as well. And when breathlessness is extreme, the patient is often bed-ridden, so it also appears very high up on the incapacity scale. However, anyone preoccupied with drawing his next breath has very little time to feel ashamed of it, so that it doesn't even appear on the stigma scale, although a sense of shame and embarrassment can survive even the most fearful emergency – I can remember patients struggling for breath, waving a weak apology for what they obviously regarded as humiliating panic.

Elderly patients often expect to have shaky hands, and if they develop a tremor, as long as they have no reason to suspect a sinister cause, they are simply frustrated, since it makes it hard for them to dress and feed themselves. But even elderly patients may be embarrassed by their tremor: they are ashamed of not being able to help themselves and also imagine that people will think they are stupid or odd or even drunk. Once again the way in which this symptom is rated depends on other factors: its severity or the age of the victim at the onset. I can remember a patient who developed a spectacular tremor at the age of forty as the result of breathing in mercury fumes. This is the illness they used to call Hatter's Shakes because of the mercury which was used to dress the felt (I think it is probably the reason why the Mad Hatter *Alice in Wonderland* is shown with a large chunk bitten out of his teacup) My patient said that there was nothing intrinsically nasty about the shakes, and since he had no reason to associate them with a dangerous industrial poison he wasn't even alarmed by them. But he was seriously incapacitated by his tremor and what worried him most was the fact that it stopped him going to work – luckily for him, as it turned out. He was also embarrassed by his clumsiness.

To sum up, then. At one time or another we have all been irked by aches and pains. We have probably noticed alterations in weight, complexion and bodily function, changes in power, capability and will, unaccountable shifts of mood. But on the whole we treat these like changes in the weather: as part and parcel of living in an imperfect world. The changes they cause in our behaviour are barely noticeable – not inconvenient enough to interfere with our routine. We may retreat a little, fall silent, sigh, rub our heads, retire early, drink glasses of water, eat less, walk more, miss a meal here and there, avoid fried foods, and so on and so on. But sometimes the discomfort, alarm, embarrassment or inconvenience begin to obstruct the flow of ordinary life; in place of modest well-being, life becomes so intolerably awkward, strenuous or frightening that we fall ill.

Falling ill is not something that happens to us, it is a choice we make as a result of things happening to us. It is an action we take when we feel unacceptably odd. Obviously there are times when this choice is taken out of the victim's hands: he may be so overwhelmed by events that he plays no active part in what happens next and is brought to the doctor by friends or relatives, stricken and helpless. But this is rare. Most people who fall ill have chosen to cast themselves in the role of patient. Viewing their unfortunate situation they see themselves as sick people and begin to act differently.

Usually this is a prelude to seeking expert advice, but falling ill can sometimes be performed as a solo act. In New Guinea, for example, the decision to fall ill is almost invariably followed by a consistent and easily recognised form of behaviour. The sufferer withdraws from the community and retires into his hut: he strips himself naked, smears himself with ash and dust, and lies down in the darkness. He also changes his tone of voice: when his friends and relatives make solicitous enquiries, he answers them in a quavering falsetto.

Such people are not merely suffering illness: they are performing it, thereby announcing both to themselves and to the community that they are sick people in need of care and attention. In New Guinea this is such a well-recognised form of behaviour that one is tempted to regard it as a formal ritual. Something similar, however, can often be found in more sophisticated communities. When someone falls ill but is not yet ready to summon expert help, he usually takes care to advertise his condition through the medium of a performance. In fact, such a performance is often demanded of him by those with whom he lives. Someone who takes to his bed when he has a sick headache, for instance, is not entirely prompted by the need for relief. It is a way of boosting his credibility as a sick person, and it may be the only way of getting the attention and concern which he thinks he deserves. In fact, the patient may have to abstain from activities he is quite capable of performing, if only to convince those around him that there is a good reason for his staying away from work.

A patient, then, is a special sort of person, rather like a recruit or a convert or a bride. By taking on the role of patient you change your social identity, turning yourself from someone who helps himself into someone who accepts the orders, routine and advice of qualified experts. You submit to the rules and recommendations of a profession, just as a novice submits to the rules and recommendations of his or her chosen order. Ordinary life is full of such voluntary transitions – changes of social role or status which are accompanied by corresponding changes in obligation and expectation. Whenever these take place, they are accompanied by rituals which mark the event and make it clearly recognisable to all who are involved. The anthropologists have called these 'rites of passage', symbolic actions which represent and dramatise significant changes in social status: they include baptisms, immersions, confirmations, all sorts of melodramatic initiations and humiliating ordeals, such as strippings, shavings, scarrings. Whenever we cross a threshold from one social role to another we take pains to advertise the fact with ceremonies which represent it in terms of vivid and memorable images.

The idea of 'rites of passage' was first introduced by the French anthropologist Arnold Van Gennep in 1909. Van Gennep insisted that all rituals of 'passing through' occurred in three successive phases: a rite of separation, a rite of transition and a rite of aggregation. The person whose status is to be changed has to undergo a ritual which marks his departure from the old version of himself: there has to be some act which symbolises the fact that he has rid himself of all his previous associations. He is washed, rinsed, sprinkled or immersed, and, in this way, all his previous obligations and attachments are symbolically untied and even annihilated.

This stage is followed by a rite of transition, when the person is neither fish nor fowl; he has left his old status behind him but has not yet assumed his new one. This liminal condition is usually marked by rituals of isolation and segregation – a period of vigil, mockery perhaps, fear and trembling. There are often elaborate rites of humiliation – scourging, insults, and darkness. Finally, in the rite of aggregation, the new status is ritually conferred: the person is admitted, enrolled, confirmed and ordained.

This idea can be applied to the process of becoming a patient. The fact that most of the procedures involved have a rational and practical explanation doesn't prevent them from playing a very important symbolic role as well. Although one can readily understand most of what happens to someone on entering hospital in utilitarian terms, there is no doubt that both the patient and the doctor experience some of these manoeuvres as symbolic transformations. Once someone has chosen to fall ill he has to apply for the role of patient: he auditions for the part by reciting his complaint as vividly and as convincingly as he can. This can also be seen in terms of religious confirmation. The candidate submits himself to a formal questionnaire in order to satisfy the examiner that he is a suitable person to be enrolled. If he passes the preliminary test he has to undertake the initial rites of separation. He is undressed, washed, and until quite recently, he often had to submit himself to a cleansing enema. Then come the rites of transition. No longer a person in the ordinary world, he is not yet formally accepted by his fellow patients – anxious and isolated in his novice pyjamas, he awaits the formal act of aggregation. He is introduced to the ward sister, hands over his street clothes, submits to a questionnaire by the houseman and registrar. Dressed with all the dignified credentials of a formally admitted patient, he awaits the forthcoming event.

Chapter 1 of The Body in Question, Jonathan Cape, 1978

States of Mind

Eight years after *The Body in Question* I was able to continue my interest in the history of ideas when the BBC agreed to broadcast a television series in which I discussed various aspects of the human mind. The distinguished individuals – philosophers, psychologists, anthropologists, clinicians and historians – who generously submitted themselves to my impudent enquiries included Ernst Gombrich, one of the greatest figures in the history of twentieth century thought, whose unique acquaintance with art history and experimental psychology was most vividly represented in his great work entitled *Art and Illusion*.

Interview with Sir Ernst Gombrich

In a lecture which he gave at the Royal Society in 1974 Professor Gombrich recalls his Sunday walks in his native city of Vienna, where the Museum of Natural History and the Museum of Art History confront one another on opposite sides of the square. He remembers his eagerness to visit the Museum of Science, and points out that it was only later that he frequently took the turn to the right and 'got stuck, as it were' in the Museum of Art History. It turns out, however, that Sir Ernst Gombrich never 'got stuck' at all, and that although he went on to become one of Europe's most distinguished art historians he never lost his original interest in science. In *Art and Illusion* he triumphantly reconciled his two concerns by dealing with the psychology of visual representation. As soon as it was published in 1956, *Art and Illusion* was universally recognised as an intellectual landmark, and since then any serious discussion of pictorial representation has had to take Gombrich's argument as its starting point.

According to Sir Ernst Gombrich, the task of setting down a pictorial likeness on a flat surface bears a startling resemblance to the method used by scientists in arriving at a theoretical picture of the natural world. In representing the appearance of things the artist does not simply trace an outline of their visual contours, but prepares instead a hypothetical construction to be matched and then modified in the light of further experience. Through an alternating sequence of 'makings and matchings' the artist gradually eliminates the discrepancies between what is seen and what is drawn, until the image on the flat surface begins to resemble a view of the world as it might be seen through a transparent pane of glass.

Gombrich's representation of picture-making coincides very closely with Karl Popper's conclusions about the construction of scientific theories. The 'makings and matchings' of the artist correspond to the 'conjectures and refutations' of the natural scientist. Both of these arguments coincide in their turn with Professor Gregory's views about the constructional character of visual perception. In all three we witness one of the most important aspects of the revolution that has recently taken place in the philosophy of mind. The traditional picture of the mind as a mirror of nature has given way to one in which active conjecture plays a leading role.

INTERVIEW

MILLER: In England where art and science are visualised as being at opposite poles it comes as rather a surprise to find an art historian considering the physiology and psychology of vision. So I'd like to start by asking you how and when you first moved from the consideration of the artefacts of art to a consideration of the way in which the artefacts of art illustrated something about the way in which we see and the way in which we represent the world around us.

GOMBRICH: Well, as you know, I studied the history of art in Vienna and the Viennese school of art history has always leaned towards a scientific, rational approach towards art. The great Alois Riegl, who wrote around the turn of the century, tried to explain the development of style in terms of various modes of perception; you may remember that Bernard Berenson talks of 'tactile values' in painting. Riegl thought that in the age of the impressionists the whole history of art had moved from touch to purely optical sensations. I don't believe that he was right but you can see that this is an angle which prepares for my direction of interest.

Now I was lucky at the time when I studied to be asked by a friend, Ernst Kris, who was keeper at the Kunsthistorisches Museum and also a disciple of Freud, and editor of *Imago*, to join him in an investigation of the history of caricature; and caricature, of course, raises many psychological problems, including problems of perception. So I was introduced very early in my life to the general problems of images rather than of great works of art; after all, nobody would claim that every successful caricature is also a great work of art.

When I came from Austria to England in 1936, I joined the Warburg Institute which concerned itself no less with the symbolic meaning of humble images than with that of great works of art. When, later, I did war work in the BBC Monitoring Service, the problems of perception, at that time of auditory perception, impinged very directly on my work of listening to broadcasts, and on the relation between what one knows, what one expects, what one believes to hear and what one actually hears. All these things were our daily bread, as it were, and having started with interests of this kind, of course I pursued them. So when I returned to the Warburg Institute and to my previous work, it was natural that I asked myself these questions with ever greater urgency. What actually is going on in the development of a naturalistic or realistic style? This was the subject I chose for the Mellon Lectures in 1956, which turned into the book *Art and Illusion*.

MILLER: And in *Art and Illusion*, if I can try to summarise the thesis, you proposed the idea that we do not have an 'innocent eye' that produces the image, which we then merely copy on to paper when we make art.

GOMBRICH: Yes, that was one of my main points. To compare the eye with the camera, which seems so obvious, is certainly misleading. We all know that painting or drawing has to be taught, that nobody who hasn't learnt it can produce a naturalistic image, a portrait or a topographical view, even though this is infinitely easier for us today than it once was, because we see images and photographs all around us. Before these aids or models came into being it was certainly very difficult to create a naturalistic image. So the first question I had to ask was how this skill was acquired in a learning process extending over centuries.

MILLER: But you point out also that there is a sort of spectrum which extends from what one would call the conventional representation of the outside world to the naturalistic. Now perhaps we could try and illustrate what is meant by the distinction between the purely conventional and the so-called naturalistic. Let us take some well-known symbols. These are conventional representations, in the sense that there is no resemblance between them and a woman and man, But nevertheless they can be read as standing for the two sexes.

GOMBRICH: These, if I may interrupt, are old astrological symbols for Mars and Venus which were very recently adapted for modern purposes but which had been adopted by biologists a little earlier.

MILLER: Yes, and yet there is absolutely no point of resemblance, no isomorphism, between these.

GOMBRICH: Well, I don't want to go into this in too much detail but there may be an element of isomorphism here after all. They might be less easily remembered if you switched them round.

MILLER: Well let's go, then, to the next stage. We have here something which is a great deal nearer to the visible difference between men and women than the conventionalised astrological signs, although no one would pretend that they were actual illustrations of men and women.

GOMBRICH: They show what in language are called distinctive features and it is these distinctive features which allow one to choose the right door in this particular situation.

MILLER: So in other words what's important about them is not so much the specific appearance of any one, but the fact that you know that one is an alternative to the other so that you don't make a disastrous mistake.

GOMBRICH: Precisely. Because there is, as you say, not a very great deal of photographic resemblance between these conventionalised signs which are conventionalised for easier reading from a distance. They are also easy to read because they are pictograms. I believe that this convention developed after the war and spread from airports, where there are many people who don't know the languages, to other such institutions. I remember having seen one in a genteel pub where the doors were marked by colour reproductions of paintings by Lawrence or Gainsborough: one representing a boy and another a pretty girl.

With the Durer *Adam and Eve*, there is now a much closer resemblance.

Adam and Eve, engraving by Durer

This I would say is what is called an idealised representation of the male and female body based on the proportions of the antique; it allowed Durer to construct the image in the right proportions which interested him so much when he came to Italy.

MILLER: And yet, although it's idealised, if this, for example, were to be included in a space capsule and launched out into outer space to convey some information of what the human race looked like, it might give some sort of information because there is a basis of resemblance.

GOMBRICH: I wouldn't bet on this spacecraft image, because they might think that human beings have curious stripes and patches on their bodies and that this arm which is in fact foreshortened is just so short. You have to learn to 'read' such an image in order to get the right information. How should anybody guess that Eve very probably had long hair flowing down her back and this isolated bit wasn't a clipped lock?

MILLER: Yes, but nevertheless within the limits of the convention of engraved representation, which has cross hatching and so forth, and within the limits of the idealisation and conventions and styles of that particular period, there would be more information conveyed about our appearance here than there would be by something which was purely conventionalised; where there was no attempt to represent our appearance.

GOMBRICH: Given that you know what the conventions are, certainly it includes much more information.

MILLER: And, of course, we're apparently already proceeding towards much more resemblance with the photograph.

GOMBRICH: The photograph not only claims to represent, it does in fact represent, one aspect of a person just as television images also represent people exactly from one particular point of view.

MILLER: Yes. But nevertheless I think the point that you make is that although one can construct a spectrum, which goes all the way from the purely conventional to what purports to be the realistic and the naturalistic, a point which you make so startlingly in *Art and Illusion*, is that even within what we take to be the idiom of realism, there are large elements of the conventional. And the artist cannot proceed in the absence of conventional schemata, to use a word you use frequently in *Art and Illusion*, when working towards representation. Now perhaps you could explain that exactly.

GOMBRICH: Yes, that is what I wanted to show. To build an image you have to start somewhere and the easiest starting point is a kind of minimal model of what you want to represent, be it a manikin or a house or a tree, which has to incorporate some of those distinctive features of which we have been talking. You can then go and correct or modify this minimal model – which I call a schema – till you approximate what you want to represent or what you see in front of you and this approximation I call matching. In this way making the model comes before matching it with reality. So you have these two formulas, 'schema and correction' and 'making comes before matching', which mean approximately the same.

MILLER: Now this, to some extent, goes against the common-sense view of what someone is doing when he or she is drawing an object. The common-sense view would be, I think, that it consists of a transcription of an image upon your own retina which you see as a privileged spectator sitting behind your eyes. And the outcome depends entirely on your manual skill rather than on some psychological skill.

GOMBRICH: It seems to me that this naive view of the 'innocent eye' is contradicted by the very fact that we have to learn to draw or paint – that you need to have a kind of language of schemata or representations in order to approximate what you can actually draw (on the canvas or on a piece of paper) to the appearance of what you have in front of you. On the other hand, I am always anxious to stress that this does not mean that there are no images which are less conventionalised than others and in particular I have never claimed that there are no such things as facsimiles or duplicates, When you speak of a three-dimensional object like a fruit it seems to me quite clear that you can make a replica of the fruit which looks very much like the real thing; in fact you may be tempted to bite into it. There is no room for relativism here because this possibility of deception exists for children and sophisticated people. We've all been foxed by three-dimensional wax images at Madame Tussaud's, so I am very anxious to stress, when discussing the development of naturalistic art by 'schema and correction', that I do not mean that the end-product cannot come pretty close to producing the identical perception we may have of the motif represented; only what we here mean by 'pretty close' differs according to the medium. Not only an artificial fruit but also a human head in the round, in other words a piece of sculpture, can be a closer imitation of nature than any two-dimensional image on canvas or paper. You cannot paint a 'facsimile' of the view from your window.

MILLER: So you're saying, then, that most of the great problems in the history of the representation of the outside world consist of choosing to try and make our facsimiles out of materials other than those that the world is made of; and particularly by trying to show it on a flat surface.

Portrait of a Young Boy, by
Giovanni Francesco Caroto

I suppose the most vivid example of that is this sixteenth-century picture in the Castelvecchio in Verona where this child gleefully confronts posterity almost as if mischievously he knew the extent to which his self-portrait will resemble his counterparts in the twentieth century.

GOMBRICH: Quite. It is also a manikin; it is a minimal model of a human being, two legs, two arms, eyes, nose, mouth, hair, but it isn't in the same sense a likeness as we presume the painter's portrait of the child must have been.

MILLER: What we have in the same picture, of course, is the painter's portrayal of the little boy which is much more of a likeness than the little boy's portrayal of himself.

GOMBRICH: Indeed, look how the gleam in the eye, the captivating smile, the texture of the hair, are rendered.

MILLER: Now you say in *Art and Illusion* that we can learn a lot about the use of schemata by looking at the way in which a child draws. This has changed very little in 500 years, even 2000 years, and I'm sure that pictures by Egyptian children were exactly the same. The boy is using a schema which is always the same at a given stage in a child's development.

GOMBRICH: Yes I think that's roughly true. Though our children are also influenced nowadays by the picture books they see or the shows they watch they are pretty impermeable to these influences. They may be more dissatisfied with what they draw and say, 'Mummy how do I draw a tree?' but they do not therefore draw trees differently.

MILLER: Yes, but the point you make is that one should never run away with the idea that because a child represents its world like this, the child is in fact seeing its world like this. If the mother were to walk in looking like the child's picture of its mother, the child would be frightened.

GOMBRICH: I think it would be very frightened and rightly so. The main point here is the one you touched on before – that we live in a three-dimensional world, we move quite effortlessly around in the world, we have two eyes, we see the world in three dimensions. The problems of transposing this experience – this visual experience of our world – on to a flat piece of paper or canvas is much more formidable than earlier students of art may have realised; and that is perhaps the reason why they spoke so glibly about primitive art not being able to represent the world as we see it. You simply can't represent the world as you see it, because the world is three-dimensional and you see it as three-dimensional. What you have to perform is a reduction of a very complex character.

MILLER: And you're saying that in the child's attempt to represent the three-dimensional world in a two-dimensional fashion, it tends to proceed by some schema which at that stage is a long way from the sort of image that it might have produced if it had had a more sophisticated education. Now what would you say was the characteristic of the schema which is used by the child in representing its world? How does it differ from a more sophisticated representation like Constable's for example?

GOMBRICH: It is, to repeat, a kind of minimal model. If a child wants to make a motorcar out of those wooden blocks children are given as toys it may sometimes be happy with any block which can be pushed along, or it may try to add wheels, but it will never incorporate all the features of a motorcar. This minimal model serves it very well on the nursery floor in very many contexts, and serves it equally well in drawings. Look at a typical child's drawing; you see the trunks, leaves, and the fruit of the tree, the house with the smoke, the sun, the blue stripe of the sky which is a separate entity and not put behind the house because it is seen as something different.

MILLER: Do you think the child's model, the child's schema, is determined by a linguistic model of its world? There is a sense, as you point out in *Art and Illusion*, in which these pictures are not really pictures in the adult sense but are really enumerations or inventories of the things which the world contains. To what extent do you think this is determined by the fact that the child is beginning to learn a language which enumerates identifiable things in the world, and that in drawing, it is listing its vocabulary rather than showing its experience?

GOMBRICH: I would very much doubt that the parallel is quite so close. I've been toying with this idea but I do think that, first of all, the vocabulary of children differs much more than their drawings do. Children may very well know about, let us say, roof tiles, which they do not represent. It depends whether they have had any experience of this or other features, such as glass panes – 'open the window', 'close the window' – all these things which are not necessarily incorporated in the model. So I would be a little careful. I know that a comparison has been made between early speech and early drawing. But things are usually a little more complicated than such comparisons indicate.

MILLER: But what do you think is the next stage in child development when it goes from a schema which is an enumeration of items towards a unified appearance of things as they look? How does the schema actually modify itself ?

GOMBRICH: I don't think we can look at it in isolation as if the child were a sort of Robinson Crusoe. The child very soon looks across the drawing surface and peers at his neighbour's work at school. Sometimes a particular trick such as how to represent eyes or lips or ears sweeps through a classroom very quickly, sometimes not to the benefit of the beauty of these drawings. But children learn from each other. They, of course, also learn from their teachers unless the teachers are determined not to show them anything (which happens), and they learn from the pictures they see around them. So they are very soon aware of the fact that a tree, by and large, hasn't got such a huge trunk and that smoke doesn't look like that and they may ask: 'How do I represent smoke?' In other words they grow up in a world of images, unlike the craftsmen of 'primitive' tribes, with whom they have sometimes been compared. The social situation is totally different and the function of images is equally different in different cultures. After all, these children's drawings which we now admire or like are produced partly to pass away the time, though they are produced particularly to impress parents or teachers who will always say, 'my, isn't that lovely', and this determines the way the child goes on.

MILLER: One of the points that you're making is that to some extent our schemata – these models that we use as stepping stones towards representation – are thieved and borrowed from our friends and our colleagues and, of course, from tradition.

GOMBRICH: Yes they are.

MILLER: And you make the point very strongly in *Art and Illusion*, that there is hardly a great artist who has not proceeded from some model or precedent which he has borrowed from others.

GOMBRICH: Yes I am absolutely convinced of the fact that what we call style is something very similar in some respects (though not in other respects) to language. That art, like science, is cumulative in the sense that one generation learns from the other but modifies and corrects what the previous generation has done. This is not true of a very static civilisation like Ancient Egypt or Byzantium where there is no desire to surpass or improve on what has been done before but rather to create an image of the same power and the same expressiveness as the one you find in the Church or the temple.

MILLER: And this applies just as much to a great genius as it does to some amateur groping his way towards representation by using an art instruction book.

GOMBRICH: Most certainly. All geniuses also had teachers they studied, and they drew after other artists. We know that during the Renaissance it was a rule that the apprentice went to draw after works of art in churches. Michelangelo went out and drew after

Masaccio's frescoes in the Carmine and, of course, though he might not have liked to admit it, he learnt a lot from his teacher Ghirlandaio. There is no other way of becoming an artist. Constable said, 'a self-taught artist is one taught by a very ignorant person', which is all one need say about it.

MILLER: This often comes as a surprise to the public, many of whom think that the mark of a genius is the solitude of his enterprise, and that what distinguishes him as a genius is his ability to create these representations without guidance. Whereas the point you're making is that this never happens at all.

GOMBRICH: I don't think it can happen, though this doesn't exclude the fact that artists may be lonely; but artists, just as they had to learn to speak and to walk and to eat, had to learn to paint, to hold a brush, to stretch a canvas and, much more important, to plan a picture. I often say that a picture is not so much invented as discovered. The artist discovers fresh effects which he can put to use in his own work. If he had never seen, let us say, a picture which looks three-dimensional, in perspective, he couldn't have even been aware that this is a possibility. What he can do is to look at a painting which is three-dimensional but a little unconvincing in the way it hangs together spatially and say, 'I must really see whether I cannot improve on this', and this is what I mean by schema and correction.

MILLER: And making first and then matching.

GOMBRICH: Then matching. Stepping back from his canvas or fresco and looking at it as if he were the beholder and saying, 'there's still something wrong here, what can I do?' Sometimes this can be reasoned out; sometimes it is through trial and error that he arrives at a better solution. The importance of trial and error is illustrated in countless sketch books of artists where you see them experimenting with postures, positions, groupings, until they get it right. This is really the experimental part of all artistic enterprise.

MILLER: And some of those sketches or experiments may include models which are borrowed from another artist. You mention in *Art and Illusion* the touching relationship between Constable and Alexander Cozens, and point out that Constable, who is always thought of as the master of clouds, copied Cozens' etchings of clouds into his notebook.

GOMBRICH: Any great artist will always be interested in what his predecessors have done and will try to learn from their work. I think this has always been the case and is likely always to be so. Even cubism which looks like an entirely fresh beginning is known to have started from an observation of certain effects in Cezanne. Cezanne didn't want to be a cubist but he faceted his pictures in a way which intrigued Braque and Picasso, so they used this device as a starting point for a completely new style.

MILLER: Now in raising the distinction between making on the one hand and matching on the other, you mention the extent to which this process in art resembles a similar process in scientific discovery. And your friend Karl Popper, of course, has made much of this relationship between conjecture and discovery.

GOMBRICH: I think one must first say that this relationship exists, but only in styles which aim at the representation, or faultless representation, of, let us say, a human body or of a distance in a landscape or of a sunlit leaf. There is a passage in Leonardo in his Treatise on Painting in which he claims that he is the first artist ever to have painted the effect of sunlight showing through a transparent leaf. Here Leonardo speaks half as an artist and half as a scientist, and it is this ingredient of science – from the use of perspective and anatomy to the use of aerial perspective and certain visual effects including, if you like, 'Op Art' – that marks the development of the Western tradition of art as so similar to the development of science.

In many other civilisations the explanations of natural phenomena resemble myths and remain static. They are traditional and are told from generation to generation. The same is true of images which remain static. In Eastern Christendom you learn how to represent the Nativity on an icon. But in the Western tradition, you have this discontent, this feeling that it isn't yet right and if I do this it looks even worse. So we have to experiment and sort out the effects by watching them. I believe that just as the scientist tests his hypothesis, the artist, as I said before, tests his own picture by looking at it. It isn't that he looks at the model or out into the world and learns how to paint, it is that he looks at his paintings and learns to paint by improving them, by finding that they do not yet pass the test he has set himself.

MILLER: So he recognises some sort of mismatch.

GOMBRICH: Some sort of mismatch. And the greater the artist, the more sure is his capacity for self-criticism in all these respects and I believe that this can be shown to be the case in more complex phenomena like learning how to represent the sheen of silk. This is not something which you learn by looking at a piece of silk. You learn it by trying out how, through a bit of white pigment carefully applied, you suddenly get this surprising effect of a sheen which looks convincing. It doesn't really look like it at all, but it has the same effect. What the artist experiments with is effects.

MILLER: Would you say, then, that one of the difficulties in representing the world around us is that we are quite naturally and understandably enslaved to the idea that it's something furnished with objects rather than 'appearances'?

GOMBRICH: Yes that is certainly the case although I find that the longer I think about it, the more the word 'appearances' seems to elude my grasp. J.J. Gibson has stressed it more than any other psychologist, that the world in which we live is a world of discreet objects which we apprehend as invariant, as he calls it; so that even to realise how little I see of a human head when I look at it from one side or exactly what an eye looks like when I see it in half profile, is something which needs trying out on paper or canvas and is by no means easy.

However, the question of 'appearances' raises some very difficult problems. What exactly is the appearance of the scenery or the landscape through the window? I can look at it in many ways according to how I focus or according to my expectations;

there's always an element of interpretation there which maybe I slightly overstated in *Art and Illusion* but I'd rather overstate it than not state it at all.

MILLER: I wonder if you could enlarge on the notion of the invariant and that favourite phrase of psychologists 'the regression to the real object'.

GOMBRICH: If you meet a friend in the street and he comes closer towards you, he doesn't appear to grow to double in size or when he goes away to shrink, because we always see the friend and not the projection of the friend on the flat surface. We discover this if we stretch out our hand and measure what we see against an upright pencil. If you are at the back of a room which has rows of chairs in it, they all look the same size because they are the same size and you are fully aware of their size. You don't think that those further forward will be too small for you and are only for dwarfs. While, of course, if we intend to draw the room realistically as seen from the back we must make the sidewalls converge and represent the front row of eight chairs as much shorter than the one close to us. These changes are normally hidden from us through the so-called perceptual constancies, the impression we have that the world is constant. This impression also applies to colour. We see the walls of a room in roughly uniform hues or colours; we abstract from the variations caused by shadows, we know these are shadows and we take this as read. The painter, of course, has to attend very carefully to the degree in which the colour is modified by the shadow or by the light, just as he has to attend to the fact that from a certain distance the scale of objects seems to diminish. I don't quite know what 'seems' is supposed to mean, but it diminishes in the projection, let us put it that way.

MILLER: So that, when you have the task of projecting something on to a flat surface, you must overcome your immediate experience of the world in which it seems to be furnished with constant objects, and concentrate instead on the image projected on the retina.

GOMBRICH: Quite. But the artist can never see his retina and therefore I believe he can only learn the trick of forgetting that the world is three-dimensional by studying other pictures and seeing what effect they make on him. For example, the surprising effect that when you photograph or paint a street with a row of receding lamp posts it will only look convincing if the fifth lamp post is reduced in height in relation to the first according to the rules of perspective. It is thus you learn to achieve the effect of three dimensions on a flat surface. As I sometimes say, to the annoyance of some of my philosopher friends, the method works, not because the world ever looks like a picture, but because a picture can be made to look like the world.

MILLER: One of the hardest problems of representation, apart from showing a world in three dimensions, has been the representation of the human face. What would you say were the peculiar problems of representing the human face, over and above the fact that it is a three-dimensional object which has to be projected on to a two-dimensional surface?

GOMBRICH: I think it is movement which is the great problem. And in particular the facial movement of expression which impresses us through its changes, through its melody. Somebody suddenly starts to smile or to frown and we are confronting a living being. To represent this constellation or configuration in a frozen form will often result in what impresses us as totally unlike. We are not aware of the various transitional phases which this mimetic or expressive movement has to go through. You as a producer are surely aware of the complexity in achieving a particular expression. There are more or less static expressions which are relatively easy to render but the characteristic of the person will always be the way they move, the melody of the expression; this can never be caught in snapshots except in lucky shots where you have the feeling 'I now can tell what he will look like in a second or two and what he looked like a second before'. Whether or not my guess is right is not so important; what matters is that this subjective conviction gives me the feeling of confronting a living human being.

MILLER: Would you say then that in representing the human face in a convincing and lively way, there are certain positions which will be chosen by an artist because they will lead the spectator to predict the way in which the model is likely to move in the next few minutes?

GOMBRICH: Oh most certainly. I mean just as the photographer asks a model to smile, so from very early on artists try to enliven a mask, as it were, or a head, by moving the corner of the mouth. You have the archaic smile of the Greeks and of early Gothic artists aiming at the same effect – of life animating the face. Later on more complex methods are used; an instantaneous turn of the head, the veiled smile of the *Mona Lisa* which is capable of so many interpretations that the image seems to change whenever you look at it. Leonardo played a very complex trick but something of this interpretability is, I think, part of the magic of some great portraits. For example, Rembrandt in particular, sometimes leaves the eyes in the shadow and, because of it, gives us the impression that here is a great intensity of gaze.

MILLER: So you're saying that the success of a representation depends to some extent on how much is under-represented or left ambiguous.

GOMBRICH: Yes, it is the suggestiveness of the image, it suggests ways in which we can supplement it: in *Art and Illusion* I call it 'the beholder's share'. Of course there is a certain amount of 'learned' response in this which may not be born with us, We learn that certain images can be supplemented and therefore brought to life. There is a cultural element but it's difficult to assign exactly what role it plays.

MILLER: So there may be, in certain portraits, an artful blurring, an artful ambiguity which invites the beholder to increase his contribution.

GOMBRICH: This is exactly what Reynolds said about Gainsborough in a somewhat backhanded compliment. He says of Gainsborough's portraits that they impress because they allow the imagination to do the rest.

MILLER: So in other words, the vitality of the portrait may be largely due to the beholder's activity, although the actual choice of what is going to be the beholder's share is strategically chosen by the artist.

GOMBRICH: Exactly. It can't be done by everyone. You have to know precisely the one distinctive feature which you must not leave out. But, just as accurately, you must eliminate that which would be an obstacle, which would look frozen if it were there.

MILLER: Presumably the same principles apply to the representation of the body's movements.

GOMBRICH: The need for these movements occurs particularly in narrative art when you represent, for example, a battle, or a fight. There are easily legible configurations like the one where one man is striking a blow and the other fighter is trying to ward it off, which allow us to understand what is actually going on. If you look at Greek representations of battles, you will see that these schemata are very much exploited; they can be made more moving and effective or more stereotyped according to the skill of the artist and to the requirements of his style. But there will always be the need to allow the beholder to read what is actually going on and therefore, on the whole, a clear silhouette is important in the representation of movement. If you think of any famous work, for example, Leonardo's *Last Supper*, or *The Creation of Adam* by Michelangelo, you will see how these famous gestures are silhouetted: you need to have clarity of all the movements.

MILLER: This statue exemplifies the same principle. By showing a fixed posture which is easily legible as a movement.

Discobolus

GOMBRICH: In this case, of course, it is an initial position rather than movement. He starts by extending his arm in order to throw the discus and therefore he could have stayed in this position, allowing the artist to study it for quite some time, before he started . . .

MILLER: Yes . . . it's in equilibrium and therefore it's a pose that could be held. And the reason why it conveys a sense of movement is that the arm is at the limit of its excursion. And therefore expresses the possibility of acceleration in the opposite direction.

GOMBRICH: Yes, it's like a taut spring, or a bow; you see that the arrow will leave immediately and will be hurled into the distance. In a similar way you find, through empathy in some of these representations of an actual moment, that the muscles are tense.

MILLER: That must be one of the reasons why the horse was so often shown in the rocking horse position, with both its front legs and hind legs extended in a position which its limbs never are in. It was done in order to convey a legible image of its movement.

GOMBRICH: Yes, that is very likely, though it did come as a surprise when artists were shown the 'instantaneous' photographs by Muybridge which showed that the horse moves its legs in different time rhythm. Ever since I discussed this example – and I was by no means the first who wrote about it; the first was the great French archaeologist, Salomon Reinach – I occasionally get a letter saying that I was wrong. Occasionally a race horse may move in this way but I think these are usually jumping rather than running, so I still hold fast to the fact that, by and large, the norm is the one which I illustrated in The Story of Art.

Muybridge horse

MILLER: But it took time for this to become a schema which was then accepted by artists.

GOMBRICH: It was much discussed in the nineteenth century; Degas and others were interested in the discovery of the camera, of what in fact we don't normally 'take in' (I wouldn't say 'see' which would be wrong) which we don't 'take in' because it's simply too fast.

MILLER: I've often wondered why the Degas images, borrowed from Muybridge's photographs, were as successful as they were in view of the fact they showed events which were invisible to all intents and purposes.

GOMBRICH: That's true but we are so conditioned by the pictures we see and once we are conditioned in this way, we don't mind any more. There's a very interesting recent development of this kind. When I was young, architectural photographers took great care always to photograph the building straight on and not to let it appear to be slanting by pointing the camera upwards or downwards. Now nobody minds. We have learnt to accept slanted shots as a way of representing a building when there is no other way of showing it; we are getting much more tolerant to certain photographic distortions which even a generation ago were considered intolerable. The same is true of the blurring due to movement in photographs. We see this in countless advertisements nowadays, and in books about cities where you see the blurred figures of people walking through them. No publisher would have published such a picture thirty years ago. So there always is a conditioning process in art. Just as we accept Picasso though we know that people on the whole do not quite look like his paintings, so we accept certain effects of the camera.

MILLER: So that an innovation in art may persuade people to see the world in a new way despite the fact that there is a mismatch between the new scheme and the world.

GOMBRICH: There isn't always a mismatch. We can see this convergence of a building when we look up and we can perhaps be aware of the blur when we see a rapid movement if we attend to it. Normally we are not attending to this, and the camera has conditioned us sometimes to attend to certain effects; like the movement of the horse to which we're not normally attending.

MILLER: But nevertheless Muybridge photographs show certain positions of the limbs which really are moving so fast that the eye couldn't possibly see them. And yet such improbable images are artistically successful; why are they successful, if they don't match up with the world?

GOMBRICH: Well I wouldn't say they don't match up with the world, they don't match up with what we can take in. I suppose we can say that we have been brain-washed up to a point by artists to accept certain things as possible.

MILLER: So is it fair to say that whereas in science there is a rigorous standard by which the model must approximate to reality, art is not necessarily in the business of creating a schema whose duty is to match reality?

GOMBRICH: Most certainly not, it very rarely is. Or only if an artist is committed to conveying the correct information. There still are, I think, medical artists who have to paint operations in the operating theatre. In their case, they are scientifically committed to make everything as clear and as correct as possible; in fact the picture must be better than the photograph because the operation is more visible as they represent it. But with this and similar exceptions where something must be represented accurately, for a police record, say, the social function of the visual image, on the whole, is not that of giving accurate information. It has many other functions – from maps to decorations, from didactic illustration to erotic titillation, from advertising to religious devotion.

Not all of them, by any means, demand attention to what we call natural appearances. I have postulated in *Art and Illusion* and elsewhere that this attention, which we quite wrongly take for granted, first came to the fore in ancient Greece in a religious context. There is a suggestive parallel, I believe, between the rise of naturalistic representation in art and the origins of the medium which you have made your own; I mean, of course, the theatre. It seems that it was in Greece that there arose the demand for the evocation of a mythical event as if it were actually happening before the spectator's eyes – what I have come to call the 'eyewitness principle'. It was this demand which, twice in history (in the ancient world and in the Renaissance) led to the process we have been talking about, the imitation of nature through 'schema and correction', through 'making and matching' by means of a systematic series of trial and error which allowed us finally to look across the flat picture surface into an imaginary world evoked by the artist.

States of Mind, British Broadcasting Corporation, 1983

Plays and Performance

The first play that I directed was *Under Plain Cover* by John Osborne. It was when I had just dropped out of the London run of *Beyond the Fringe* and had a couple of months to spare before leaving for New York. I had yielded once again to an unsolicited invitation, this time from George Devine at the Royal Court Theatre. I warned Devine that I was completely unacquainted with theatrical direction and that I was therefore unqualified to undertake the task, but he assured me that I would pick it up as I went along. I was relieved to discover that the diagnostic skills that I had acquired during the course of my clinical training were effortlessly applicable to the task of getting actors to pretend convincingly that they were someone other than themselves. Over the years I have been consistently preoccupied by the nature of human action, and what psychologists and philosophers have to say about this subject seems to me deeply relevant to the task of theatrical representation.

Directing a play – Robert Lowell's *Old Glory*, July 1964

The actors keep pleading for props and I begin to realise how much physical objects occupy the performers hands and how much they direct his performance. We seem to be nothing without objects. We're looting the tangible world for artificial limbs – anything will do: pencils, hankies, cups and matchboxes. We are like carnivorous amoebae, gliding about and engulfing things – holding them, warming them and then discarding them before we pass on and take up something else. It is as though our body image was made of protoplasm, pouring itself down our arms and into the objects we handle until, warmed by our touch, they become briefly incorporated.

The James-Lange theory seems to apply to acting. One of the actors asks today what one of the lines means. No one seems to know – until he just says it and finds out by doing so. Meaning is often locked up in the performance – or rather performance unlocks the meaning. Actors sometimes won't say a line until they know for certain what it means. It's sometimes necessary to persuade them to just say it. It's as if performance is the Prince Charming kiss with which the actor stirs the sleeping line into existence.

The importance of trivial half-conscious movements in a performance. I bring a quotation from *The Rise of Silas Lapham* into rehearsal. The shyness of one of the characters is epitomised by her absent-minded poking of a wood shaving with the point of her parasol. As she comes to the conclusion of a line of thought, "She gave the shaving a little toss from her and took the parasol up across her lap."

The green umbrella

The story of a performer blocked or frustrated until given some prop or even mannerism is part of theatrical folklore, but unlike most of the other hearsays and myths of the theatre, the story of the green umbrella has more than a grain of truth in it. Again and again one sees actors released and enabled by a prop. This works in one of two ways:

1. having such an object in his hands leads him to do what people normally do with such an object, and then one thing leads to another, in which the completion of one action with the object inevitably sets the stage for the next action;

2. apart from the train of actions which are naturally suggested by having this or that object in his hands, there are metaphorical implications. I give someone a handbag and ask her to clutch it tightly with both hands, which makes her into the sort of person who would turn out to do other things, temperamentally related to handbag-gripping.

Novels into films

There are many reasons why good novels won't "go" into films. One of these is the delicate relationship of dialogue to narrative prose. The narration is not simply a disposable support for what would otherwise be dramatic dialogue.

In any serious work of fiction the narration and the conversation are inseparably reciprocal. If, in narrating a scene, an author abstains from direct speech in favour of a reported summary of it, this must be what was meant; once you try to film the scene in question, inventing the dialogue which is merely suggested in the text, the fictional artwork is irreversibly deformed.

A character in a novel is not *in it* in the way that someone real might be *in Birmingham* or *in a cubicle*. He can't be taken out of the book, as some people suppose, and put into a film since he is made out of the same sort of material as the book he is in. Mr. Carker, for example, is undoubtedly a peculiar individual. Perhaps his most interesting peculiarity is the fact that he is in *Dombey and Son* and can't get out of it.

When TV or film versions of novels "fail", the "failure" is often attributed to the contradiction between the creations of the director and the images which the novel has conjured up in the mind's eye of the individual reader – "that's not how I see Mr. Rochester". But there is more to it than that.

The experience of reading a novel more or less precludes a filmic version of what it represents. And yet, on the face of it, the idea of a filmed version seems to have every possible advantage. Words, after all, often fail to convey the full details of a scene. For example, it's difficult and usually impossible to recognise someone from a verbal description – unless of course there is some dramatically distinguishing mark such as a scar, Cyrano's nose, etc., whereas even a bad photograph will serve to pick someone out of a crowd.

So one might expect a film to fill in all the things that the novelist's words fail to convey. But that misses the point, because a novel is not something which makes the best of a bad job as far as visual representation is concerned, *i.e.*, with lots of stuff missing that a film version could fill in. In a good novel what the author *gives* is what there *is*. The text somehow fills the fictional space created by the novelist, and if the reader has read the text properly, he or she would find it difficult to identify the gaps. In other words, in an important work of fiction the text doesn't even admit the possibility of further details. For example: when Conrad describes the governess in *Chance*, he alludes to her hair and its greyness and not much else. On the other hand, this does not mean that the reader necessarily supplies what Conrad has left out. She somehow seems to be complete as described and the shock of seeing her realised in a film is not that of seeing one's own visualisation contradicted by someone else's, but rather of seeing the described depicted.

It's often said that the difficulty of portraying a well-known character from literature on the screen is that each reader has his own mental image of that character. But that's not really the problem. It's not that any one particular realisation is bound to fall short of so many different imaginings, but that no realisation can possibly match an imagining. That's because mental images are a different sort of thing altogether. For one thing, they can have lots of missing parts without seeming to lack them.

Solving dramatic problems, April 7, 1976

The beard in the fourth act of *Three Sisters*. It could just be a moment of bathos to counterbalance Masha's grief at the departure of Vershinin. In fact, we weren't actually thinking about it at all – the issue of what was meant or what might have been meant by it only came up as a result of trying to work out the subsidiary problem of exactly when Kuligin – Masha's husband – was to take the false beard off. By rights, or at least by common sense, he should take off what was only meant as a joke at the moment when Natasha comes in and seems to be frightened by it. For some reason, though, I told AB (playing Kuligin) to keep it on – to brazen it out, both as an actor and as the character – and suddenly we discovered a better and more touching use for what had previously been a comic device on Chekhov's part. Immediately after Natasha's exit I asked JS (playing Masha) to go across to Kuligin, say, "It's time to go," and then to tenderly take off the beard for him. In other words, to unmask him and to discover under the woolly absurdity of this comic prop, the serious, concerned face of her hitherto neglected and despised husband – as if by having concealed himself under a deliberately assumed absurdity he could for the first time reappear free (in her eyes at least) of his natural and inadvertent foolishness. It was as if, under the beard which he had put on after all only as a joke, he had changed for her, Masha, and his natural dignity had unexpectedly become apparent. God knows how it worked, but he went into that beard as an insensitive clown and emerged from it as a man of dignity and patient forgiveness. But we had to find all that out, and we only did so by solving the apparently trivial problem of when to take off a false beard.

Nowhere in Particular, Mitchell Beazley, 1999

Paying attention

My preoccupation with action, intentional or sub-intentional, has overlapped with an equally intense interest in vision and the exercise of attention. Travelling on buses and trains my own attention has been consistently directed towards the gaze of others and activities of which they are largely unaware.

Most of the short pieces reproduced in these pages were scribbled down at odd moments in notebooks which I almost always carried with me.

Sketchy perception

In a lecture devoted to the achievement of the 17th century painter Claude, J.M.W Turner doubted that his French predecessor "could have attained such powers but by the continual study of the parts of nature". He was referring to the sketches in which Claude alluringly records his informal observation of natural detail. And yet as far as Turner was concerned, the idea of dignifying such studies as free-standing works of art was more or less inconceivable, because although he conceded that finished landscapes were, in a sense "pictures made up of bits", he saw no justification for exhibiting "pictures of bits" as such.

The irony is that while Turner himself rarely, if ever, painted what he would have described as a *bit* of a scene, many of his contemporaries did. The fact that such sketches were increasingly rendered in oil indicates that they were produced as an end in themselves and not necessarily with a view to a more "serious" painting, imaginatively composed of such bits.

Thirty years before Turner's lecture, the French artist Pierre-Henri de Valenciennes had painted unusually "beheaded" pictures of Roman rooftops in which the normally subsidiary details of chimneys and tiles assumed a monumental significance. At the same time, the previously conventional landscape painter Thomas Jones re-framed his own vision and composed a series of disconcertingly eccentric canvasses representing the overlooked and undervalued backs and tops of Neapolitan houses. The serious attention thus given to the negligible aspects of the visible world gathered momentum in the years that followed, and in works from 1820 onward, it is possible to recognise a genre of self-sufficient "pictures of bits". This, as Peter Galassi, curator of photography at New York's Museum of Modern Art, points out, "is true even in the rare cases where the sketch apparently served only to record a motif for a later composition". By panning up to frame the disintegrating eaves of an old barn, John Linnell created a painting that is much more vigorous and memorable than the public painting in which he later included this "trivial" motif. With this exception, none of the oil sketches which figured in Galassi's 1981 exhibition *Painting before Photography* can be identified as parts of or preliminaries to more important canvasses. On the contrary, they are independent works of art which "take forthrightly as their subject a single, nameable thing: the trunk of a tree, a cloud, a humble gate". As Galassi states in his catalogue, Constable expressed the new mood when he confessed his love for "old rotten banks, slimy posts and brick work".

Turner's antithesis between "pictures of bits" and paintings imperceptibly made up of them has its natural counterpart in vision itself. The reason is that the capacity to resolve fine detail is confined to a surprisingly small area of the retina, the fovea, around which visual acuity falls off so steeply that it's impossible to take in the details of a whole scene at a single glance. Try fixing your eyes on the last word of this sentence and see how difficult it is to read the surrounding text.

The result of this restricted acuity is that our perception of the visual world has to be assembled in discrete instalments. Although we are not explicitly aware of doing so, we are constantly flicking our gaze from one part of the visual field to the next, and by bringing the specialised centre of the retina to bear on one sector of the scene after another we collect an anthology of sporadic snapshots from which we build up an apparently detailed picture of the world around us. In order to achieve this effect the brain has to overcome at least two representational problems. For one thing, it is necessary to suppress the distractingly smeared imagery which inevitably accompanies rapid eye movements from one fixation point to the next. The method by which the nervous system does this is not fully understood, but one way or another, vision is briefly switched off whenever the eye disengages itself and flicks to the next position. To all intents and purposes the subject is conveniently blinded during these potentially disruptive episodes.

Although the efficiency of this mechanism is a necessary condition, it is not enough to guarantee the characteristic coherence of visual experience. In addition to extinguishing the blur that occurs between fixations, the visual system has to integrate the consecutive series of snapshots into an instantaneous panorama. Once again, the mechanism by which the brain achieves this remains almost entirely obscure, but it presupposes the existence of a short-term storage device capable of retaining and logging each shot. Even so, it's difficult to understand how the compilation is implemented and how the discontinuities between adjacent bits are smoothed out. Although the finished picture is unarguably "made up of bits", that's not how we see it. It doesn't look like one of Hockney's photographic collages; we witness the scene as a continuous whole.

It's tempting to visualise this process in terms of a hypothetical work space, something like a studio in which the artist lays out and surveys his informal sketches before putting them together to make up an imaginative landscape.

But the analogy is misleading. Apart from the fact that the artist's sketches take some time to "do", the process by which they're elaborated into a formal picture takes even longer, whereas the "bits" with which the brain has to work are recorded in a fraction of a second and the act of composition is just as rapid.

Besides, in contrast to a piece of art work, which requires no such thing, it simply gets done and it makes no sense to ask by whom. As the American philosopher Daniel Dennett has argued, we must shake off the idea of a Cartesian viewing theatre to which retinal information is delivered for conscious consideration. If there were such a place, we would have to imagine it occupied by a phantom spectator; once we let that genie out of the lamp, philosophical chaos ensues.

Associated movements

In the darts matches we see on television these days, you can see that each player displays a characteristic facial twitch at the moment when the dart leaves his hand. A quick raising and lowering of the eyebrows, a rapid dropping of the jaw with the lips closed, an abrupt pursing of the mouth. What's going on? None of these movements have anything to do with helping the dart on its way to the target. This makes me wonder about some of the expressions which pass across the face of a conductor during an orchestral performance. Are they expressive instructions to the orchestra or are they involuntary responses to what the orchestra is playing?

Bernie's baby

She smiles each time I look at her – whatever "looking at her" means. But smiling's not all she does. In some sense it is the least she does. Each time she smiles she raises both arms and rubs the side of her smiling face with her hands, wriggling and twisting her body the while. The whole gesture, of which the smile is a relatively small part, looks like an expression of coy evasion, as if she is embarrassed by the encounter and is doing her best to escape from it.

Actions

Vis-à-vis Wittgenstein's question about the difference between my arm going up and my lifting it. Is the difference something mysteriously added to my arm merely going up? Is it my doing something – x, say – which then causes my arm to rise? And is this prior event x something which might happen *without* it causing my arm to rise?

Think about the factors which might prevent voluntary arm-rise:

1. a heavy weight in the hand;

2. the arm bound to the side;

3. severed tendons in the shoulder;

4. severed motor nerves to the shoulder muscles;

5. spinal transection;

6. an injury to the motor cortex.

With 1 and 2, the event x, which supposedly precedes and causes my arm-rising increases as a result of the frustration caused by my failing to raise my arm. In the case of 1 – the heavy weight case – arm-rise might eventually take place as a result of increasing the intensity of x. In the second case, I'd say, "Try as I might, I was unable to get my arm to go up". But it would be wrong to say that x – *i.e.*, my trying – had increased without anything happening. On the contrary, a great deal has happened but none of it has had any effect on arm-raising. A great deal of effort happens, much more than is needed for unimpeded arm-lifting. In this particular case, trying and failing is not the experience of doing x (whatever that is) and discovering that nothing happens, but rather of having to exert more mechanical effort than one would expect to under normal circumstances and then finding that the required result doesn't happen. And yet, that is not quite it. Failing to get one's arm to go up in cases 1 and 2 is not a question of doing x, then 2 times x and finding to one's horror that the arm fails to go up. The trying is somehow part of the failing. In fact, I don't feel tempted to use the word *try* unless some sort of failure happens.

I don't *try* to lift my unimpeded arm; I just lift it. So failing to raise my arm and failing to raise my heavily weighted arm are two entirely different things.

Failure to raise my weighted arm is a case of failing to raise a weight.

The point is that unless I am mysteriously ignorant of the fact that my arm has been surreptitiously weighted – in my sleep, say – raising my weighted arm is always a case of lifting a weight and not of lifting the arm plus a weight.

More actions

I can't clench my fist without contracting the flexor muscles in my forearm.

But would I really want to say that the contraction of my forearm muscles was the cause of my fist clenching? The thing is that *causes* come before the events that they bring about, but my fist clenches at the same time as my forearm muscles contract. Besides, I don't *get* my fist to clench by contracting my forearm muscles. On the contrary, the only way in which I can get my forearm muscles to contract is to make a fist with my hand.

So the two are not related to one another as cause and effect. Contracting my forearm muscles isn't something I have to do first and then, God willing, my fist clenches! This is not very helpful!

Another way of looking at it: I don't seem to be able to move any of my muscles as a basic action. A given muscle, my biceps say, can be moved or contracted by making a gesture which requires the contraction of that muscle, so that, although the muscle's contraction is unarguably a necessary component of a particular action, its contraction is not part of what one does in performing the action. To move my muscles *as* muscles, I have to do something else,

I have to *act* in such a way that certain muscles are bound to contract in order to achieve the result I am aiming at.

A game of snap

The game of snap requires the player to react to two identical formats or pictures. How about this variant? Instead of having *identical* pairs you might have the following similar types of pairs:

1. a photograph of something – a cow, say – versus a line drawing of it seen from the same angle and the same size;

2. a photograph of something from one angle and a photograph of it on the same scale but from a different viewpoint;

3. a photograph of something – a bottle, say – versus a photograph which, though different, belongs to the same category – a flask, say;

4. a photograph of something versus a heavily degraded but otherwise identical photograph of the same thing.

The present tense

Why is it that the present tense is used in the narrative summaries at the beginning of chapters in 19th century novels, whereas the narration itself uses the past tense? Presumably it's because the chapter in which the narrated events occur has a current existence: that is to say, the summary or synopsis points out the receptacle or container in which the narrated events have a present existence. A counterpart to this summarising present occurs in the description of the contents of a picture: "In the picture, Jesus *goes* into the wilderness where he is tempted by a devil." So, although Jesus actually *went* into the wilderness, in the pictorial representation he is currently doing so. We also say "what happens in *Hamlet*" and not "what happened in *Hamlet*". What about the present tense of stage directions? "Konstantin goes to his desk, opens the drawers, and looks through his papers." Whereas in the account of an actual production one would probably say: "Konstantin went ever so slowly over to his desk and reluctantly looked at his papers." Perhaps one might even mention the name of the actor who played it that way, since it was his performance which distinguished the action from the one that customarily happens when Konstantin goes over to his desk. Etc., etc.

Mental states

We talk about beliefs, wishes, hopes, etc. Are we to assume that these words refer to determinate, numerable states of mind and that for each one of them there is something distinctive which differentiates it from all the other ones, and that there is a series of brain states to which each of these mental states corresponds? Can that be so?

Social constructions

Positive: promotion, baptism, confirmation, qualification, enrollment, registration, initiation, coronation, ordination.

Negative: disqualification, demotion, disbarring, defrocking, abdication, unconditional surrender, conviction, resignation, sacking.

Compare these with: solution, crystallisation, fracture, freezing, melting, evaporation, germination, fertilisation, metamorphosis (insect).

Apes and men

In the *Jungle Book*, which he published in the same year as Gustave le Bon's treatise on *The Crowd*, Kipling describes the fickle impulsive apes who occupied the ruined buildings of an extinct aristocratic civilisation:

> "They would sit in circles in the hall of the king's council chamber scratching for fleas and pretending to be men; they would run in and out of the roofless houses and collect pieces of plaster and old bricks in a corner and forget where they had hidden them and fight and cry in shuffling crowds, then break off to play up and down the terraces of the king's garden. They explored all the passages in the palace and the hundreds of little rooms, but they never remembered what they had seen and what they had not.
>
> They drank at the tanks, made the water muddy and then they fought over it and then they would all rush together in mobs."

It's unlikely that Le Bon knew anything about Kipling or vice versa, but the fact that the two authors, writing in the same year, virtually paraphrase one another is a coincidence that requires an explanation.)

Although the *Jungle Book* is fondly regarded as a harmless tale of forest folk, it is easy to recognise its hidden agenda and that Kipling's disparaging account of the Bandarlog is prompted by political sentiments similar to the ones which led Le Bon to write so contemptuously about the human crowd.

Le Bon would have approved of Kipling's choice of apes to epitomise social behaviour of this sort. As an evolutionist, he recognised the primate ancestry of the human species, and since he regarded the crowd as an evolutionary throwback, representing it as a pack of monkeys would have struck him as a biological truth rather than a literary metaphor. He regarded the members of a crowd as pathetic impersonations of men, brought to this regrettable condition by egalitarian ideas inherited from the revolutions of the 19th century.

What are you looking at?

Surely there are two possible answers to this question. One answer is, whatever it is that intercepts my eye-line. Someone other than me could just as easily answer this question by simply tracing (in the geometrical sense) the line of my conjugate gaze to the first thing it encounters. There might be some errors here, in that a few degrees could make all the difference between my looking at that barn on the horizon and my seeming to look at the house just to the left of it. All the same, it is a question that can usually be settled by pointing along the line of my gaze, in the hope that my extended arm and finger will pick out what I am looking at better than my mere look would do.

But there is also a sense in which the question "What am I looking at?" cannot be answered either by taking my eye-line into consideration or by my pointing. What if I say, "I am looking at the most beautiful picture in the Uffizi"? Now, as it happens I am standing right in front of Simone Martini's *Annunciation*, and there is no doubt that the large oblong picture that bears that name is the object at which my gaze is directed. But my companion, whose eye-line is directed at the same picture, might not agree that she was looking at the most beautiful picture in the Uffizi.

So how about a somewhat less contentious claim? I might say,

"What I am looking at is its style." In this sense of "looking", I am looking at an "aspect" of the picture, something about it that cannot be distinguished simply by following my eye-line.

Visual information

The amount of significant information that has to be put into a painting is less than one might suppose. In "doing" faces, for instance, you might think that each millimetre requires a distinctive change of shading or colour in order to show the modelling, and as an amateur you're baffled by the technical subtlety that this seems to demand. But when you come to think about it, the problem is rather different. What you have to do is to make decisive changes in shading or colour at certain crucial points, and let the spectator's imagination fill in the intervening gradients. I always imagined that the left cheek of Botticelli's Venus was modelled with infinitesimally small changes of shading, but this turns out to be an illusion. In fact, if you mask out the sharp edge of the cheek, the steep gradients of the nostril and the eye sockets so that all you see is the broad expanse of the cheek itself, it becomes surprisingly apparent that there's no visual modelling whatsoever.

Over a space of about ten to twelve square centimetres the colour of the paint is more or less uniform, and yet as soon as you unmask the rest of the face, the cheek appears to be modelled once again.

Seeing *as* and seeing *in*

When he discusses representation, Richard Wollheim talks about seeing the depicted object *in* the paint – meaning presumably that we recognise that it's *apples* which are thus depicted and that it is nevertheless a *depiction* of them. Recognising them as a depiction implies that we acknowledge that someone, *i.e.* the artist, intended us to recognise that that is what he intended when he made the picture – because we can recognise things in something where there is no such intention. We can "see" an image of the Virgin in the discoloured heartwood of an apple tree, or we may perceive the silhouette of a city in the polished cross section of a piece of variegated agate. In contrast to depictions, we simply marvel at the accidental likenesses, and if we are Hapsburg Archdukes we keep such specimens in our *Schatzkammer*.

When I mistake someone for someone else, once I learn the truth I suddenly see the extent to which he is unlike whoever it was I took him for.

But I am not tempted to call the original experience an illusion. I can see how I made the mistake, and my subsequent seeings are no longer mistaken.

Compare this to illusions which lead me to see things which I have good reason to believe are not in fact what they seem to be – but the illusion persists nevertheless. For example, when I go to the cinema I am fully aware of the fact that I am confronted by a sequence of still pictures alternating with extremely rapid periods of darkness. But I can recite this fact to myself without being able to escape the experience of moving pictures.

More about seeing in

Wollheim talks about seeing apples *in* the paintwork (as opposed to the traditional expression of seeing the paintwork *as* apples). It may seem obvious and trivial but there are all sorts of "seeings in" and it would be nice to be clear about the differences.

1. Seeing apples *in* the foliage. In this situation the identity of real apples is compromised by the fact that the otherwise unambiguous contours of the fruit are occluded by the overlapping contours of equally real leaves.

   But when I see apples in the paint, the brushwork isn't something which gets in the way of my seeing the apples more clearly.

2. Seeing something in a container. Apples *in* a bowl or *in* a box or indeed *in* a bowl *in* a room.

3. Seeing faces in leaves, in clouds or in the dying embers of a fire. This is not an example of mistaken seeing, because I know perfectly well that I am looking at whatever it is I am looking at. What I see, rather, is another *aspect*.

   What about seeing leaves in a forest or embers in a dying fire? That's what forests and dying fires consist of, dammit! It's just that something about the configuration of the leaves, clouds or embers *lends* itself to the perception of another aspect.

4. How about seeing something in a completely cloudless blue sky, when there is nothing which could even begin to lend itself to the seeing in question? This is a free-standing visual experience which owes none of its properties to anything that is actually to be seen. "Why do you bend your eye on vacancy?"

5. All right, back to seeing apples *in* a painting. In the case of real apples, everything about them is a property of the apples themselves and there is nothing left over to contradict this. Whereas in the case of

the painted apples, only certain visual features of the configuration lend themselves to the impression. There is an awful lot of paint around, for example. The reason why we talk about seeing apples *in* such a set-up is that not all of it lends itself to apple appearances. On the other hand, you wouldn't want to call this experience an illusion. When I recognise and see apples in a painting, it's not a question of my supplying the fruity details which the painting somehow leaves out, nor is it a question of my suppressing the pigmenty details which the painting cannot eliminate. As Wollheim rightly stresses, I see it all in all, apples and paint inseparable.

When I look at one of Cezanne's apple paintings and recognise apples in it, I would be very offended if someone said that I was just "seeing things".

It's certainly not an hallucination. After all, other people see the apples, too, and you wouldn't want to call this a mass hallucination – the Apples of Mons.

But nor is it an illusion. In the case of an apple painting what I am seeing is sufficiently like real apples to trigger apple recognition – or to be more accurate, an apple-painting recognition.

The situation is not altogether different from the one in which I say, "I can see his mother in his face." When I say something like this, I obviously don't mean to imply that I can see something other than his face in his face, in the way that I see a tiger looking through the foliage. It's just that I am struck by certain aspects of *his* face which resemble certain aspects of his *mother's* face. Where else but in his face would I expect to find such features?

Words and pictures

Experimental psychologists have shown that their subjects' ability to recall items mentioned in a passage of descriptive prose is made easier by showing them a picture of the situation – an illustration which explains "what's going on". Presumably the converse applies: the memory of a picture might be made easier by the subjects being allowed to hear the reading of the story that the picture illustrates.

Reproduction

I must get some new spectacles to replace the ones I broke last week.

What does that mean exactly? I want to reproduce the ones I broke. But that doesn't mean that I want them to be held together with a paper-clip like my old ones were. What I need, obviously, is spectacles that will let me see in the way that the broken pair once did.

So how do we go about that? One method might be to copy the old ones – *i.e.*, to measure the size and curvature of the lenses, grind new glasses to those specifications and set them in frames of the original design. Such a replacement would automatically meet the needs of my eyes, since that is what the original glasses were prescribed to do. The alternative method is to get the optician to prepare some glasses to the refractive specifications recorded from the original consultation. In other words, it isn't a question of copying the object as such, but of reproducing the functional intention of the original object.

An alternative replacement might be found by sorting through a box of second-hand spectacles and trying them one by one until I found a pair through which I could read small print. Hermit-crab optics. So how about biological optics, then? Each of us grows eyes which, with considerable variations, meet normal visual needs. These eyes are indistinguishable, both in design and in visual function from the ones which were grown by the previous generation and by the generations before. Copies? In one sense they are. But the process by which the eyes of one generation get to be like the eyes of the preceding generation is not one of copying. Genetic instructions are followed and in each generation a satisfactory pair of eyes is the inevitable result. The previous pair of eyes plays no role in either the structure or function of the subsequent pair.

In neither case do the eyes shape themselves according to the refractive requirements of their particular owners. They may be better or worse as eyes – after all, some people have to wear spectacles and others don't – but they are all examples of eyes. But they are neither copied nor prescribed as such.

Attention

I am listening to the radio in bed this morning, hearing every word that is spoken. Suddenly the TV at the other end of the room switches itself on and my attention transfers itself to what is being said by the figures on the screen. I attend to what they are saying with the result that I no longer take in what is being said on the radio.

It is not a question of the radio becoming inaudible. I can still hear, for example, the alternation between male and female voices. But in paying attention to what the TV presenters are saying, I lose the intelligibility of the radio broadcast. In other words, my attention seems to be distributed between two sources of *meaning* rather than between two sources of sound.

Reading

Chardin has a portrait of a philosopher reading. But we wouldn't want to say that he was seeing a page of print, although "seeing" print is a necessary condition of reading it. So it doesn't sound right to say that Chardin's philosopher is looking at his book, but simply that he is reading it.

A typographer might be looking at the book, but in the act of appreciating the type, he would somehow have to exempt himself from the experience of reading the text.

The spared glance

While being photographed I am asked to turn my head away but to keep my eyes looking towards the camera. This sidelong glance is very popular with modern photographers, but you can see the same thing in many paintings. It undoubtedly has a peculiar vitality – it seems to imply that the glance has just alighted and that the subject has merely spared the look whilst otherwise engaged.

Another spared glance

In the *Portinari Altarpiece* in the Uffizi, the glance which St Margaret seems to "spare" in order to look at the ointment jar held by the Magdalene standing beside her. From the position of her head on her neck you can recognise that she will return a moment later to her pious reading.

Portinari Altarpiece

But if you isolate her as a pictorial detail, so that you can't see what her spared glance is directed at, you could easily confuse her appearance with that of the Virgin in Flemish Annunciations.

Detail of Portinari Altarpiece

Like St Margaret, the Virgin disengages her eyes from her book, but in this case she refrains from reading the better to hear what the angel is saying.

Vacant gazes

There are many pictures and of course real-life situations in which the eyes though open are not seeing anything. Not because they are blind but because their owner is, as we say, off in a world of his own.

One of the most familiar examples of this is the look of people talking on the telephone. As they chatter away, their gaze is raised obliquely, not necessarily because they are half-attending to something on the ceiling but because they are wholly absorbed by what they are listening to and have therefore unhooked or disengaged their eyes from the world around them.

Averted gazes

Strictly speaking, the averted gazes we often see in paintings are ones in which the person actively *refrains* from looking at what is self-evidently the principal subject of the painting. For example the shocked diners at Herod's feast who deliberately turn their eyes away from the dreadful spectacle of the Baptist's severed head. Another example is the young girl who turns tearfully away from the asphyxiated bird in Joseph Wright of Derby's *Experiment on a Bird in the Air Pump*.

Experiment on a Bird in the Air Pump,
by Joseph Wright of Derby

Such averted gazes are to be distinguished from ones in which the represented figures pursue their own interests, apparently unaware of the dramatic event referred to in the title of the picture. In other words they are not turning away from anything – they are simply otherwise engaged.

But there is another sort of averted gaze to be seen in paintings.

It's one in which the subject appears to disengage visual attention to this or that, the better to concentrate on something non-visual. For example, in Frans von Mieris' *Doctor's Visit to the Sick Girl* the physician conspicuously turns his gaze away from the patient's wrist the better to concentrate on the pulse which he *feels* there.

Doctor's Visit to the Sick Girl, by Frans von Mieris

You can see something similar in Caravaggio's group of young musicians. The young man tuning his guitar looks skyward as if to concentrate on the sound of the plucked strings, the sight of which might distract him.

Types of gaze

a. **Perceptual.** Looking in order to see. Directing the eye-line in order to examine, inspect, observe. All of these are examples of looking at what is there. But then there is searching – *i.e.*, looking with a view to finding or recognising something not yet seen.

b. **Indicative.** Ostentatiously directing one's gaze with the purpose of getting someone else to direct his or her gaze to the same thing. This is often accompanied, of course, by pointing. But when there's a question of confidential secrecy and there is one person and one person only whose attention you wish to attract to the area in question, when pointing would draw the unwanted attention of others, A looks secretly at B and swivels his eyes towards the object or person of interest, in the hope that B and B alone will be privy to the indication.

c. **Expressive.** Gazes by means of which someone silently tries to influence the mood or the actions of someone else. In Tintoretto's *Venus and Adonis*, the Goddess fixes her eyes upon those of Adonis thereby imploring him not to leave for the hunt. The silent exchange of glances between two people who thus tacitly express a shared opinion about the behaviour or statements of a third party. Mutually adoring looks.

The legibility of such expressive looks obviously depends on something more than mere eye contact. The context is obviously important. But the meaning of a "look" is also determined by the facial expression that accompanies it. A love-lorn look at someone won't necessarily be read as such unless the face as a whole wears the appropriate expression. All the same, mutual glances may be a necessary component of acts such as inquiring, threatening, regretting or apologising. In other words they are the non-verbal equivalent of what John Searle calls "speech acts".

Visions

The traditional motif of St Luke painting the Virgin might not be exactly what the title implies. In Rogier van der Weyden's version, St Luke is unarguably painting the Virgin, but if you look carefully at his eye-line, it's not actually directed at her. In fact, his gaze doesn't seem to be directed at anything in particular. Perhaps, then – and more interestingly – he is painting not what he sees but what he *imagines* or *visualises*, which means that Rogier has included *his* portrait of the Virgin to help us understand what *St Luke* is envisioning.

St Luke Drawing the Virgin, by Rogier van der Weyden

So that the visual experience represented in Rogier's picture is subtly different from the one which is represented in Fillipino Lippi's painting in the Badia. In this picture there is no question of St Bernardino *imagining* the Virgin as St Luke seems to be doing in Rogier's painting. Nor is he seeing her in the conventional sense; rather he is having a *vision* of her.

Apparition of the Virgin to St Bernardino, by Filippino Lippi

More visions

Official notice on a London bus: "PLEASE DO NOT SPEAK TO OR OBSCURE THE DRIVER'S VISION WHILE THE BUS IS MOVING."

Someone went to the trouble of writing these words and getting them printed on hundreds of plastic placards. It evokes a driver who has visions which can be spoken to – say, of the Virgin Mary – and does not want anyone to speak to her, or obscure his view of her, while he is driving the bus.

Further thoughts about looking

Looking at what one is doing. This is a distinctive form of looking at something, in that one can be completely blind to almost every visible aspect of whatever it is that intercepts one's eye-line, because the eyes are here employed in guiding action and nothing else. For example, in Manet's *Execution of the Emperor Maximilian*, it sounds rather odd to say that the soldiers are looking at the victim, and this is not entirely to do with the fact that their gaze is fastened on such a small and uninteresting part of the unfortunate man.

What they are doing is *aiming* so that what they are looking at is something that one wouldn't normally attend to at all – *i.e.*, the distance between the muzzle of the gun and the supposed position of the Emperor Maximilian's heart. And the same goes for any picture in which people are shown looking at what they are doing. They're keeping track of their own actions, guiding them with the aid of attentive vision..

Photographic smiles

William came back from school today complaining that the photographer refused to snap him until he smiled and it seems that the poor fellow had to pull faces before he could get what he wanted from William. But why did he want a smile in the first place? Why are photographers so eager to get smiles and go to the length of getting people to say "cheese" in order to obtain them? It seems to have something to do with photography rather than portraiture as such. After all, there aren't many smiling faces in painting – so few, in fact, that they are generally noted for their smiles. The *Laughing Cavalier*, the *Mona Lisa* and so on. To some extent, of course, this is because no one could hold a smile through the length of a pose – it would soon become a *rictus*. And when painters did catch a smile, that is to say without the sitter having to hold it for hours, it was a proof of the artists' skill rather than an illustration of the subjects' personality. And the same goes for Victorian photographs: the film was too slow to catch anything but a rictus. No one smiles in Julia Margaret Cameron's plates. But did anyone feel that they were missing smiles at the time? Did everyone breathe a sigh of relief when film eventually became fast enough to capture a grin? And yet for some reason the introduction of fast film coincided with the request – no, the demand – that the subject prepare his or her face for photography by giving a smile.

Why is a smile so important that the photographer will even put up with an artificial version of one? I wonder if it has something to do with friendliness, and that modern snapshots are not simply records of the subject portrayed, but rather a representation of the relationship between the subject and the invisible photographer... the hope being that when the photo is discovered years later, perhaps the smile conjures up the image of an encounter between two people, one of whom departed without leaving a visible record of himself.

Representation

When we say that something is a representation, the assumption is that it somehow falls short of whatever it represents, although the way in which it falls short of it depends on the function the representation is expected to serve. At one end of the scale we have things we regard as substitutes or replacements rather than representations; *i.e.*, some substance, object or person which replaces a missing ingredient, part or role. In some cases the substitute is indistinguishable from whatever it replaces. The repair, as we say, is as good as new. When I say that the substitute is indistinguishable, this may just mean that it's *functionally* indistinguishable, though distinguishable in many of its other properties. An artificial kidney has none of the visible properties of the organ it replaces. It's a large machine that stands on the floor outside the body of the patient. But it functions at least in some respects like the missing kidney. We wouldn't want to say that it was a representation of the missing organ, though. On the contrary, we would be more likely to regard a functionally useless plastic model which *looked* like a kidney as a representation of one.

How about a working model of a kidney which reproduced some, though not perhaps all, of its physiological functions? It is not serving a patient nor does it look like a kidney, but since it illustrates the function of that organ we would have no hesitation in calling it a representation. What one would *want* to say, then, is that it represents the function of a kidney as opposed to its appearance.

Ways in which a person can be represented

By a deputy – that is to say, by someone appointed to act, as we say, on behalf of the person in question. As, for example, when the vice-president represents the president at a state funeral. He doesn't represent the president by virtue of his resemblance. He doesn't represent him any better by being his twin or by wearing his clothes, nor is his function compromised if he happens to have only one leg. He represents not the man but the office, by being formally declared as such. In other words, although he represents the president he is not a *representation* of him but rather he is his *representative*. And what makes him a *representative* is some legislative act to that effect. In other words, his competence is created by fiat and it has little or nothing to do with his personal character. But there are other types of deputy in which the competence is a matter of skill rather than appointment – an understudy, for example. An actor who replaces a sick star does not fulfil the role by being declared a deputy; in fact, he is not really a deputy at all. He doesn't represent the missing actor in any sense. He represents rather the person he is now fortunate enough to play.

Both presidents and vice-presidents represent their country in that some, though not all, of their actions are taken on behalf of the country as a whole. But the president doesn't eat, drink and sleep on behalf of his country, and not all of his publicly visible actions represent his country either. When the president sends condolences or congratulations to another head of state, he does so, as we say, *officially,* and the action is recognised as being done on behalf of the country he represents.

An understudy doesn't act on behalf of a missing actor, he replaces him in the role. Nor does the understudy *pretend* to be the actor who is off for the night. But there is a sense in which both the star and his understudy are pretending to be the person in the play. Vis-à-vis pretence in this context, there is an obvious difference between pretending to be Othello and pretending to be a doctor in order to get ladies to take off their clothes.

In pretending to be Othello, the actor is not trying to convince the audience that he is someone actual called Othello, but that he is someone called Othello who fictionally exists in a make-believe world. And even when an actor plays an actual living character, he's not pretending to be that person in the sense that he would expect, if his pretence was successful, to be personally praised or blamed for the pretended versions of the actual behaviour that he played. On the other hand, what about an actor who was secretly invited to pretend to be a living head of state in order to reassure the public that the sick or possibly dead statesman was alive and kicking.

If his impersonation were successful, who would get the praise or blame for his pretended actions? In the case of an actor standing in for his sick colleague, he would, if successful in the role, accept the praise on his own behalf for a performance as good as (if not better than) the person he was standing in for. He wouldn't have to accept the applause on behalf of the invalid since his performance is a functional replacement and not a ceremonial substitute.

Upside down

I write down someone's initials MW and only later become aware of the fact that the second letter is simply the first one upside down. Now, although I wrote them both effortlessly, thinking of one as M and the other as W, I would have found it difficult to write down the second one while thinking of it as an M upside down. In other words, although the character W is the character M rotated through 180 degrees, it was only by thinking of it as a W the right way up that I could write it without thinking.

Flemish narrative

In *Marriage of the Virgin* by the Master of the Tiburtine Sybil, the events of the Virgin's life leading up to the marriage, including the miraculous details of her birth, are to be seen on the far side of a balustrade, out in the open air, beyond the framed porch in which the marriage itself is taking place.

We are to understand (though how?) that beyond the balustrade does not mean "outside the house and at the same time" but something previous to the main scene.

Roles

Someone can be a body, a cloud of atoms, an assembly of cells, an organism, a person, a father, a Frenchman, a villain or a candidate. Only certain things can happen to each of these entities. You can't execute a cloud of atoms and you can't run an election campaign on behalf of an assembly of cells.

Dreaming

It's possible to wake quite slowly from a nasty dream and it may take some time to recognise the fact that one has been unhappily awake for several minutes. You can roll gently in and out of restless sleep, imperceptibly passing from the imagery of dream to the train of wakeful thought, like a half-drowned sailor washed backwards and forwards in the shallow breakers at the low-tide line – gradually and unnoticeably left high and dry by the retreating waters of sleep so that one can only tell from one's exhausted misery that one was recently afloat in sleep and dreaming unhappily.

Offence versus insult

The two are not necessarily identical. For certain offences to be taken as an insult it may be necessary for the offended person to take account of a third party who has witnessed the incident. Last night I was standing at a bus-stop in Camden Town. Just ahead of me stood a respectable old lady.

Within earshot of both of us there were two vigorously swearing labourers.

The old lady could scarcely avoid hearing what to her must have been offensive words. But she showed no sign of it until she accidentally caught my eye. She now knew that she had been overseen overhearing and that she was therefore obliged to take up the option of feeling insulted, and blushed.

Time present and time past

In realistic painting, the juxtaposition of people or objects within the same pictorial frame implies that they are co-existent: a group portrait of the members of the Linen Drapers Guild, for example, or a still life by Chardin.

So how about the Giovanni di Paolo in the Kress Collection? Within the loggia, whose alcoves recede realistically into the distance, we can see the Annunciation. But in the park just outside, Adam and Eve are being driven from Eden, an event which cannot be co-existent with the Annunciation.

The Annunciation and Expulsion from Paradise,
by Giovanni di Paolo

And yet the painter leaves us in no doubt as to the *spatial* coexistence of the loggia and the park outside. The park can be seen behind and through the colonnade on the left-hand side of the loggia. On the right-hand side of the loggia, however, just behind the seated Virgin, there is a blank wall, partly cut away so that we can see Joseph warming himself at the fire in what is presumably another room. So that on the left-hand side of the picture, in the parkland just outside the loggia, we see events which are historically antecedent to the Annunciation. But on the opposite side, just as realistically, Joseph is obviously sitting in another room at the same moment as the Annunciation.

Seeing as

When I talk about seeing something as something else – say, seeing a cloud as a weasel – it's only because I recognise that the thing at which I am looking has an official identity and that any other way of seeing it is in some sense at least a misidentification. But that doesn't mean that I am taken in by the misidentification. Thus, when Polonius agrees with Hamlet that the cloud is backed like a whale, he takes it for granted that Hamlet will not assume that he, Polonius, mistakes it for a whale. So how about Picasso's sculpture in the Minneapolis Art Institute in which the head of a baboon is represented by a battered racing car?

Advice about shadows

Having failed miserably to represent the shading in a group of objects arranged on a table, I am advised to look at the scene through the fine metal mesh of a tea strainer, and try to focus not on the scene itself but on the mesh.

Interesting! The scene is slightly blurred so that shadows appear in relatively simple blocks and you are not plagued by innumerable details of shading.

More about shadows

In a chance encounter with some amateur German painters, Renoir pointed out that the shadows that they represented were invariably much too dark, that no shadow is black but always has a colour. So why does the amateur painter so often get it wrong? It must mean that they have reasons for thinking that shadows are black and that this overwhelms the visual evidence to the contrary.

So where do we get the belief that shadows are black? It has something to do with the influence of language. Language makes a distinction between light and dark and (derivatively) between black and white, so that in viewing a scene in which some parts of it are lit and the other parts are in shadow, the amateur artist is biased in favour of blackening the apparently unlit areas.

Identifying colours

In the *Elements of Drawing*, Ruskin points out the difficulty of naming the colours that appear in a good painting:

> "You thought it was brown, presently you feel that it is red; next there is, somehow, yellow in it... If you try to copy it you will always find your colour too warm or too cold – no colour in the box will seem to have an affinity with it."

You could say it was the paint-box that created the problem of finding the right colour; with its fixed set of named colours, it gives the misleading impression that these are the hues that occur in the natural world. In this sense, the paint-box is not unlike a dictionary that lists (or seems to list) the colours that are to be seen. In other words, paint-boxes and dictionaries compromise our ability to see the actual colours of Nature itself.

Sunday in the park (circa 1965)

The hawthorn trees are covered in blossom, sprouting inflorescences of eyes. A branched, attentive periscope.

A man with his eyes closed in a deck chair. His head is turned to one side and as we pass unseen next to him I can just make out the blunt pulse of his carotid pumping dreams into his head, but not a drop of the dream leaks out of him.

Out of the park and into the zoo. The gazelle and antelope house. The animals in these fragrant stalls have all the sacerdotal dignity of their ancient role as victims. Watchful and jumpy, with large eyes permanently darkened with fear. Across the way, carefully separated from their traditional prey, are the lions: relaxed, arrogant and mangily superior. They lie on their shelves, one foreleg thrust out, bent indolently at the wrist.

Air miles

Striding along the moving walkway at Frankfurt airport I get the enigmatic impression of weightlessness. Presumably this is because the speed at which visual images stream across my retina is much greater than it would be if I were walking unaided. It's as if one weighs oneself by comparing the muscular effort that one puts into an action with the visual displacement that results.

Overheard

"I think television is the curse of the age. I used to think it was the aeroplane."

"I travelled on an American boat – though, speaking personally, I've never had any faith in American seamanship."

"I've never been much good at looking down steep ravines. How about you?'

"I can remember the time when you couldn't give snooker tables away."

"They've got beautiful sands in Douglas. They just don't know the meaning of dangerous beaches"

"On our way down to Alfriston the other day we got held up by a policeman who said there was cows in the lane. I reckon the lead cow was the black sheep of the family"

Overseen

Through an aircraft window on coming into land, a banner over the passengers' entrance: "SPOKANE WELCOMES METHODIST MINISTERS". As a general principle?

Notice in the lobby of the Hyatt Regency Hotel: "WINNING IN DENTISTRY"

A view

From a high embankment the train passes a row of suburban back gardens. One leg of a huge electricity pylon rises out of someone's vegetable garden and carries the drooping cables off and away to another distant tower.

The owner has leaned a bunch of gardening tools against the foot of the pylon. Small domestic implements leaning against the arrested stride of something vast going elsewhere, beyond the knowledge and even the possible imaginings of the gardener himself. Perhaps he doesn't even know what he's propped his tools against and it's only from the privileged view of the embankment that we can see the dreadful truth.

Radio astronomy

In the hot, midsummer fields outside Cambridge, planted among the buttercups and the ox-eye daisies are two mechanical dishes tilted at the empty sky – silently attending to events infinitely distant from and totally different to the comfortable buzzing going on in the meadow.

Reflecting surfaces

As we fly over the flat fields near Bologna, the lakes and ponds reflect, or I suppose they reflect, the cloudy sky above the aircraft. I say *suppose*, because it's only in the belief that these gaps in the textured fields are reflecting something from somewhere else that I credit the otherwise invisible surface with a glassy sheen. For some reason I see the clouds *in* rather than *on* the surface of these lacunae and I automatically see the surface as something optically different from the matte furrows all around.

With an effort – whatever that means – I can see the fleecy images of the reflected clouds not as virtual images in some virtual depth, way below the level of the fields, but simply as blue and white patches coplanar with the surface of the fields.

The vision thing

My interest in the dramatic representation of human movement co-existed with a preoccupation with vision, a topic to which I had been introduced while still at Cambridge through my contact with William Rushton, Horace Barlow and other physiologists working on the subject. At the same time I came into contact with the distinguished art historians Michael Jaffé and Francis Haskell who directed my attention to the problems of pictorial representation. As the result of many friendly discussions on this subject, not to mention my increasingly frequent visits to the Fitzwilliam Museum in Cambridge, I developed a life-long interest in the distinctive artificiality of pictures and sculptures, my attention alternating between representation of human movement and the varieties of individual gaze.

After giving a series of talks on the varieties of looking in paintings I suggested to Neil McGregor who was at that time the Director of the National Gallery that it might be interesting to mount an exhibition on the distinctive peculiarities of mirrors and all those other reflective surfaces which appear so frequently in the history of Western art. I little suspected when I undertook the task how vast and varied the topic would prove to be., and that I had committed myself to a subject in which the complex varieties of visual experience immediately made themselves apparent.

The following piece was based on the introduction to the richly illustrated catalogue to the exhibition which opened in 1998.

Reflection.

Some years ago I was struck by the behaviour of our cat on the edge of the pavement in front of our house. An hour or so earlier, a downpour of rain had left deep puddles in the gutter. Normally the cat would have hurried across the street without pausing to consider the supportiveness of the ground underfoot, but now she sat hesitantly on the side of the curb apparently disconcerted. From time to time she cautiously dabbled her paw in the otherwise invisible surface of the water and fastidiously shook off the droplets. After a while she crept along the pavement to a point where the gutter was dry. Here she scuttled across the road. Evidently pawing the puddle had confirmed her reluctance to entrust her full weight to such a paradoxical surface. What had prompted her to test the puddle so cautiously? Something about the appearance of its questionable surface enabled her to distinguish it from the safely supportive surface of the brickwork. What could that have been? One answer might be that, in contrast to the matt surface of the dry ground, the puddle was disconcertingly reflective. But what exactly does that mean? In what way does a reflective surface disclose itself as something fundamentally different from the unreflective surfaces which surround it? The problem is that unless it's ruffled by the wind into a pattern of noticeable ripples, the surface of a puddle or a pond, like that of a flawless mirror, is more or less invisible.

Though not quite. Pools of motionless water, like mirrors, afford the observer a 'view', but in contrast to the 'actual' view to be seen through a window or an open door, this view is virtual. Things are not where they seem to be. Looking at the puddle from the opposite side of the street I could see what I knew to be the reflected image of the cloudy sky above.

I doubt if the cat saw it as such or that she was disconcerted by seeing clouds and foliage where they had no business to be. Still, she must have experienced the puddle as something fundamentally different from the surrounding dry ground, and although she may not have recognised what she saw as a paradoxically displaced sky, let alone that the submerged image of another cat looking at her from the lower depths was actually herself, I suspect that she *did* see something at a disconcerting depth below the otherwise invisible surface of the puddle.

In other words the cat reacted to the virtual view of the sky above as if it were the actual view of a dangerous depth below.

As J.J. Gibson has repeatedly pointed out, one of the most important functions of the visual system is to represent the supportiveness of the ground underfoot and the ability to distinguish it from yielding watery surfaces protects terrestrial mammals from the risk of drowning.

In the natural conditions under which the visual system evolved, horizontal sheets of still water would have been the only surface whose enigmatic reflectiveness represented an interpretive challenge. In nature there are no vertical surfaces which offer comparably deceptive views of a world beyond. So the invention of artificially reflective materials complicated the scene considerably, and although human beings have adjusted themselves to a world which includes mirrors and transparent windows, it is easy to underestimate the cognitive problems created by surfaces which are reflective enough to provide misleading views.

As we know, it takes some time for a human infant to recognise the difference between what it sees in a mirror and what it sees through an open doorway or indeed a transparent window. The reflected image which she sees in a mirror is not recognisable as such until she is able to discover a way of testing its peculiar representational relationship to her own presence

The surfaces which afford the experience of seeing oneself in the mirror, are ideally invisible and in some cases they can be confused with the equally impenetrable glass surface of a window through which we can see to an actual beyond. And we can occasionally mistake one for the other. And the ability to identify one's own reflection can often play a crucial part in recognising a mirror as such.

Some years ago I visited a palazzo in Ferrara. I entered the vestibule and stood at the bottom of a grand staircase, on the first landing of which I saw what seemed to be a framed doorway leading to the back of the house. As I mounted the staircase I was surprised to see my own image approaching in what I immediately understood to be the surface of an equally large mirror. What I had taken to be the framed entrance of a corridor leading ahead of me, turned out to be the reflection of the vestibule behind me. To all intents and purposes, my seeing it as a rear view depended on my recognising it as a reflection.

As soon as I recognised it as a mirror I became aware of other tell-tale signs which should have been visible from the outset. And when I retraced my steps and stood again at the bottom of the stairs I was surprised to discover that I could see after all what I had previously overlooked, i.e. the blemishes and dust on the otherwise invisible surface of the glass, and the unmistakable gleam of its bevelled edge. Any one of these clues would have been enough to give the game away and yet for some reason I had failed to notice them until the appearance of my reflected image told me that I was looking at a mirror.

Under normal circumstances, mirrors betray themselves as such without the assurance of a personal reflection, just as they do in paintings where for obvious reasons, we are denied the opportunity of seeing ourselves reflected. But in contrast to a sheet of plate glass with which we can painfully collide without any advance warning, it's impossible to get that close to a mirror without meeting yourself coming in the opposite direction.

It's this encounter that Lewis Carroll leaves so artfully un-described when he smuggles his heroine from her own room into its reflected counterpart on the far side of the mirror.

Alice, you will remember, amuses herself by entertaining the idea that the reflected room is an actual one and that by pretending the glass has conveniently softened enough to let her through, she can visit the looking glass world. What Carroll conveniently forgets to mention is the indescribable shemozzle that would have occurred as soon as the real Alice collided with her reflected self, coming in the opposite direction. In fact, considering how observant Lewis Carroll allows her to be about all the other contents of the looking glass room, it is decidedly odd that she fails to notice that the room in question is occupied by someone who looks and acts exactly like her. Apart from the fact that the two individuals in question are gazing in opposite directions, one apparently looking at the other.

Two sides of the mirror

Are we to assume that Alice thinks the reflected Alice is as actual as the reflected room? If the reflected room was sufficiently actual to allow the real Alice to visit it, she would have had no reason to believe that the reflected occupant is any less actual. If both Alice's are actual, how are we meant to visualise their collision? It's all very well to pretend that the otherwise impenetrable glass which separates them can soften, but that wont do when it comes to getting through each other, because if one Alice politely dissolves in deference to her mirror image, the courtesy will be symmetrically reciprocated leaving no Alice's at all.

In order to be sure that his story can continue, Carroll has to gloss over the difficulty of reconciling the apparent actuality of the reflected room and the self-evident virtuality of her appearance in it. Until she caught sight of her reflected self she could sustain the admittedly pretended belief that the room she could see on the far side of the chimneypiece was just as real as the one on the near side. But this illusion would have been shattered as soon as she saw herself, because in contrast to everything else shown in the mirror, which could after all have been a reverse duplicate of the real room, Alice had incontrovertible first person knowledge of where she, the one and only Alice, was standing. And unless she made the deeply counter-intuitive assumption that the looking glass world included a continuously updated replica of herself, she would be bound to recognise that the 'other Alice' was a virtual image of her own actual presence on the near side of the mirror. And in conceding 'that' she would have had to concede that the looking glass world was just as virtual and that the apparently distant wall beyond her own reflected image was none other than the one behind her own back.

Familiar though we are with the experience of seeing things, ourselves included, in the mirror there is still an undeniable sense that the experience is an illusion since what we see or rather where we see it is not where it seems to be.

But even when we recognise it as an illusion the frequency with which we decorate our walls with mirrors is prompted by something more than the opportunity to see ourselves represented. It also provides the intriguing illusion of an alternative world which might be visited if only we could, like Alice, go through the impenetrable looking glass.

Lecture, 23 May, 2013

The psychology of vision continued to excite me, and after conducting a week-long seminar at New York University devoted to imitation and the varieties of optical illusions, my attention was directed to the complex subject of camouflage and disguise in the animal kingdom and its application in human warfare. I was delighted to have the opportunity to explore this

further when the Imperial War Museum invited me to
collaborate in an exhibition devoted to both the natural
and the artificial expression of visual pretense.

Camouflage

Long before its military usefulness had been recognized and
exploited under the now familiar but surprisingly recent title
of 'camouflage', naturalists had repeatedly drawn attention
to the biological use of visual subterfuge and to the fact that
the form and colour of many animals serve the purpose of
concealment and disguise. Throughout the 19th century
the reports multiplied but there was no comprehensive
analysis of the subject until British zoologist Sir Edward
Poulton published his fundamental work on *The Colours
of Animals* in 1890 by which time three decades after the
publication of Darwin's *The Origin of Species* it was almost
unanimously accepted that these profitable adaptations were
the unplanned results of natural processes, and not, as was
once supposed, the products of purposeful design.

Like many of his predecessors, Poulton recognized that
the colours and forms developed by living organisms could
be either *protective* or *aggressive*, depending on whether
they served to defend from attack or to assist in capture,
and he went on to argue that in each case there were two
relatively distinct ways of achieving the desired effect. The
first of these he described as a *general resemblance* to the
variegated colours of the environment. Such a creature
would, to some extent at least, blend in as if it had become
transparent, thereby affording an apparently uninterrupted
view of the background. In fact, although Poulton doesn't
refer to it in any detail actual transparency is occasionally
employed to achieve this cryptic effect. For optical reasons,
it only works under water, but there are certain species

of fish whose tissues have become so rarefied that their refractive index approximates to that of the surrounding medium, with the result that light passes through their bodies without noticeably betraying their slightly prismatic presence. But even their true invisibility is compromised by the light-absorbing pigments of the eye and by the opacity of food in the gut.

'Silvering' of their bodily surface produces a comparable reduction in the visibility of certain fish, although in a completely different way. By reflecting, as opposed to transmitting, light the shiny scales project an image of the foreground. At certain depths this image is relatively blurred and more or less indistinguishable from that of the background, with the result that the creature which furnishes this hazy reflection becomes conveniently inconspicuous.

Such effects involve modifications of the creature's body, but many animals achieve the same end by *constructing* whatever is required to hide themselves out of material salvaged from their environment. The caddis fly larva, for example, encrusts itself in a makeshift shroud of sand grains, small shells and vegetable *bric-à-brac*, as do certain sea urchins. Another example of such 'adventitious' concealment was reported by the pioneering geneticist William Bateson. He described a species of crab which "takes a piece of weed in his two [claws], and, neither snatching nor biting it, tears it across... He then puts one end of it into his mouth, and, after chewing it up, presumably to soften it, takes it out and rubs it firmly on his head or legs until it is caught by the peculiar curved hairs which cover them."

Purposeful though they seem, it would be a mistake to suppose that such disguises are assembled, in the way that military camouflage is, with the conscious intention of concealment. Because although there is an undeniable sense in which Bateson's crab constructs its artificial covering, just as the caddis worm does, there is neither intention nor ingenuity involved. In both cases, the actions which create the artefact are impulses dictated by genetic instructions inherited from the creatures ancestors – the same type of instructions that determine the creature's equally distinctive morphology. Like the spider's web or the bird's nest, they are examples of what Richard Dawkins calls the 'Extended Phenotype.' That is to say, they are the extended expression of the creature's inherited genotype. In contrast to these kinds of disappearing tricks, there are certain creatures, especially insects, which remain perfectly visible, but disguised as something else. They assume what Poulton termed a special resemblance to a particular item on the scene. That is, they appear as something other than themselves – a dead leaf, say, a lichen-covered twig, or even a bird dropping. Ideally, such disguises render a defenceless creature uninteresting to a hungry predator, and when employed by a predator give it a better chance of ambushing its prey undetected.

Dead leaf butterfly

For example, whereas ordinary caterpillars possess five pairs of legs, the so-called 'stick caterpillar' has only two at the rear end, with which it attaches itself to a twig, while its long thin body, which is corrugated with humps and bumps resembling irregularities of the bark, sticks out an acute angle from the stem, thus resembling an inedible branch. The stick caterpillar practises protective mimicry; as an example of aggressive mimicry, Poulton cites a Javanese spider which takes advantage of the fact that butterflies in that region are attracted by bird dung. According to the reports of a local naturalist, the spider resembles this alluring material in extraordinary detail. As soon as the unsuspecting prey alights on what it supposes to be its meal, it is trapped and devoured.

The success of such disguises depends on the ability of a creature to maintain a convincingly lifeless stillness, since any sign of liveliness would automatically give the game away. Nevertheless, given that it is not in fact a stick or a bird-dropping, the creature must occasionally risk mobility in order to forage and mate. Hence stick caterpillars pass themselves off as motionless twigs during the day and only relax their statuesque pose and crawl about to feed unseen under cover of darkness. Compared to the often remarkable deceptions which can be achieved by mimicking the appearance of particular items in the environment the alternative strategy of pretending not to be there at all is fraught with difficulties. Because even if the creature is sluggishly confined to one particular habitat wearing patterned colours which blend into those of its immediate surroundings a careless movement will immediately betray its presence. Species which assume a general resemblance to their chosen environment therefore frequently reinforce their concealment by developing the ability to stay motionless for long periods. Creatures can achieve much more effective concealment by actually changing their appearance according to their setting. Poulton identified two ways in which this is achieved. *Discontinuous variations* are periodic transformations, often involving radical redesigns of bodily structure, which afford a creature the opportunity to blend in with a different setting. Such a strategy is more or less confined to butterflies and moths whose characteristic metamorphoses from larva through chrysalis to winged adult may coincide with abrupt changes in habitat. These episodic adjustments sometimes involve switching from a *special resemblance*, in which the larval grub mimics the appearance of a twig or a rolled-up dead leaf, to a subsequent *general resemblance*, in which the winged adult assumes the overall colours of its background.

Certain fish, amphibia and reptiles possess the ability to change colour with remarkable speed and fluidity. Poulton categorized such rapid changes of appearance as *continuous variations*. Although the detailed mechanism by which these transformations are achieved was not fully understood at the time, Poulton and his contemporaries recognized that they were not, as might easily have been suspected, the direct result of variously coloured light 'imprinting' itself reversibly on photosensitive pigments in the skin. Experiments had proved that blinded animals lost the power of altering their colour to correspond with the surrounding hues, indicating that the effect was mediated indirectly through the eye, from which, according to Poulton, 'differing nerve impulses pass along the optic nerve to the brain. The brain, being thus indirectly stimulated originates different impulses, which pass from it along the nerves distributed to the skin, and cause varying states of concentration of the pigment in the cells.'

In Poulton's day, as he admitted, 'the highest powers of the microscope have failed to detect the connection between the nerves and the pigment cells in the skin.' These connections can now be clearly viewed, yet the precise means by which a pattern projected onto the retina brings about a corresponding alteration of colours in the skin still remains a mystery.

The ability to realize such rapid changes of appearance, however they may happen, is confined to species whose versatile skin is sufficiently exposed to display them. The fur and feathers with which mammals and birds are clothed rule out the possibility of such conveniently prompt responses. Nevertheless. seasonal climatic changes are almost invariably accompanied by alterations in the colour of pelts and plumage. These often occur before there is any visible change in the appearance of the landscape, making it seem reasonable to assume that they are brought about not by visual stimuli but by a change in temperature. Once these seasonal coats have been established they remain unalterable until the time comes for them to undergo their replacement. The result is that the colours which succeed one another from one season to the next are inevitably generalized, and although they undeniably afford a significant degree of concealment – why else would they have been selected? – the extent to which they resemble each of the particular backgrounds in which the creature happens to find itself is inevitably limited. So again there remains a tendency to exploit stillness or stealth, sometimes both.

Certain predators for example await motionless until their victim comes within reach of an easy snatch. Others actively stalk their prey, occasionally freezing if they have reason to suspect that their stealthy approach has been detected.

But there is another problem, and it applies, or so it is claimed, to any creature whose bulk is sufficient to expose it to the potentially revealing effects of being illuminated from the sky above. With its top side brightly lit and its underside in shadow, its three-dimensional presence, motionless or otherwise, becomes perilously apparent, regardless of correspondence, however close, to the colours and patterns of the environment.

Poulton believed that nature had developed an effective way of minimizing this particular risk of detection. By exploiting mutations which darken the illuminated topside while bleaching the dimly lit underside he argued that natural selection had created a strategy to diminish the otherwise noticeable bulk of the creature. Although Poulton is rightly credited with the first account of this supposedly concealing device of 'counter-shading', the subject was broached at about the same time by the American naturalist and painter Abbott Thayer, who represented its usefulness with almost obsessional enthusiasm. According to him, artists knew better than anyone that differential shading was the most effective way of rendering the three-dimensional bulk of an object, so that it was only to be expected that nature would protect creatures by favouring variations which worked in the opposite direction. As far as he was concerned, counter-shading brought about a flattening effect which reduced a creature's otherwise bulky visibility. The fact that it was conspicuously absent in animals that lived in the dark confirmed his belief. And yet the extent to which this principle achieves the flattening, let alone the concealing, effect which Thayer claimed is somewhat questionable. In many cases the transition from dark to pale takes place so far down on the creature's flank that the pallor in which it terminates is almost invisible. The result is that when the creature is viewed from the side, the counter-shading, such as it is, is all but hidden and so can make no significant contribution to its concealment.

Even when the gradation of tone is more clearly apparent, its flattening effect is debatable. Its advantage is certainly clear in the case of fish, which because they live suspended in water may be viewed by potential predators from above or below. When viewed from above, a fish's dark top side will blend into the dimness of the unilluminated depths; conversely, a white underside seen from below will blend into the brightness of the sky above. The same principle applies to the colouring of certain birds.

But in fact neither of these are true examples of counter-shading, for the simple reason that a dark back or a light underside is only effective in helping to conceal the creature when the other is not visible. They make independent contributions to concealment; the fact that there happens to be a graded transition between them is all but irrelevant.

In spite of these and other objections, the concept of counter-shading continued to play a prominent part in the various theories of cryptic coloration and its importance was repeatedly stressed by the naturalists who succeeded Poulton and Thayer, especially by the distinguished British zoologist Hugh Cott in his classic 1940 study *Adaptive Coloration in Animals*. Cott also emphatically stressed its practical importance in his subsequent work on military camouflage during the Second World War.

During the years that Thayer continued to publish his overstated claims with regard to counter-shading, his attention was drawn to a less questionable type of natural concealment – one which would shortly play a significant part in the subsequent development of military camouflage. He observed that the variegated colours which afford many creatures a generalized resemblance to their surroundings are often supplemented by patches, stripes and blotches whose abrupt shapes break up the contours by which they would otherwise be identified. Given the fact that the concealment achieved by resembling the background is unavoidably partial, these 'disruptive' patterns provide a helpful note of confusion, if only because they serve to divide the attention of the observer between a number of conflicting shapes among which it is less easy to distinguish that of the creature itself.

Thayer's recognition of 'disruptive coloration' anticipated its theoretical formulation by the Gestalt psychologists of the early 1920s. These German investigators were preoccupied with the principles which determine the recognisability of natural objects and abstract shapes. According to them, one of the factors which make a 'figure' distinguishable from the 'ground' against which it is seen is its coherent unity and the fact that its contours enclose an unambiguous 'form' or 'Gestalt'. Anything which competes with the legible continuity of its outlines would compromise its salient identity.

It's easy to see how suggestive these ideas would have been to anyone who was interested in the ways in which animals conceal themselves, though as it happens, Thayer died just before the fundamental works in Gestalt psychology were published and discussed. But even if they had been published earlier it is unlikely that he would have acquainted himself, let alone sympathized, with these somewhat abstract arguments. For as far as he was concerned the truth of the matter was self-evident to anyone who worked in the visual arts. In the introduction to the 1908 edition of his *Concealing Coloration in the Animal Kingdom* he announced that the subject had got into 'the hands of the wrong custodians' and that 'it properly belongs to the role of pictorial art, and can be interpreted only by painters, for it deals wholly in optical illusion and this is the very gist of a painter's life.'

As a result of this proprietory attitude, Thayer failed to take any account of the by then widely reported fact that 'disruptive colours' sometimes made creatures more rather than less conspicuous, and that this was not necessarily to their disadvantage. For example, in 1867 Alfred Russell Wallace had already explained to Darwin's satisfaction that colourful ostentation was sometimes a beneficial feature. If a species happened to combine conspicuous coloration with prickles, poisons or a repulsive taste, predators would eventually learn the costs of attacking it. By bearing the tolerable loss of a few individuals, the species as a whole, and the bold colours that singled its members out, would eventually gain a protectively deterrent reputation.

A few years later Wallace's colleague H.W. Bates drew attention to an interesting variation on this theme. He reported the existence of edible species whose conspicuous appearance mimicked that of unpalatable ones. Without having to incur the biochemical expense of developing poisons, their striking resemblance to species which *had* done so would, in the course of time, lend them the vicarious reputation of being too risky to attack. However, the efficiency of this device presupposes that the palatable species are outnumbered by their unpalatable counterparts.

In 1879 the German naturalist Fritz Muller drew attention to an alternative version of the mimicry which Bates had recently described. He identified a number of equally unpalatable insect species, all of which displayed the same conspicuous uniforms, thereby spreading the risks of educating hungry predators.

Although Poulton took some time to accept the statistical evidence in favour of Mullerian mimicry he immediately recognized the importance of Wallace's findings, not to mention those of Bates. Unlike Thayer, he acknowledged the fact that concealment was not the only way of reducing the risk of being attacked, and that as long as there was a memorable correlation between the *appearance* of a creature and its unpleasant *taste*, the very fact that it was conspicuous would play a significant part in the defence of its fellows.

In contrast to the various forms of concealment and mimicry mentioned earlier – for which, there are many recognizable counterparts in human warfare – it is difficult to identify any military equivalents to the 'warning colours' described by Wallace, Bates and Muller. Although a conspicuous show of armed strength does often play a significant part in disconcerting the enemy, the threat which is represented by such displays is intended to create alarm, whereas in the case of 'warning' colours there is nothing intrinsically deterrent about their appearance. On the contrary, they positively invite the greedy attentions of a predator, whose subsequent reluctance to attack such self-advertising prey depends on the ability to remember the unpleasant consequences of doing so. And even then, the tutorial effect is confined to the individual predator unlucky enough to suffer such a bitter experience. Meanwhile Wallace had already identified yet another benefit to be gained by undertaking the risks of being conspicuous. But in this case the value lay in attracting the attention of individuals of the same species as opposed to that of its enemies, 'Gregarious mammals' for example, 'while they keep together, are generally safe from attack, but a solitary straggler becomes an easy prey to the enemy; it is therefore of the highest importance that the wanderer should have every facility for discovering its companions with certainty at any distance within the range of vision.' In other words, the vividly noticeable colours shared by members of a particular species make it easy for them to recognize one another, so that if a particular individual strays into vulnerable isolation, it can readily identify the distant presence of its fellows and return to the collective security of the herd.

In this particular case there is, surely, a military equivalent to what Wallace describes. In traditional warfare at least, the existence of vividly recognizable uniforms and flags undeniably helped to maintain the disciplined coherence of the action. But since they also provided the enemy with a conveniently visible target, it's not surprising that with the introduction of smokeless powder and more accurately aimed firearms, conspicuous uniforms were soon replaced by drably inconspicuous khaki.

There was another example of conspicuous coloration which taxed naturalists during the 19th century. The frequency with which the males and females of a species differ in their appearance had many times been noted. In birds and insects especially, the females are reticently coloured, whereas their male counterparts display flamboyantly ornamental liveries. For Darwin, such differences were inconsistent with his theory of natural selection, because although there was an obviously protective advantage in the modest dress of females, it was difficult to understand why the male of the species exposed himself so flagrantly. As evolutionary historian Helena Cronin points out, Darwin came to the conclusion that natural selection was powerless to account for such apparently pointless splendour. His solution was his theory of sexual selection. He held that male ornamentation evolved simply because females preferred to mate with the best-ornamented males. This obviously gives these males a mating advantage and ultimately the likelihood of greater reproductive success.

Thus over evolutionary time, males develop ever-more exaggerated, immoderate flamboyance. To begin with, Wallace went along with this idea, but since it conflicted with what he regarded as the more fundamental truths of natural selection, he became increasingly reluctant to recognize the equivalent reality of sexual selection, and as time went on his disagreement with Darwin became more and more explicit.

Argus pheasant displaying

As far as he was concerned, bright colours were the natural expressions of health and vitality – witness the vivid tints of blood, bile and fat – and it was only when, in the case of brooding females, they were vulnerably exposed to the necessities of concealment that natural selection suppressed them in favour of more reticent appearances. Wallace was by no means alone in this respect. In the years which followed its publication in the *Descent of Man* (1871), Darwin's theory of sexual selection was subject to widespread criticism and ridicule. Meantime the role of *natural selection* itself was also increasingly called into question, especially after 1900, when the rediscovery of Gregor Mendel's plant breeding work inaugurated the explosive growth of experimental genetics.

For the practitioners of this new science, mutation – that is to say abrupt and often large-scale change in the hereditary mechanism – was regarded as the driving force of evolutionary change, and the effect of selection was confined to the elimination of harmful novelties.

It took more than thirty years, but eventually there was a reaction against this attitude, epitomized by the polemical introduction contributed by Julian Huxley for Hugh Cott's *Adaptive Coloration in Animals*, published in 1940: 'Among a certain section of experimental biologists... it has been fashionable and indeed almost a matter of professional conscience to display a radical scepticism on the subject of adaptations, especially colour adaptations and most particularly mimetic adaptations. Upholders of the theories of protective and warning coloration and of mimicry have often been attacked as armchair theorists, insufficiently acquainted with modern work in genetics, which for some unexplained reason is held to do away with adaptive interpretations.' According to Huxley, 'Dr. Cott, in this important book has turned the tables with a vengeance on objectors of this type... far from genetics in any way throwing doubts on their adaptive interpretation, the facts of cryptic, warning and mimetic coloration pose searching questions to the geneticist, and demand a recasting of many current views on the efficacy and mechanisms of selection.'

Cott's book is, as Huxley writes, a worthy successor to Edward Poulton's earlier work. It retains and adds to the categories established by his predecessor, and since natural history had flourished in the intervening years, undeterred by the condescension of laboratory scientists, Cott's text contains a wealth of previously unrecorded detail, copiously illustrated with many of his own accomplished drawings and photographs. In contrast to Poulton, his analysis is characterized by repeated reference to the optical principles involved in concealment and disguise:

'When we recognize anything by sight... the means by which the eye is enabled to distinguish it are fourfold and it is essential for the proper understanding of our subject that these should be clearly appreciated. Firstly the object appears in the field of vision as a continuous area of colour, differing more or less markedly in hue and purity and depth from its immediate surroundings, against which it is therefore seen to stand out in contrast.

Secondly, the (object) is not seen simply as a wash of flat colour – even when in actual fact it may be uniform in colour. For it is thrown into relief by the effect of light and shade, which enables the eye to detect surface curvature, modelling and texture.

Thirdly, although natural objects are not, or are but rarely bounded by lines – in the way that an outline drawing is – nevertheless the surface of every visible body is framed by a contour [which] has a characteristic shape, enabling the form of a familiar object to be recognized.

Fourthly, under certain conditions of illumination a shadow will be thrown by the object upon its background... By framing the outline of the object, as well as by virtue of their own shape and conspicuousness, shadows tend to facilitate recognition.'

It is interesting to see how Cott applies some of these principles to what he regarded as the most important type of natural concealment, 'Disruptive Coloration' – a concept which had already influenced the development of military camouflage:

> Provided an animal is seen against a broken background, it is probably true to say any pattern of darker or lighter colours and tones will tend to

hinder recognition by destroying to a greater or less degree its apparent form.... but in order to achieve effective results the colours, tonal contrasts and patterns employed must conform to definite optical principles .... In the first place the effect of a disruptive pattern is greatly strengthened when some of its components closely match the background while others differ strongly from it. Under these conditions, by the contrast of some tones and the blending of others, certain portions of the object fade out completely while others stand out emphatically.

As a result of this interaction between strongly contrasted adjacent tones, some of which blend into the background, the creature's recognizable identity is effectively disintegrated, so that instead of seeing one recognizable animal the observer is confronted by a clustered array of apparently discontinuous surfaces. The effect is enhanced by disruption of the contours of the creature or stripes which cut across as opposed to running parallel to its all too recognizable edges.

In 1935 Cott read a paper to the British Association for the Advancement of Science in which he reported an important but previously unnoticed variation on this theme. He referred to it as *Co-incident Disruption*. During fieldwork in Portuguese West Africa, he had noticed that certain species of frog could increase the confusion created by their disruptive colours by bringing their striped limbs into close contact with comparably coloured stripes on the side of their body. With its thigh hugged close to the flank, 'the silvery stripe on the exposed part of the hind limb exactly coincides with, and forms an extension of, the similar stripe on each side of the back.' In this attitude, against a dark background, all that can seen is a dim blob with two parallel white stripes, Something similar happens when the common frog bends and folds up its hind legs; blotches and stripes which seem to have no relationship with one another when the limbs are extended line up to create a bewilderingly disruptive pattern. The same principle is frequently exploited to reduce the conspicuousness of a vertebrate's eyes. As Cott observed, 'Of all shapes a round disc is the most striking and easily seen and recognized – hence the use of the "bull's-eye" for target practice' Small though it is, the vertebrate eye with its dense black pupil stands out from the most jumbled background and thereby draws attention to its owners vulnerable front end, where it can least afford the risk of injury. It's not surprising that nature has evolved a variety of 'disruptive' solutions to this problem. 'Animals belonging to many widely different families and orders have the eyes camouflaged in precise detail .... Sometimes an irregular dark disruptive area includes the whole orbit. Sometimes the upper margin of an elongated patch of dark pigment crosses the iris exactly on the top of the pupil...or again, the eye may be crossed by a stripe exactly the width of the pupil itself, and so on.

Since the creature's front end is the one at which a predator's attack is most likely to prove fatal, Cott demonstrated that nature often provides a conspicuous false eye at the rear end, where injury would be somewhat less devastating. Poulton had, in fact, already identified such deflecting eye-spots in many species of butterfly. Other naturalists had demonstrated the frequency with which areas of the wing bearing such false eye markings show signs of damage from predators' attacking beaks.

And so it goes on for almost five hundred pages of such carefully analysed detail that it seems uncharitable to question Huxley's claim that it represents the last word on the subject.

Nevertheless, to the modern reader it seems slightly odd that Cott expressed so little interest in how these adaptations might have come about during the course of the creatures development. To some extent of course such considerations would have been irrelevant to the task he had set himself. As a dedicated naturalist he was concerned to analyse the usefulness of the various features he described; the question of their embryological origin was a distraction that in any case remained at that date unanswerable.

Biologists in the 1930s were already acquainted with the reproductive significance of chromosomes, and with the fact that the information which dictated the structure and function of the forthcoming organism was distributed throughout the length of these divisible filaments in the form of discrete, albeit invisible entities called genes. However, the biochemical medium in which this productive information was represented and the process by which it was translated into developmental effects remained obscure. In recent years the relationship between molecular biology and experimental embryology has become so complex that it is impossible to provide a reasonable summary here. But research in this area has been so productive and so precise that scientists can now ask what were previously unanswerable and indeed inconceivable questions about the origins of the adaptations that Cott described sixty years ago.

Introduction to *Camouflage, Thames and Hudson, 2007*

Visualising Action

In a later exhibition, *On the Move*, at the Estorick Collection in London, I addressed myself to the pictorial representation of action, animal and human, and I introduced the visitors to the way in which the topic underwent a revolutionary transformation as a result of what photography was able to represent.

Among the various events that attract our attention in the world around us, we can distinguish two types. There are those that we recognise as the unmotivated effects of equally unmotivated *causes* and, on the other hand, those to which we give the name of *actions*. The latter are peculiar to what we regard as living organisms, which distinguish themselves as such by characteristic forms of mobility, and by the fact that they tend to do things to their own advantage – something conspicuous by its absence from the behaviour of inanimate objects, which have no interest in their continued existence. When we see a billiard ball move immediately upon being struck by another, we visualise the event as a mechanical ricochet and have no inclination to regard the movement of the first ball as one of aggression or that of the second ball as one of escape. The distinction I am trying to make is exemplified in a poem by Robert Frost entitled 'A Considerable Speck'.

> A speck that would have been beneath my sight
> On any but a paper sheet so white
> Set off across what I had written there.
> And I had idly poised my pen in air
> To stop it with a period of ink
> When something strange about it made me think,
> This was no dust speck by my breathing blown,
> But unmistakably a living mite
> With inclinations it could call its own.
> It paused as with suspicion of my pen,
> And then came racing wildly on again
> To where my manuscript was not yet dry;
> Then paused again and either drank or smelt –
> With loathing, for again it turned to fly.
> Plainly with an intelligence I dealt.
> It seemed too tiny to have room for feet,
> Yet must have had a set of them complete
> To express how much it didn't want to die.
> It ran with terror and with cunning crept.
> It faltered: I could see it hesitate;
> Then in the middle of the open sheet
> Cower down in desperation to accept
> Whatever I accorded it of fate. [...]
> I have a mind myself and recognise
> Mind when I meet with it in any guise
> No one can know how glad I am to find
> On any sheet the least display of mind.[1]

---

[1]   R. Frost, 'A Considerable Speck', *Robert Frost's Poems* (New York: St. Martin's Press), p. 251.

The behaviour that Frost observed in what he at first thought to be an inanimate 'speck' of dust blown by his breath, led him to believe that it was after all a living organism with interests in its own survival. However, the extent to which this 'speck', whose behaviour had earned it such consideration, was conscious of its predicament, and that it actually *wanted* not to die, is somewhat questionable. And Frost was mistaken when he suggested that he was witnessing a 'display of mind' analogous to his own. Serviceable though its behaviour seemed to be, it would be wrong to assume that the creature harboured what we would regard as conscious intentions. On the contrary, we know that organisms as primitive as this are hard wired to behave as expediently as this considerable speck did. As we ascend the tree of life, living organisms become increasingly versatile in their ability to serve their own interests, and the repertoire of their opportunistic actions becomes richer and more variable. But the extent to which they are conscious of the risks and opportunities to which they react is impossible to determine.

The situation is completely different when we come to consider human actions, for the almost self-evident reason that most of the things we do are prompted by intentions to which we can refer using the medium of language, so that more often than not we can explain to others what we are trying to do.

But not everything we do is prompted by the conscious urge to bring about a foreseeable result. In fact, as the American philosopher John Searle pointed out: 'Many of the actions one performs, one performs quite spontaneously without forming, consciously or unconsciously, any prior intention to do those things. For example, suppose I am sitting in a chair reflecting upon a philosophical problem and I suddenly get up and start pacing around the room.

My getting up and pacing about are clearly intentional actions, but in order to do them I do not need to form an intention.'[2]

The point is that even when we act idly, without any conscious intentions, we can recognise our movements or actions as ours. If I lift my arm for no apparent reason I can, as Wittgenstein pointed out, distinguish between that and its mysteriously going up of its own accord: I am acquainted with the fact of raising my arm without having to see it happen because, even when it occurs for no particular purpose, I know that I am the author of the action. And it is such actions – rather than events – which I am writing about.

When photography first made its marketable appearance in 1839, the sensitivity of the silvered plates used by Louis Daguerre required lengthy exposures that precluded the possibility of recording anything which happened to be on the move, so that although motionless buildings and bridges were represented with remarkable finesse, the brightly lit streets were disconcertingly empty, apart from the occasional pedestrian who was standing still for long enough to register on the photographic plate.

In the course of the next twenty years or so the efficiency of lenses and shutters steadily improved and, with the introduction of increasingly sensitive plates requiring much shorter exposures, urban photographs began to include signs of life which had previously been conspicuous by their absence. In Adolphe Braun's stereoscopic snap of the Pont Neuf in Paris, pedestrians and vehicles are now clearly apparent, just as they are in George Wilson's photograph of Princes Street, Edinburgh.

---

[2] J. R. Searle, *Intentionality: An Essay in the Philosophy of the Mind* (Cambridge: Cambridge University Press, 1983), p. 84.

Paris street photograph by Louis Daguerre

Edinburgh street photograph by George Wilson

Objectively speaking, the figures in these photographs are motionless, but since they are sufficiently focused to be recognisable as exponents of lively action, there is an unarguable sense in which we see them on the move. Of course the same principle applies to the equally static configurations of painting and sculpture. As long as the represented figures are known to be active and purposeful, the observer automatically credits them with the probability of their being on the move, especially if they are portrayed in attitudes and positions from which it is relatively easy to infer both the previous and the subsequent movement. For example, in a fifteenth-century engraving of the Death of Orpheus by Durer we can tell, from the admittedly static positions of their arms, that the assailants have just raised them and that in all probability they will strike a downward blow a moment later.

The point is that we underestimate what Ernst Gombrich famously referred to as 'The beholder's share' in vision, and we carelessly assume that what we see is exclusively determined by what is in front of our eyes. Whereas the truth of the matter is that although there is an undeniable correspondence between what we see and whatever happens to be in view the experience is strongly influenced by what we know, remember, believe or expect. In other words, the intelligence and experience that we bring to a picture, unconsciously or otherwise, has a significant effect on what we take it to be a picture *of*, and what – if anything – might be going on.

Paradoxically, this principle can be profitably applied to what early photographers once regarded as a regrettable failure of the medium. Lengthy exposures that sometimes resulted in the disconcertedly blurred images of whatever happened to be on the move were subsequently exploited for the very purpose of representing rapid movement, and in the twentieth century smear and blur became pictorial idioms of choice.

By the time photography had developed to the point where it began to include figures whose activity could at least be inferred, the public was already familiar with optical toys which went one better, affording as they did the undeniable illusion of continuous movement. In 1832 the Belgian physicist Joseph Plateau introduced what he called the 'phenakistoscope', a device which presented the viewer with a succession of static pictures, each of which represented an arrested moment in the otherwise continuous development of a natural movement. The figures were arranged around the circumference of a rotating disc which was to be viewed through another in which there was a radial sequence of slits.

Phenakistoscope

If the rotation of the pictorial disc was viewed without the slitted disc in front of it, the viewer saw nothing but a whizzing smear. But as long as the two discs were mounted, fore and aft, on the same spindle so that the visibility of the pictorial disc was repeatedly interrupted by that of the slitted disc in front of it, the streaming blur resolved itself into individually recognizable figures that visibly danced, ran and galloped without seeming to go anywhere. On the contrary, they appeared to be exercising their limbs on an invisible treadmill.

The stroboscope, independently devised by the Austrian mathematician Simon von Stampfer, was almost identical to Plateau's mechanism. George Homer's zoetrope was somewhat different. Instead of a pair of discs it consisted of a rotating, open-topped cylinder. The pictures were arranged around the lower edge of the inside, to be viewed through a row of slots just above. In each of these devices the illusion of movement was somewhat compromised by the distracting visibility of the rotations which brought the pictures, one by one, into view. It was not until the 1870s that there was any noticeable attempt to overcome this difficulty.

In 1876 the English barrister Wordsworth Donisthorpe suggested an arrangement in which the movement that delivered the successive images was effectively concealed, so that the visibility of each one was confined to the brief moment when it was actually in view. This was to be achieved by taking prints of the exposures and fixing them one after another onto a long strip of ribbon or paper. This strip was wound from one bobbin to another so that the photographs were made successively visible at the same rate that they had been exposed. Although this device was never actually realised, with the benefit of hindsight one can recognise the extent to which Donisthorpe had unwittingly anticipated some, but not all, of the basic principles of the movie projector, in which the viewer is completely unaware of witnessing a succession of still pictures, for the simple reason that each frame is brought into view under cover of darkness, held motionless for a moment before it is invisibly removed, and equally invisibly replaced by its successor. This complicated process is achieved by coordinating the intermittent advance of the sprocketed film with the alternating action of a shutter which conceals both the arrival and the departure of each frame. Mechanically this is indistinguishable from the operation of a machine gun, where a succession of bullets is intermittently brought into position, held still for as long as it takes for the firing pin to strike the cartridge and then moved on to be replaced by its successor. Both of these, in turn, bear a striking resemblance to the mechanisation of the industrial production line, in which the conveyor belt moves intermittently, stopping for as long as it takes for the worker to perform his or her task.

Why, you might ask, does the intermittent succession of almost identical pictures afford the experience of continuous movement? The traditional explanation invokes the so-called persistence of vision, according to which, when the human eye is presented with such a succession, there is a brief period, after the removal of one picture, during which an after-image of that picture persists upon the retina, allowing it to blend smoothly with its successor. This theory, which seems to have originated from the experimental work of Michael Faraday and Peter Roget, and was revived by Plateau and his colleagues, is repeatedly cited by modern theorists of the cinema who seem to overlook the fact that, if it were literally true, far from affording the illusion of movement it would result in the overlapping of several still pictures comparable to Marcel Duchamp's *Nude Descending a Staircase.*

But since that is not what we actually see, one can only assume that the illusion of continuous movement is due to something other than the persistence of retinal imagery. In any case, even if we accept the claim that retinal images outlast the moment of their optical projection, it would be a mistake to regard this as a case of persistent vision for the simple reason that vision does not actually occur in the retina. Although it is difficult to say exactly where it does occur, it becomes increasingly apparent that what we see is actively constructed by the visual system as a whole and that the experience of movement, real or apparent, is a complex neurological process which even now is not fully understood.

There were intimations of this constructive notion towards the end of the nineteenth century. In 1875 Sigmund Exner performed an interesting experiment on the illusion of movement. He briefly flashed a light on the left-hand side of a screen and, a moment after it disappeared, flashed another light on the right-hand side. The observer reported that instead of seeing two separate lights going on and off, one after another, he saw one light moving from left to right. However, if the interval between the appearance of the lights was either too short or too long, or if the distance between them was increased, the illusion might be lost. These results are conspicuously at odds with the traditional theory, because if the image of the left-hand light had outlasted its extinction, then the observer would have seen two lights, the first of which might have faded gradually. The apparent movement was self-evidently created or constructed by the observer. And in a much more complicated way that is what happens in the cinema.

The versatility of this constructive process was shown in a number of subsequent experiments. For example, in 1916 Vittorio Benussi discovered that if a visible obstruction – a black square for example – was placed between Exner's two lights, the observer tended to report that the apparent movement hopped over the obstruction in a curved line. Other observers reported that the light disappeared behind or sometimes passed in front of the black square. But none of the apparent movements were either fanciful or elaborate. In other words our visual intelligence, unconscious though it may be, creates the simplest possible illusions of movement.[3]

It is interesting to consider how implicit knowledge determines what we actually see. For example, in the 1970s the Danish psychologist Gunnar Johansson put small lights onto the joints of actors dressed in black in a darkened room. Until the actor moved the observer reported nothing more than a constellation of motionless lights, but as soon as the actor started to move, the observer immediately knew what he was looking at. One can only assume that the visual system was exploiting its unconscious knowledge of the body image.

The first person to achieve widespread celebrity for his photographic study of animal locomotion (especially that of the horse) was a self-promoting Englishman who had shown no previous interest in the subject. But having yielded to a flattering request to investigate the gait of the horse he embarked on a career that was to earn him lifelong international fame.

Born in England in 1830, Edward Muggeridge migrated to America in 1852, by which time he had begun to redesign his name in an effort to dramatise his supposedly Saxon pedigree. As Eadweard Muybridge, he worked for several years as a successful bookseller in and around the east coast of the United States. He returned to England in the early 1860s, having just recovered from a nearly fatal stagecoach accident. During his lengthy convalescence he began to

---

[3] For further reading see D. D. Hoffman, *Visual Intelligence: How We Create What We See* (New York: W.W. Norton & Company, 2000).

devote himself to the study of photography and when he returned to the United States he rapidly established himself as one of the most accomplished landscape photographers on the west coast. In 1868 he published a major series on the scenery of the Yosemite Valley, extolling his technical virtues under the pseudonym of Helios. He drew attention to the heroic efforts required to prepare, fit and then expose the cumbersome collodion wet-plates.

After publishing another series of remarkable photographs, his achievements came to the attention of the former Governor of California, Leland Stanford, who was now a chairman of the Pacific Railroad. Like many of his sporting colleagues, Stanford was preoccupied with the controversial claim that there was an unobserved moment during its rapid trot when the horse had all four feet off the ground. In the hope that high-speed photography might capture this invisibly unsupported moment, Stanford invited Muybridge to apply his skills to the problem. What he wanted was a high-speed picture of his champion horse Occident trotting at full speed. Muybridge was predictably excited by this request. He recognised immediately that it could only be done – if at all – if the horse were to trot past the camera seen from the side, so that the position of all four legs would be apparent.

As it happened, the photograph was too indistinct to be publishable, although it was clear enough to prove Stanford's point. Muybridge tried again but the picture was never published.

In 1874 Stanford had become much more ambitious. This was almost certainly the result of his having read the recently translated version of Etienne-Jules Marey's *Animal Mechanism*, a remarkably subtle account of the French physiologist's long-standing studies of terrestrial locomotion. As we shall see, Marey's research method was graphic rather than photographic. For example, in studying the gait of the horse, he fitted the underside of each hoof with a rubber bulb that was connected by an air-filled rubber tube to a recording device which traced the pressure changes onto a revolving smoked drum.

Marey realised that it might be difficult for the untutored eye to read this somewhat technical calligraphy. But with the help of a gifted military artist, Emil Duhousset, these records were translated into a series of pictures illustrating the various positions of the horse's limbs. In a brief afterthought, Marey suggested that consecutive photography would be a more truthful representation, especially if the images could be animated by some of the optical instruments which we have already mentioned.

However, as far as Marey was concerned the fanciful drawings to be seen in these popular toys were not fit for the purpose of scientific analysis. They were frivolous and inaccurate. He was unaware of the fact that photography was about to supply a realistic alternative. And, as it happens, Stanford and Muybridge were already on to something that might solve the problem. They were in fact independently about to embark on an ambitious programme of research when Muybridge was arrested and indicted for the murder of his wife's lover. After a lengthy trial in which his counsel pleaded not guilty on the grounds of insanity, citing the serious head injuries which Muybridge had suffered in the stage coach accident more than ten years earlier, he was acquitted.

During a self-imposed exile in South America, Muybridge resumed his photographic studies and on his return to San Francisco announced that he was now prepared to take photographs with an exposure of less that 1/1000 of a second. In August 1877 he published another shot of Occident trotting along the Sacramento track. The press greeted it with some enthusiasm although one journalist complained that its truthfulness was compromised by extensive retouching. And the fact is of course that Muybridge had fiddled with the image, but he was confident that it was a truthful representation.

In the early summer of 1878 he made the first serial photographs of the horse in motion. With the help of Stanford's mechanics and electricians he set up a row of twelve high-speed cameras equipped with electrically-controlled shutters, and in the presence of a large number of journalists two of Stanford's prize steeds were snapped as they trotted or galloped against a carefully prepared white background. One of the horses was harnessed to a sulky whose wheels struck wires laid on the ground at twenty-one inch intervals, thereby releasing the shutters of the cameras, which were arranged at the same interval along the open front of a shed facing the track. For the unharnessed animal the trigger took the form of thin threads which were stretched above the track at the same intervals so that she effectively took her own pictures in rapid succession.

THE HORSE IN MOTION.
Illustrated by
MUYBRIDGE.
"SALLIE GARDNER," owned by LELAND STANFORD; running at a 1.40 gait over the Palo Alto track, 19th June, 1878.

Stanford horse

In the following year, the number of cameras was doubled and the intervals between them more or less halved, and by this time other animals were introduced. By 1881 a large number of these instantaneous photographs were published under the title of *The Attitudes of Animals in Motion: A Series of Photographs Illustrating the Consecutive Positions Assumed by Animals in Performing Various Movements.*

In fact the achievement had already been recognised by *Scientific American* in June 1878, and in December of that year the French scientific journal *La Nature* published several reproductions of the photographs. As one might have expected, Marey asked the editor to put him in touch with Muybridge, insisting that this was just what he had been waiting for and that these truthful images could replace the ones that had so exasperated him in the optical toys he had rejected earlier.

Meanwhile Muybridge himself was determined to animate his sequence of photographic stills and he soon came up with a machine that combined the phenokistascope and the magic lantern – the zoopraxiscope. It was an interesting variation on the device that had been created by Plateau fifty years earlier, but in this case the now realistic images could be projected onto a screen that was large enough to be viewed by a number of people at the same time. Muybridge described it as 'the first apparatus ever used or constructed for synthetically demonstrating movements analytically photographed from life'.[4]

An interesting reciprocity! Muybridge's photographic enterprise had been initiated under the influence of Marey's publication of *Animal Mechanism* and now Marey had been impressed by what Muybridge and Stanford had produced.

---

4   A.V. Mozley, introduction to *Muybridge's Complete Human and Animal Locomotion: All 781 Plates from the 1887 'Animal Locomotion', Volume 1* (New York: Dover Publications, 1980), p. xviii.

By 1881 Muybridge had become an international celebrity, and shortly after his arrival in Paris he was invited by Marey to demonstrate his slides and animated projections to an impressive group of guests including Marey's colleague Colonel Duhousset, the editor of *La Nature*, Gaston Tissandier, and the distinguished photographer Nadar. A few months later Muybridge received an enthusiastic reception at a party to which he had been invited by the famous artist Meissonier, who was shortly to modify his military pictures under the influence of Muybridge's striking animations. Early in the year, he repeated his Parisian performance at the Royal Academy in London with an audience including Thomas Henry Huxley and Alfred Lord Tennyson, as well as several members of the royal family.

In the course of these lectures Muybridge repeatedly insisted that his photographic 'stills' proved how inaccurate the traditional representations of animal movement had been, and that since antiquity artists had consistently misrepresented the equestrian gallop. He cited a large number of reproductions in which the creature was almost invariably shown in the so-called 'rocking-horse' position, in which both forelegs are extended out to the front with the hind legs stretched out in the rear. The frequency with which this attitude was repeated in the course of art history gave it an undeserved reputation for truthfulness, so that when they were confronted by the more complicated attitudes to be seen in Muybridge's photographs the public often concluded that it was the *camera* that had lied. This was the moment at which Muybridge exploited the zoopraxiscope to prove his point. By animating the succession of seemingly untruthful stills, thereby restoring the continuous action with which everyone was already familiar, Muybridge was able to convince them that far from lying, the camera was the only reliable source of pictorial truth. If, as his critics repeatedly insisted, the photographs were false, why was it that when animated they represented movement so truthfully.

By this time, Muybridge had developed an almost missionary zeal and although he was disappointed by his repeated failure to obtain sponsorship for an ambitious project devoted to the relationship between the photographic representation of movement and that of traditional art – in which he had hoped to get contributions from both Marey and Meissonier – when he returned to the United States in 1882 he renewed his efforts by issuing a prospectus for *The Attitudes of Man, The Horse and Other Animals in Motion.*

In 1883 his luck suddenly changed when the University of Pennsylvania in Philadelphia invited him to pursue his investigations in a more systematic fashion. Apart from its long-standing scientific distinction, the university was extremely wealthy; but the most significant fact was the presence of two men who had already expressed an informed interest in Muybridge's earlier work in Palo Alto. Fairman Rogers was the head of the Pennsylvania Academy of Fine Arts, a civil engineer and an extremely prosperous sportsman. Thomas Eakins on the other hand, was an accomplished painter and photographer who had corresponded with Muybridge six years earlier. Both men were apparently eager to recruit Muybridge and after extensive negotiations with the academic establishment funds were promised on the understanding that Muybridge was to be supported and above all instructed by physicists, anatomists and engineers. In other words, it was to be a serious academic exercise. But it took longer to establish than anyone expected, and it was not until 1885 that the outdoor studio was up and working; even then there were unexpected failures. But with the technical assistance of university chemists and electricians who helped to devise what was needed to synchronise the exposures of three separate batteries of cameras arranged at varying angles to one another, thereby affording foreshortened and oblique views in addition to the conventional row of cameras parallel to the line of action, Muybridge was now able to print an enormous number of photographic sequences.

He started with human subjects and in August of that year moved his equipment to the Zoological Gardens in order to take pictures of birds and animals. Until recently the photographic plates that he compiled as a record of this project have been widely regarded as a scientific database for the study of human and animal locomotion. But, as the distinguished historian Marta Braun[5] was the first to point out, the extent to which this pictorial compendium should be regarded as a scientific enterprise is extremely questionable. Apart from the fact that we have to 'read' the images in order – ignoring the black frames that contain each one and which make it difficult to visualise the continuity, let alone the trajectory, that they supposedly represent – the intervals between each exposure are not reliable enough to allow one to draw any quantitative conclusions. In any case, careful examination of these assemblages shows how much Muybridge fiddled with their arrangements and that when, for some reason, frames were either missing or blurred he was quite prepared to replace them with a duplicate of the *previous* frame or even with frames taken from different photographic sessions. Even when they are undoubtedly consecutive – that is to say, when each picture truthfully occupies its proper place in the sequence – the recognisable individuality of the figures and the visible peculiarities of their physique distract one's attention from the dynamics of their movement. In other words, it is difficult for the observer to suppress his interest in who these people are and what

---

5   Marta Braun, *Picturing Time, the Work of Etienne-Jules Marey*, U. Chicago Press, 1992

they are up to. We seem to be witnessing a story rather than a scientific demonstration. This is particularly obvious when Muybridge addresses himself to female movement. More often than not these sequences are distractingly picturesque, condescendingly domestic, trivially playful and in some cases teeter temptingly on the edge of soft pornography. In fact it is difficult to imagine anyone looking at these pictures with anything other than a narrative interest.

This is much less apparent in his *animal* sequences, in which we have no personal interest in the individuals represented. We are witnessing nothing but flight or gait so that we can concentrate on the consecutive positions of the wings and the limbs. And in the case of the avian photographs, the pictures certainly disclose with remarkable accuracy what the unaided eye could never succeed in capturing. But in contrast to Marey, Muybridge makes no attempt to describe, let alone analyse, the dynamics involved.

Until Governor Stanford prompted him to read the recently published *Animal Locomotion* it is unlikely that Muybridge would have known anything about the distinguished French physiologist Etienne-Jules Marey. In fact, as I have already pointed out, there is nothing to indicate that the English photographer had any interest in animal locomotion, whereas by 1874 – when Stanford and Muybridge first took note of him – Marey had already earned an impressive reputation for his amazingly varied papers on the subject of animal movement.

Marey was born in Beaune in 1830. As a schoolboy he had already shown a remarkable talent for making mechanical toys, and if his father had not insisted on his studying to become a doctor he would almost certainly have followed his own inclinations and applied for entry to the École Polytechnique. The chances are that his achievements as a civil engineer would have been just as impressive as the ones for which he is now celebrated, but it is not as if his originality was stifled by the training he had been forced to undertake. On the contrary, by the time he entered medical school in 1849 the subject of experimental physiology, which was just beginning to flourish in France, immediately aroused Marey's interest. As a radical materialist he was convinced that the movements and actions of the living body were closely related to those of engines and machines, and that because of their undeniable complexity the unaided senses failed to capture the subtle continuity of their natural action.

It soon became apparent to Marey that the mechanical ingenuity which had already earned him the admiration of his medical colleagues could be profitably employed in devising physical instruments which were a) sensitive enough to capture the variables in question, b) able to faithfully transmit what was captured, and c) capable of recording the transmission in a legible graphic form.

While he was still an intern he began publishing on the subject of what he referred to as the hydraulics of the *circulation*, and by 1860 had devised an astonishingly subtle instrument that recorded the continuous variations of the radial pulse. By this time he had given up whatever ambition he might have had to become a clinical practitioner and until 1867 addressed himself exclusively to the *internal* movements of the living body: that is to say, to actions and processes that were scarcely noticeable to the unaided senses, such as the contractions of the heart, the pressure variations in the blood vessels and the variable contractions of muscle.

In 1867 he directed his attention to the *overt* movements of both the human and the animal body and, by exploiting the tripartite system he had devised previously, tried to systematise the rhythms of locomotion. In his studies of the human gait he attached an air-filled tambour to the soles of the shoes, connecting them by a pneumatic tube to a recording device held in his hand by the pacing subject. He used a comparable set-up for recording the four-legged movements of the horse. Two years later he took on the much more difficult task of analysing the flight of birds. The graphic technique that he had successfully used for humans and horses now had to be modified to allow for the fact that the creature was airborne and that the movements of its wings were so rapid and so complicated that it required an elaborate set of sensors that was impossible to harness to anything but a large bird.

Marey bird

In fact, by the 1870s Marey was beginning to recognise some of the shortcomings of the hydraulic technique he had created, such as the fact that the apparatus was forbiddingly cumbersome and often failed to detect some of the subtler variables of animal locomotion, especially in the case of birds. The graphic results required expert reading and gave no impression of what the creature actually looked like as it engaged in its action. Marey began to suspect that photography might be a satisfactory alternative and that as long as the plates were sensitive enough to record a succession of rapid exposures, the camera could capture the continuity of a particular action with pictorial accuracy, without having to use skeins of pneumatic tubing.

The photographic technique to which he eventually committed himself was recognisably different to the one Muybridge exploited. In fact, two years before he became acquainted with the Californian results he was already expressing interest in what his astronomical colleague Pierre-César Jules Janssen had achieved in recording the transit of Venus across the face of the Sun.

In 1873 Janssen described a photographic revolver fitted with a lens in the gun barrel. At the butt end there were three discs, the circumference of one of which was photo-sensitive. The intermittent rotation of this disc was coordinated with that of a pair of slotted discs which allowed a section of the photographic disc to be briefly exposed to the incoming light at regular intervals. When the plate was developed it revealed an orderly succession of stills arranged around its circumference. In 1876 Janssen published an article in which he suggested that such a device would 'allow one to approach the interesting question of physiological mechanics related to the walk, flight, and various animal movements'.[6]

Marey immediately recognised the possibility of such an arrangement, and although he was intrigued by the article which Muybridge published in *La Nature* in 1878, it was apparent to him that a photographic gun was technically preferable to the somewhat unreliable battery of twelve cameras that Muybridge had employed.

By the time the English photographer was revelling in his Parisian acclaim, Marey had already begun to develop a portable counterpart to Janssen's device, a weapon that

---

[6] Braun, p. 55.

was light enough to be held in the hand so that it could be pointed at birds in flight. Instead of having to co-ordinate the exposures of twelve separate cameras, the accurately timed sequence was achieved with a single machine.

Fusil photographique

There were, however, two serious disadvantages. The images were too small to be easily legible and since, like Muybridge's 'snaps', the successive stages of the movement in question were confined to widely separated frames, there was little sense of their energetic continuity. In the effort to overcome these problems Marey introduced a completely different photographic technique. He abandoned the gun in favour of a different type of camera altogether, one that was fitted with a motionless horizontal plate so that the successive exposures now disclosed themselves one after the other within the same frame. As Marta Braun rightly points out, the results represent a fundamental change from pictorial convention, in which 'we read what occurs within the frame as happening at a single instant in time [instead of looking] at several men moving in single file [we see] a single figure successively occupying a series of positions in space'.[7]

Marey now had a versatile process to which he gave the general title of 'chronophotography', by means of which the trajectory of locomotion became apparent. Photosensitivity had now reached the point where it was possible to multiply the number of exposures per second and in many photographs the figures begin to overlap. Although these configurations gave a vivid impression of energetic action, there was a point at which the resulting overlap made it difficult to read the position of the limbs. In order to eliminate this confusion and to allow a more detailed analysis, Marey introduced an extremely ingenious way of simplifying the imagery. His subjects were dressed in black so that the bulky outlines of their physique blended into the dark background. Meanwhile, narrow lines of reflective material were stitched onto their clothing in positions which corresponded to their jointed limbs. The successive exposures now disclosed the pure geometry of the action. This, in turn, could be translated in a graphic form on paper and submitted to analysis.

In the early 1880s Marey's work attracted the attention of the French government whose military officials, dismayed by France's humiliating defeat in the Franco-Prussian War, suggested that the systematic study of human locomotion might play a significant role in designing exercises that would guarantee fitness and endurance. With the aid of a talented and patriotic assistant, Georges Demeny, and with generous grants from the French government, Marey was able to establish a physiological station in the Bois de Boulogne. Here, against a carefully designed arrangement of blackened hangars their subjects, dressed contrastingly

---

[7] Ibid., p. 66.

in white costume, were photographed as they walked, ran, leapt and jumped.

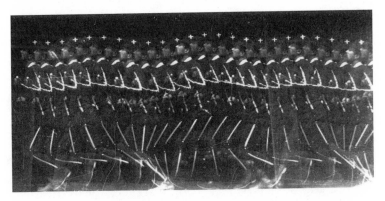

Multiple image of man running, by Marey

In 1886 Marey resumed the photographic study of bird flight which had previously defeated his technical ingenuity and, with the aid of cameras representing a considerable improvement on the 'gun' that had proved to be so disappointing three years earlier, he was at last able to picture the detailed trajectory of airborne movement. Once again, the extent to which the images were separated or overlapped depended on the frequency with which the plate was exposed. Marey was so interested in the results that he commissioned bronze sculptures based on both sets of images.

Throughout these studies Marey displayed his characteristic versatility and he continued to devise ingenious improvements of the camera so that the images became increasingly clear and easy to read. In many cases he supplemented the photography with the graphic techniques that he had exploited a few years earlier. For example, in his repeated studies of the jump he attached tambours to the soles of the athlete's feet so that he could measure the variable impacts associated with such ballistic efforts.

In contrast to Muybridge – whose influence on art was largely confined to corrections of the pictorial representation of animal movement, particularly to the all too often misrepresented gait of the horse – Marey unknowingly laid the foundations for one of the most significant developments in twentieth-century modernism, although it was not until several years after his death that this influence expressed itself in the dramatic appearance of Italian Futurism.

By the time Marey died in 1904 the understanding of the relationship between space and time was undergoing significant transformations. In addition to the fact that the mechanisation of transport and communication had altered the subjective sense of distance, the traditional concepts of space and time had been extensively modified and reconstructed by physicists and mathematicians so that the relationship between distance and duration had become much more complicated. And although it is unlikely that anyone in the artistic community was deeply acquainted with the details of non-Euclidian geometry, not to mention the subtleties of Relativity, there was a widespread belief that the structure of visible reality was not what it seemed and that the conventional ways of picturing it had to be reconsidered.

With the introduction of Cubism by Picasso and Braque, the representation of three-dimensional reality underwent a startling reconstruction, subverting as it did the traditional notion that picturing something was inconceivable from anything other than a single point of view. In other words, seeing someone from the side precluded seeing him from the front. By jamming the profile and the full face into a single configuration the Cubist challenged the impossibility of representing both aspects simultaneously.

A year or two later, Futurism was to do something comparable to the pictorial representation of *action*. And this is where Marey's enterprise was so influential. Movement, whose progressive continuity had traditionally been represented at one particular moment from which the observer could do no more than infer what was about to happen, was now dynamically represented in an overlapping succession of stills. In the many paintings that were clearly inspired by Marey's laminated images, actions that would have taken time to complete disclose themselves on a single frame.

Of all the Futurists, Balla's work is most recognisably indebted to the model of Marey's chronophotography. Works such as *Dynamism of a Dog on a Leash*, *Girl Running on the Balcony* or the *Hand of the Violinist* reveal the full extent of this influence. Luigi Russolo was in fact the first Futurist painter to use repeated, overlapping forms to evoke movement in his large work *Music*, where the figure of a pianist is endowed with five hands in order to suggest rapid movement up and down the keyboard. Russolo's use of this pictorial device perhaps owes more to the early Futurist interest in optical illusions and the mistaken belief in the phenomenon of the 'persistence of vision', in accordance with which they maintained that for the attentive observer 'a running horse has not four legs, but twenty, and their movements are triangular'.[8]

Dramatic though it was, the painterly influence of Marey's chronophotography was relatively short lived. However, photographers have continued to exploit such imagery right up to the present day. The most systematic modern exponent of this idiom was Harold Edgerton, professor of electrical engineering at the Massachusetts Institute of Technology. During the early 1930s, he developed and expanded stroboscopic principles that had been at the

---

[8] U. Boccioni and others, 'Futurist Painting: Technical Manifesto' (1910), in U. Apollonio (ed.), *Futurist Manifestos* (London: Thames and Hudson, 1973), pp. 27-31 (p. 28).

root of nineteenth-century chronophotography through the use of a high-speed electronic flash. Ranging from twenty, to a hundred, to a million times a second, these flashes enabled Edgerton to make images in the style of Marey but with far greater accuracy and clarity. Edgerton's iconography, too, is immediately comparable to Marey and Demeny, including images of fencers and other sportsmen

By the end of the nineteenth century it had become increasingly apparent to Marey and his colleagues that the results of his physiological research could be profitably applied to the growing demands of the industrial work space and that in all probability they could help to determine the most productive and the least wearisome use of the labourer's limited resources of personal energy. Marey realised that the photographic techniques that he had previously used to analyse the movements of *military* athletes could be gainfully employed in the workshop, and that it might be possible to recommend the most efficient use of tools.

From the enormous volume of his learned publications, not to mention the unprecedented ingenuity of the mechanical devices with which he recorded physiological processes, one gets the somewhat misleading impression that Marey is to be seen as a major contributor to scientific knowledge. And yet it is almost impossible to identify a fundamental *theoretical* principle which he derived from his records and observations. This is largely due to his reluctance to undertake experimental intrusions into the living body of animals. He was convinced, without any theoretical justification, that vivisection interfered with biological function and to all intents and purposes destroyed what the observer might be trying to explain. He failed to appreciate the inescapable necessity of intelligent interference and that although one might give memorable representations of this, that or the other biological process, it was impossible to understand them without a discriminating sequence of theoretically-directed experimental destructions.

The irony is that his failure to leave a significant scientific legacy is closely related to his *seemingly* scientific commitment to the idea of the body as a machine. In fact it is difficult to find any interesting references to those aspects of the body that are peculiar to living organisms and the basic features by which they *differ* from machines – the contractile material from which muscles are made, the elaborate nervous circuitry by which their action is co-ordinated and of course the peculiar chemistry of muscles and nerves. In that sense it is interesting to compare Marey's work with the monumental legacy of Sir Charles Sherington (1857-1952) whose minutely detailed experimental work on the integrative action of the nervous system still defines modern ideas about the mechanisms of locomotion.

On the Move, Visualising Action, Estorick Collection, 2010

The Afterlife of Art

Throughout my career as a director of operas and plays, the frequency with which I have engaged in the revival of works, most of which were written and composed in the distant past, raised the controversial issue of authenticity, and I became interested in the questionable responsibility of dealing honourably with the subsequent performances of works which had outlasted their author's wildest dreams of posterity.

In a very important sense, great plays can be said to exist without being theatrically performed, and I cannot deny the fact that each time a play is staged the production is inevitably a limited version of the range of possible interpretations. But if the principle that plays should be read rather than performed were to be taken seriously it would dissolve the distinction between drama and all the other forms of literature, and make it difficult to understand why a writer had chosen to cast his ideas in the form of a play at all. In fact, the suggestion that plays are best left unperformed is comparable to the belief that novels can be successfully dramatized. In both cases, there is a fundamental misunderstanding about the structure and purpose of the genre. A play that has been kept unperformed has been aborted, whereas a novel that has undergone dramatization has been irreversibly mutilated. As long as we recognize and accept the argument that performance is, necessarily, a limitation, then the destiny of a great play is to undergo a series of performances each of which is incomplete, and in some cases may prove misleading and perverse. By submitting itself to the possibility of successive re-creation, however, the play passes through the development that is its birthright, and its meaning begins to be fully appreciated only when it enters a period that I shall call its *afterlife*. In the case of Shakespeare's plays, for example, what is often disputed is the form that their continued existence should take (and who should determine that form) when the works have outlived their original performances.

This applies not only to plays but to other works of art that survive the period in which they were conceived and first realized. I have borrowed the word 'afterlife' from Aby Warburg, the founder of the Warburg Institute, which he described as a place where scholars could study 'the afterlife of the antique'. He was referring to the process by which classical culture was revived following its long neglect after the fall of the Western Roman Empire. This process took a peculiar course, described by one of Warburg's colleagues as 'an undulating curve of estrangements and rapprochements', culminating in the triumphant restoration that we now recognize as the Renaissance.

I find the phrase useful because it draws attention to the peculiar transformation undergone by any works of art that outlive the time in which they were made. If they are rediscovered after a long period of being lost or neglected, they are perceived and valued for reasons somewhat different from those held originally so that they change their character and to some extent their identity. In other words, there comes a point in the life of any cultural artefact, whether a play or a painting, when the continued existence of the physical token that represents it does not necessarily mean that the original identity of the work survives. In some examples of painting or sculpture the re-evaluation is the paradoxical result of physical deterioration; the object may be recovered in a form that would no longer be acknowledged by its maker. The classical Greek sculptors, for example, would have had to allow for the natural process of weathering, and some of them might have even welcomed the patina that their creation acquired in later years. But we cannot assume that they would have been delighted by the mutilation that befell so many of these works as a result of years of burial and neglect. When pieces of classical sculpture were recovered and collected during the Renaissance, however, part of their appeal was undoubtedly associated with their mutilation. There is little doubt that some of the appeal of the Belvedere Torso can be attributed to its suggestive incompleteness, and that the work is now being appreciated for features that would have been regarded as faults by the artists of antiquity. A sculpture, originally made to conform to certain standards of finish and perfection, resurfaces in a culture that puts a distinctive premium upon its damaged format.

There is another reason why we cherish works that have been bequeathed to us in a damaged condition. In fact, when certain ancient monuments are restored the refurbishment induces public indignation, in the belief that the object no longer looks like an antique work of art.

The situation is made more complicated by the fact that restoration is frequently carried out insensitively so that the finished work is seen as a travesty. And yet even when performed with all the available resources of skill and scholarship we are left with the uneasy sense that a diaphanous hood of *interpretation* has been slipped over the repair and that, far from being restored to its original state, the object has merely provided an armature on to which the modern craftsman has imposed his own ideas about the distant past. As we shall see, this is analogous to the sense of disapproval expressed in criticisms of the interpretation imposed upon the classics by contemporary theatre directors. Yet it is difficult to see how plays, operas, paintings or sculptures can be restored to their original condition without risking the imposition of re-interpretation.

As well as the physical effects that can be inflicted upon an object, comparable social and institutional influences affect the subsequent life of a work of art. The work may be transferred to a place or setting that bears no resemblance to the one where it had a recognizable social, aesthetic or religious function. It would be nonsense to talk of the work merely continuing its life; it has a new one – an afterlife. The equestrian statue of Marcus Aurelius, for example, was originally a triumphant effigy of this Roman emperor. It was then lost, or simply lay around Rome, was recovered during the Renaissance, misidentified as a portrait of Constantine, and finally placed by Michelangelo on the pedestal in the centre of the Piazza del Campidoglio in Rome as a demonstration of the Christian Imperial theme. Even if we now know its real identity, we can no longer visualise the statue as it would once have been seen. Apart from the fact that it is placed in a strange, and previously unthinkable, setting, a modern observer might be puzzled, for example, by the rider's dangling feet although these would have seemed perfectly natural to its original audience for whom stirrups did not yet exist.

Marcus Aurelius

Some works of art are *deliberately* dismembered in the course of their subsequent revival and this, as I have already pointed out, has an irreversible effect on the way in which they are now perceived. Plunder and commerce often led to the dispersal of certain Renaissance altarpieces, for example, with the result that works that were once appreciated for their carefully designed entirety are now distributed between widely separated galleries. The visibility of these disconnected fragments is altogether different from that which they would have displayed as part of the original integrated art work; they begin to acquire unintended attributes as the subjects of an unforeseen type of scrutiny. For example, when a predella is removed from the altarpiece to which it belongs and is displayed as an independent object in its own right, the illustrated strip acquires a significance it would never have had when subordinated to the image for which it supplied a decorative border. Visitors to the ducal palace at Urbino have become acquainted with Uccello's *Profanation of the Host,* unaware of the fact that when originally attached to the lost altarpiece for which it was painted it would have dwindled to a marginal ribbon of ornament. In its afterlife it has enlarged to become a masterpiece in its own right. An even more vivid example is Mantegna's *Crucifixion* in the Louvre. Wrenched from its rightful place in a predella belonging to the great altarpiece in S. Zeno at Verona, this phosphorescent panel has assumed monumental proportions.

The fact that these works are now exhibited in galleries rather than churches has had an important part to play in transforming their identity. Apart from any decay or restoration they may have undergone, they have been changed by social re-allocation. Something that was once intended to guide and intensify religious experience is now being enjoyed as an example of aesthetic achievement. The spectator cannot exempt himself from the role in which he has been cast by the act of entering a gallery, and the secular gaze that now falls upon the picture changes it just as much as the dust and smoke of time. Even if the picture were confronted as an aid to religious devotion today, it has entered its afterlife and many of the signs that are there as aids to the original congregation can no longer be read by a modern audience.

Michael Baxandall has pointed out the specific information that is conveyed by the various positions of the Virgin's hand in quattrocento Annunciations. There are, according to him, five successive phases of the Angelic Exchange or Colloquy and each position of the Virgin's hands characteristically registers one of these. For an audience who knows nothing of this, the positions of the Virgin's hands are no more than trivial variations on the single theme of the Annunciation, vaguely expressive perhaps, but not especially significant. The original audience, familiar with the possible alternatives, however, would have automatically known which of the five phases of the angelic colloquy they were being invited to meditate on: the semaphore was recognized. If a modern congregation were now to use that object as an aid to devotion, it would face it merely in a mood of generalized piety, unaware of the specific code it was there to show. Even if the language were understood, as it might be by the art historian code-breakers, the picture would still not be read as it was when first presented. We are no longer a pious audience; if we distinguish one of the five phases we do so as informed tourists.

The predicament is made even more complicated by the different policies that determine how a picture is displayed in a gallery. When a painting is exhibited alongside other works by the same artist, its appearance is altogether different from the one that it has when hung next to works done by other painters of the same period. When a painting is displayed as an instance of a *genre* – in an exhibition devoted to still life, for example – it looks altogether different from the way it would appear in an exhibition devoted to the many different works of a particular period. The way in which a painting is perceived is also influenced by the way in which it is reproduced. The appearance of many great works has been irreversibly changed by being introduced to the public in the form of photographic copies, most of which represent the work on an incorrect scale. Visitors to a gallery or a church are often shocked to discover that a picture is either much larger or much smaller than it seemed in a book of reproductions. The viewer's confusion is increased by the custom of reproducing enormously blown-up details, some of which become more attractive than the whole painting, which may seem quite disappointing by contrast.

For all these reasons it seems right and proper to describe the renewed existence of these works of art as afterlives, and to see them not simply as faint or attenuated versions of their *previous* existences, but as full-blooded representations of their *subsequent* existence. This unforeseen hereafter that we inhabit, and in which we perceive such objects, departs so much from the time of the work's original conception that it seems advisable to think of the work as a separate entity with its own peculiar conditions.

The concept of an afterlife can be usefully applied to plays and operas on a rather different logical level. This is because there is no particular object, perishable or otherwise, with which a play or opera can be identified. What is being referred to when someone talks about the existence of such a work?

The continued existence of *Hamlet*, for instance, does not depend on the existence of any particular copy of the text since any old version will do as long as it is a reliable transcript of the original. The contrast with a painting is self-evident. Piero's *Flagellation* can be said to '*exist*' only if the authenticated handiwork of the artist survives. Neither copy nor forgeries will do. This is a distinction that Nelson Goodman makes in *Languages of Art*, between what he calls *autographic* works of art, which are identified with handwork, and those he calls *allographic*, which have to be re-created in performance. An autographic work, like the *Flagellation* by Piero, is one whose identity presupposes the continued existence of the physical artefact that left its maker's hand, and only with the destruction of the work itself does it cease to exist, although it may survive by imitation or copy in a forgery. The very existence of an autographic work makes forgery possible – but there cannot be a forgery of an allographic work, such as a play, which does not physically exist as an *object* in the way that a painting or sculpture does. You might forge a manuscript but how could you counterfeit a production?

These problems apply to any work in which performance is recognized as a constitutive part of the art. As Nelson Goodman points out, an unperformed play is not quite so forlorn as an unperformed symphony. *King Lear* could have had an intelligible existence without ever having been staged, whereas the very notion of an unperformed *Winterreise* seems unintelligible. Yet there is a sense in which a play can be said to have been completed only when work has been supplied by someone other than the playwright. This does not mean that playwrights are slipshod artists, constitutionally incapable of finishing their own work, or that their relationship to the actors who perform their plays is in any way comparable to that of a great painter who leaves his assistants to apply the finishing brush strokes as, for example, Verrocchio who left Leonardo to finish his *Baptism* by painting in one of the angels' heads. The craftsmanship supplied by the theatrical profession belongs to a different category from the work that went into making the script, whereas the effort that goes into revising or finishing a painting is merely a continuation of that which brought it into existence in the first place.

Of course, in a purely practical sense the continued existence of *Hamlet* depends on the survival of at least one reliable text, but since it makes no difference which one, it may be tempting, as Richard Wollheim points out, to identify the play with the class of all its reliable copies. This suggestion is open to several objections, one of which is that the fortunes of *Hamlet* would then fluctuate with the number of copies in existence. If there were twenty thousand copies would the play be more substantially *in existence* than if there was only one? It also ignores the possibility of performance. The alternative expedient, of identifying a play with *one* of its performances, will not work either, because it would follow that any faults in that particular performance would apply to the play itself. And what would one want to say about a play that had never been performed?

In the effort to discover *something* in which the existence of a play could be said to consist, the suggestion is sometimes made that each work should be identified with an ideal performance, that is to say with no *actual* performance but with the best *imaginable* one. But it is always logically possible to imagine a better performance than any particular one claiming that status. This concept cannot supply the wherewithal for a play's continued existence. Besides, the notion of an ideal performance begs the very question that I am trying to explore. It implies that an ideal performance would be unanimously recognizable if and when it occurred.

This, of course, is the point at issue. Not everyone agrees with Dame Helen Gardner that the best imaginable production of *Macbeth* was the one in which Laurence Olivier performed the title role; those who were satisfied by Trevor Nunn's production of the play would almost inevitably disagree with Dame Helen. Great plays seem to be capable of an almost infinite number of alternative performances and, unless we make the improbable assumption that successive productions have a built-in tendency either to improve or to degenerate as time goes on, it is impossible to predict when and where the ideal is likely to realize itself.

The allographic work of art introduces all the ambiguities and open-endedness that give rise to the debate about the role of the director. You have a *text*, the purpose of which is to provide the instructions from which it is possible to produce a *performance*; but that, as Nelson Goodman points out, is not the text's only function in allographic works. It is also an authenticating device, the purpose of which is to provide a system of identification that allows you to say, on any given occasion, that this performance is an instance of the work in question.

It seems to me that the scripts of plays are ineffective in regard to both of these functions. The text of a play is surprisingly short on the instructions required to bring a performance into existence. Playwrights do not include – and cannot, because of a shortage of notation – all those details of prosody, inflexion, stress, tempo and rhythm. A script tells us nothing about the gestures, the stance, the facial expressions, the dress, the weight, or the grouping or the movements. So although the text is a *necessary* condition for the performance it is by no means a *sufficient* one. It is short of all these accessories which are, in a sense, the *essence* of performance. The physical act of *reading* the words of a script does not constitute a performance. Words are nothing more than the bare minimum when staging a play. Similarly, the script is defective as an identity card unless we accept that a play is fully performed simply when all the words are given in the right order. In the phylogenetic history of an evolving organism it is always possible to recognize the existence of a morphological prototype, and while this may undergo extensive transformation, with the unexpected enlargement of one part accompanied by a proportional shrinkage of another, the structural relationships are preserved so that it is easy to recognize the underlying affinity of many different examples. As Darwin pointed out, careful analysis shows that the fin of a porpoise, the paw of a lion, the hoof of a horse and the wing of a bird or bat are all related to one another by their common descent from a prototypical vertebrate limb, The successive performances of a play or an opera can be compared to this process; and although the works may undergo changes that are sometimes tantamount to anamorphic distortions, something equivalent to topological propriety is preserved from one instance to the next.

Another model that I find useful is the procedure used by cartographers when transferring a map of the world from a *spherical* globe on to the *flat* surface of a page. The oceans and continents preserve the topological continuities of the original but can do so only at the expense of considerable changes in their relative proportions. The point is that as long as the director observes some intuitive sense of topological decorum, his own production, albeit different from those of his predecessors, can be mapped on to them and through them can be mapped finally on to the structures of meaning that are inherent in the original text.

In recent years these proprieties have often been set aside to allow productions in which there would seem to be no limits to the director's imaginative energy. In the kind of production that I have in mind, many of which seem to originate in Germany, it is difficult to identify any organic continuity between the production in question and its predecessors, and the work appears to be quoted rather than produced.

These productions are so fractured that it becomes impossible to map them on to anything inherent in the text. When that happens I feel as if I am confronted by something that resembles a foetal abnormality – in which the orderly process of emergent development has been arrested and distorted by morbid processes working against the long-term interests of the work in question. Unfortunately critical fashion has often favoured these bizarre aberrations, and productions that have developed along more organic lines may be dismissed as boringly obvious.

In fact, if the theatrical illustrations of any one Shakespearean play were to be arranged in chronological order they would look so different that it may be easier to recognize the period of the picture than the identity of the play. Yet all these performances were generated by the same script and its failure to give rise to identical productions means that its status as a set of instructions is somewhat ambiguous. Scripts may contain clearly instructive passages, such as stage directions which prescribe certain physical actions – *Konstantin moves rapidly upstage, opens the French windows and vanishes on to the verandah. He returns accompanied by Nina'* – but the bulk of the text is made up of speeches, and the sense in which these should be regarded as instructions is much less clear. This becomes more apparent when you contrast such notation with, for example, the score of a passage assigned to the clarinet in Mozart's Quintet in A, K581, where it is difficult to regard the symbols as anything *other* than a set of instructions.

While a script is an example of a notation, and in that sense at least resembles the inscriptions in a knitting pattern or a musical score, it is very important not to be seduced by this analogy between words and music. Angered by a floridly conceptual production of a play, critics sometimes point out that no one would ever dare to take such liberties with the performance of a Mozart symphony and that the modern director should pay as much respect to a script as a conductor does to a great classical score. According to those who exploit this analogy, re-staging *Hamlet* in modern dress is comparable to re-scoring the 'Haffner' for brass band and Moog synthesizer, and, since no one in his right mind would dream of doing *that*, why should anyone take the liberty of vandalizing the work of a great playwright? The frequency with which this argument recurs suggests that there is an illuminating similarity between symphonies and plays and that, because the performance of both depends on the obedient following of scripted instructions, the decorum that is observed in one is indistinguishable from the etiquette that applies to the other. This view is misleading and unhelpful. It assumes that successive performances of any one musical work are much more standardized than in fact they are. But the important point is that the so-called *language of music* cannot be usefully compared to the language of human discourse. People speak glibly of the language of music, and although this is only a figure of speech, I think it has encouraged a critical assumption that words and music lie on the same level of interpretability. The extent to which music can be regarded as a language at all is highly questionable.

We might accept that a score, like a script, relies on notation, the forming of 'phrases', a syntax, and that music can conjure up images – the third movement of Beethoven's 'Pastoral' Symphony skillfully re-creates the impression of a storm. It can evoke moods and, in its own idiosyncratic way, it can also represent colourful scenes and natural events but, since it can neither assert nor deny, there is no way in which music can be said to *describe* the scenes that it represents.

Nor is there anything in music, for example, that corresponds to a word: there are no recognizable units or segments for which one can substitute alternative bits with equivalent meanings. Perhaps the best way of highlighting the differences is that you cannot even imagine a paraphrase in music. We talk about phrases in music and we talk about phrases in language, but it is central to language that phrases *can* be paraphrased. The meaning that is expressed by a sentence can remain more or less constant under paraphrase, whereas it is impossible to imagine what would count as a paraphrase of the opening bars of Beethoven's *Hammerklavier*, because there is no central, underlying proposition that would remain constant and survive an alternative expression in another series of notes. Music is syntactical but not semantic.

Despite the fact that we talk about 'the composition of music' there are no *rules* of composition; what one composes in music are its elements. Those elements can, in fact, have significance by being composed but they do not refer to another domain of propositions that survive transformation into a different composition.

This is not the only reason why the comparison between scripts and scores turns out to be unworkable. In contrast to the phrases in a musical *score* the phrases in a dramatic *script* represent the utterances of a particular character who means something by uttering it. Recognizing what the character *means* by a particular phrase calls for something over and above *linguistic* knowledge. It is necessary to take into account *who* spoke it, to *whom* and under what circumstances. Whereas the artist who plays the solo instrument in Haydn's Cello Concerto in D can successfully perform the part without having to imagine being anything other than a cellist; she does not have to pretend to be Haydn or some person imagined by Haydn. The actor who plays the part of Claudius, on the other hand, can expect to succeed only if he imagines a person who consistently means something by the lines that appear opposite his name in the script.

Claudius's speeches could be said to have a meaning that is independent of any particular person who might utter them, but their full significance becomes apparent only when put into the mouth of a recognizable character who cannot be identified on the evidence of the scripted speeches alone. For example, on one level it is quite easy to recognize the meaning of Claudius's famous soliloquy which begins with the words, 'O! *my offence is rank*', and it would be perverse to deny that these were the thoughts of a remorseful murderer. It is only by disregarding this and other written evidence that Cavafy was able to represent Claudius as an innocent victim slain by his deluded nephew. But the fact that the script leaves us in no doubt as to

Claudius's resourceful villainy, by showing us his readiness to commit further crimes in order to cover up the original one, does not mean that his character is unquestionably determined. On the contrary, there are several alternative ways of personifying him and with each of these portrayals the speeches begin to assume a different significance.

Similarly in *King Lear* it may be possible to identify what I can only describe as a sea level of meaning from the sentence, '*O! reason not the need*' and that irreducible level may remain unaffected by uttering this line in a hoarse whisper, in a guttural French growl or the electronic tones of the computer Hal in the film *2001*. Yet the purpose that this sentence serves in the play demands a more subtle identification of its meaning, and the inscription that Shakespeare provides to represent this line does not give enough phonetic instruction to identify its further reference in the domain of meaning. The point here is that although the meaning of the sentence may not be altered very much by the changed tone of voice, what Lear meant by speaking the sentence undoubtedly is. He could speak the line as if to say, 'Oh, for God's *sake*, let's not go into hair-splitting assessments of necessity' or as if to say, 'Jesus Christ, don't let's get into a discussion about *need*'. And yet Shakespeare's written script contains no explicit marks referring to the prosodic features that would make this difference clear. There is nothing referring to stress, pitch or intonation and, since the line is spaced according to the printer's conventions, there is nothing to indicate a pause or a crucial syncopation. There is no reference to facial expression or manual gesture, and yet all of these variables have a bearing on the sense or tone of the line.

The differences that I am referring to are not just colourful variations. They can alter the meaning of what is said and the character of the person who speaks. A relatively small change in pitch, stress and timbre of the way in which 'melt' is spoken in Hamlet's '*O! that this too too solid flesh would melt*' can make all the difference between exasperated disgust at being 'too too solid', and palely interesting melancholy. An actor who commits himself to the first reading has automatically biased his choice when it comes to the alternative readings of other lines, since a character who is angrily disgusted by the situation in which he finds himself will act and speak differently from someone who beautifies his despair.

The point is lucidly demonstrated by John Searle, when he invites the reader to imagine a situation in the Second World War in which an American soldier is ambushed by Italian troops and wishes to give them the impression that he is one of their German allies. What he would like to do is to express the meaning that is conveyed in the German phrase '*Ich bin ein deutsche Soldat*' but, unfortunately, the only German phrase that he knows – one he remembers from a freshman course in modern languages – is '*Kennst du das Land wo die Zitronen blühn?*' His intention in using this sentence is to make his non-German-speaking Italian captors believe that what he has actually said is: "I am a German soldier' but this is not what the sentence itself means. As a well-formed German phrase, it means what Goethe meant it to mean, namely: 'Knowest thou the land where the lemon trees bloom?' Nevertheless, although the meaning of the phrase is *constrained* by the rules that determine the reference of its constituent words, its force varies according to the circumstances in which it is used and cannot be retrieved by parsing it.

Let me give another example. The phrase 'This room needs painting' has an intelligible meaning regardless of the circumstances in which it is uttered. This means that, even taken out of context, it can be understood by anyone who speaks English. It cannot, for example, be used to express the idea 'This room needs demolishing' or, 'I could do with a drink'. But the *force* that it has is quite a different question. If it is spoken by an estate agent who is trying to convince a reluctant client that an apartment is worth leasing in spite of its dingy appearance, the phrase might well be taken as an apologetic recommendation, tantamount to saying, 'This room could be quite attractive if it were painted. Disregard its dingy appearance and try to imagine what it would be like if it were redecorated.' But if it is spoken by a commanding officer in the course of a routine inspection, his underling would be wise to take it as an *order*. The same phrase is used to achieve two altogether different types of *speech act*: an apologetic recommendation on the one hand, and a menacingly veiled command on the other. And, although the circumstances are enough to distinguish the two types of speech act, the speaker of each one would reinforce the distinction by using the appropriate intonation. If all that was required to extract the speaker's meaning from a phrase were the rules of English composition there would be no room for irony or metaphor.

When someone says: 'Can you pass the salt?' – and you apply the rules of grammar as a merely competent speaker of English rather than a competent member of the English-speaking community – you would extract nothing other than a phrase that could be paraphrased: 'Are you able to pass the salt? Are you competent at salt-passing?' The rules of English would enable you to extract from that phrase only something about competence. Whereas you know that a speaker who asks this question is not inquiring about your ability to pass the salt, but is actually asking you to *pass* the salt. In other words, he's not making an enquiry, but a request. The humorous schoolboy answer is to say 'yes' to such a request, and this itself is a joke about the difference between utterance's meaning and speaker's meaning. This is an extremely simple example, and there are all sorts of very complicated elaborations of which metaphor is one. If you hear the advice: 'Put a Tiger in Your Tank' and you were to extract the meaning on the basis of English composition alone, you would in fact have to undertake an elaborate programme of cramming a striped carnivore into a motor-car petrol tank. It is only a knowledge of the English community, car-owners, and assumptions about tigers having a fierceness that might apply to the power of petrol that enables us to see that this is not, in fact, an order to go out and track tigers for the boot of the car.

The theory of speech acts is directly relevant to the problem of theatrical performance. Despite the fact that the speeches included in a script can be spoken more or less intelligibly, without having to take into account who uttered them, to whom and under what circumstances, knowing how to perform them so that the audience can recognize what the character means calls for something over and above a sensitive understanding of Tudor English. The lines that Claudius addresses to Hamlet in Act 1, scene 2, for example, have a meaning that can be identified without having to consider the context in which they occur:

> Though yet of Hamlet our dear brother's death
> The memory be green, and that it us befitted
> To bear our hearts in grief and our whole kingdom
> To be contracted in one brow of woe,
> Yet so far hath discretion fought with nature
> That we with wisest sorrow think on him
> Together with remembrance of ourselves.

Recited as an isolated poem, the lines may be taken to express the proposition that death comes to everyone and it is inappropriate to over-indulge a grief. In order to express these sentiments unambiguously, the speaker would have to distribute the stresses in the right way with the help of the poetic metre. But when it comes to speaking the lines *in the play*, and especially in a particular *production* of the play, the diction is much less determined than some critics seem to suppose. How the actor delivers the speech depends not only on the sentiments that it expresses but also on the effect that Claudius wishes to have on Hamlet at that particular moment in the play. And that, in turn, depends on what sort of person the actor and director suppose Claudius to be. Yet the argument that an accurate recognition of the character's personality will specify how the lines should be delivered is at best impractical. Claudius is a *fictional* person and his character is not decidable as it might he if it were based upon someone actual. As the play unfolds we learn all there is to know about him. Since all that exists of the character is in the play Shakespeare wrote it is pointless to ask for further biographical details. However, the actor who is cast in the role cannot afford to luxuriate in this interesting indeterminacy. Fictional though Claudius may be, the actor who plays him must convince the audience that his actions and speeches are determined by actual motives and must improvise his characterization on the understanding that the portrait that he then offers is, at best, an interesting and plausible conjecture.

The actor's performance as a particular character requires *hypothesis*. Critics often object to the introduction of hypothesis without realizing that far from it being some kind of *contaminating* influence, it is in the nature of *all* perception. There are no perceptions without hypotheses, although some may strike us as more outlandish and unacceptable than others.

What happens when an actor approaches a part is something rather like the process used by scientists when they improvise and test a theory. In other words, although the text fails to portray the character that it is said to represent it will usually suggest some sort of hypothesis on the basis of which the actor can make a start. More often than not, the hypothesis goes a long way beyond the information that is given by the *text* and cannot, therefore, be justified by straightforwardly referring to the lines that the author has written. This applies also to the conjectures that must, at one time, have formed the basis of the traditional and widely accepted theatrical representations of the character in question. The difference is that the conjectural model that the modern actor uses as the basis of characterization is recognized as such and, instead of sticking to it through thick and thin, he or she consistently modifies and redesigns it in the name of some *emergent principle*. To borrow Karl Popper's phrase, process is one of conjecture and refutation alternating with one another as the rehearsal develops. This is presumably what underlies hostile critics impatient dismissal of modern productions for being unduly influenced by 'ideas'.

What do people mean when they say that one actor's performance is not an acceptable characterization? One answer, of course, is that that they dislike the breaking of precedent. In the history of a frequently performed classic, certain characters speak and behave as if the profession had signed some sort of agreement with respect to his or her personality. Naturally the impersonations vary quite widely from one production to the next but none the less leave the impression that they cluster round one broad hypothetical prototype. And although no single performance of the part displays each and every feature of the prototype, it is so easy to recognize a family resemblance amongst them all that it is tempting to conclude that the profession as a whole shares a collective image of the ideal representation. It is with the help of this model or scheme that the actor approaches the task of deciding how to deliver each of the lines that has been written for the character he is to play. And each time a performance is given in accordance with this scheme it becomes more and more difficult to dislodge it from the imagination of the regular theatregoer. After a time, the actor in the role of Claudius, together with most audiences, becomes reluctant to accept any version that departs too widely from the inherited prototype. It is as if the *fictional* identity of the character has been replaced by an *actual* one, and novelties are criticized for being breaches of biographical truth.

Claudius is not the only Shakespearean character who has fallen victim to this process of dynastic consolidation. Hamlet himself has shared the same fate; so has Ophelia. In fact, the more often a play appears in the repertoire the more likely it is for each of its characters to become stereotyped, and when a contradictory performance is given it is often treated as an impudent pretence, like one of those people who pop up from time to time claiming to be the Grand Duchess Anastasia.

It is sometimes argued that many of the answers to these problems, as to how to deliver a line or play 'in character', are implicitly represented, and that an intelligent reading of what is *written* supplies all the necessary information. Shakespearean scholars, for example, often insist that the metrical structure of the verse automatically distributes the stresses to convey the meanings that Shakespeare had in mind, and to eliminate the unacceptable alternatives. Now, while there is a great deal to be said in favour of this argument, in so far as a disregard for metre usually leads to a misconstruction of meaning, the structure of the verse does not specify as much as the scholars believe, and playgoers are often startled to discover that metrically indistinguishable readings are, none the less, enjoyably different. The question all these points raise is: *why do playwrights submit their work in such a remarkably indeterminate condition?* Musical scores, after all, leave much less to the imagination of the sight-reader. Over and above the accurate specifications of pitch, key and rhythm, composers often make detailed references about loudness, energy and overall phrasing. Changes of pace are indicated and the tone of a passage is often identified by reference to a rich, descriptive vocabulary. Nothing comparable is to be found in the text of one of Shakespeare's plays.

There are at least two possible reasons for these glaring deficiencies: one technical and the other cultural. The technical reason is connected to the difficulty of devising a notational system rich enough to represent all the variables I have just mentioned. In the area of prosody, for example, the phonetic distinctions that can make a difference to the meaning of a sentence are so small that it would take an almost infinite set of written characters to represent them all. Such a notation would be so dense that it would be difficult for the eye to distinguish the different characters from one another. It would be like trying to tell the time on a clock dial that depicted nanoseconds. And since prosody involves several independent variables, each one of which would probably require its own dense notation, the script would become well nigh illegible. It is difficult to imagine any actor sight-reading such a 'score'. The problem becomes even more complicated when one takes the gestural aspects of language into consideration. Choreographers have tried, with varying degrees of success, to evolve notations for representing the essential aspects of a dance routine. Apart from the fact that most of these schemes pose a serious problem of legibility, it is questionable whether they successfully represent anything more than the crude outlines of a dance. Choreographers who make use of these schemes, in order to revive dances that have dropped out of the repertoire, succeed only when they are able to consult their memory of the original version.

When it comes to devising a notational scheme for facial expression, the problem seems almost insoluble. Experts in 'body language' have tried to analyse facial movements in to a set of discrete particles – so-called 'kimemes' – in an effort to identify some gestural counterpart to the phonemes of spoken language. But these systems are comparatively crude

Problems begin to arise after the last performance of the play's inaugural run and, unless the playwright is available to supervise the revival, the advice that he gave to the original cast will have been lost. While a conscientious stage manager often keeps a detailed prompt copy, the stage directions that it includes fall a long way short of what is necessary to reinstate everything that was in the premiere unless, of course, it is consulted by people who participated in the original production. When the playwright is associated with a company, the details that are conspicuous by their absence from the *written* text are often conveyed from one revival to the next in the collective memory of his faithful colleagues.

This tends to happen when the author has been celebrated as a daring innovator. The colleagues who were closely associated with his pioneering efforts often appoint themselves as custodians of the orthodoxy and ensure that all the remembered details of the inaugural production are preserved from one performance to the next. In many cases, this board of guardians is headed by a close relative who tries to police the performances long after the playwright's death. Such pedantic custody is not necessarily an advantage. Personal intimacy may or may not imply a privileged understanding of the author's intentions. And the inflexible determination to preserve the play in the image of its first production can sometimes do the author a terrible disservice. The play can become mummified by dogma; there is evidence to show that the works of Chekhov suffered in this way. After his death in 1904, Chekhov's colleagues at the Moscow Arts Theatre succeeded in establishing a canonical production of each of his plays. The proprieties were supervised by his widow who extended her vigilance to the smallest detail. But the style of the company was superseded by developments in every other area of the European theatre, with the result that the orthodox production began to look quaint and even irrelevant. Something comparable happened to Wagner and to Brecht.

Inevitably with time there comes a point when the human link between the first production and any subsequent one snaps, and the bridge of reminiscence and anecdote is irreparably broken. When that happens the detailed additional instructions that had been written down in the prompt copy become curiously unintelligible, since there is no one available to explain the generative principles on which they were based. It is at this point that the play begins to enter its afterlife and the indeterminacy of the text begins to assert itself. By the time the language has become recognizably archaic, the process has become more or less irreversible.

There is an alternative scheme for recording and preserving the details of a dramatic performance; one that involves neither notation, nor description, nor personal memory – *electronic recording*. Instead of annotating or paraphrasing what happens on the stage, this technique provides a visible and audible example of it. It is, to all intents and purposes, an imperishable replica and seems automatically to overcome the deficiencies of a written script. But following an example or copying is fraught with as many difficulties as obeying a linguistic instruction, although the problems are of a different order. These can be understood only by analysing the somewhat bewildering concept of exemplification itself or what it is for something to *be* an example. The most useful account is the one provided by Nelson Goodman and the argument that follows is based closely on his. As an example of an example, Goodman refers to a tailor's booklet of textiles. Each little swatch exemplifies some of its own properties but not all of them. The customer knows, when he is offered the booklet, that although each swatch illustrates colour, weave, texture and pattern, it does not provide an example of shape or size. Each piece of cloth undoubtedly has both a shape and a size but that is not what it is illustrating for the purposes of the deal. How does this apply to a video tape? How literally should one take the instruction: 'Regard every aspect of this tape as exemplary and follow it slavishly'? We know from experience that each performance contains not only regrettable flaws, but incidental features that are neither here nor there. How can we discriminate? When the tape is reviewed shortly after recording, the issue can usually be settled by straightforward common sense. Or, to be more accurate, by relying on the fact that the sensibility of the viewer coincides, to a large extent, with that of the performers; so that the features that the viewer regards as exemplary are likely to be the same as the ones regarded as such by the production team. There is usually someone available to correct the mistakes – a stage manager, for example, who might point out: 'Look, that turn of the head, which you seem to like so much, was something we kept asking him not to do.' As time goes by, however, the process of discrimination becomes more and more difficult and, without the help of a personal consultant, it becomes harder to tell which aspects of the recorded performance are to be taken as exemplary and which are not.

Eventually, the sensibility of the viewer will be so different from that of the original production team that the discriminations that he or she makes are quite likely to contradict the ones made by a distant predecessor.

A performance reinstated on the basis of this judgment would be recognizably different from the one that it claimed to be copying faithfully, The process of reproducing a performance by copying an electronic replica is fraught with the same problems as forging a painting. When the forger is a contemporary of the painter, he shares so many of his victim's aesthetic standards that he automatically recognizes which features of the work are to be regarded as exemplary. As long as his technical skill is sufficient, he can create a fake that is almost indistinguishable from the original. But when the forgery is done at a much later date, the aesthetic principles and features that the copyist regards as exemplary, and emphasizes, would be different from the ones identified by a predecessor.

This is vividly illustrated by the difficulties of maintaining the repertoire in a large international opera house. Productions are expected to defray their original expenses by a long series of profitable revivals. But since it is impossible to run any one production continuously over many years, it is usually necessary to reinstate the performance after a considerable lapse of time. By then, the original cast has almost certainly dispersed and, more often than not, the producer who was responsible for the premiere is no longer available to supervise the revival. Before the development of video tape, the prompt copy and the model book were the only available sources of information and, as I have already pointed out, such instructions are notoriously unreliable. The development of mechanical reproduction held out the hope of a more accurate record. But practical experience has shown that there are unforeseen disadvantages.

When the tape is consulted less than a year after the first performance, there seems to be little difficulty in reproducing a passable replica of the original. When several years have passed, a curious problem of visibility begins to arise: what the tape shows is not necessarily what the new assistant director sees. The vision of the aspiring copyist is now so recognizably different from that of the original production staff that, even when the most conscientious efforts are made to duplicate what is to be seen on the screen, the resulting performance departs more and more from the original. In other words, the extent to which an electronic record can be regarded as a model is limited by the perceptual capabilities of the person who tries to use it for this purpose.

If we had a video copy of the first performance of Shakespeare's *Twelfth Night*, it is no good saying it exemplifies everything that it shows because people would disagree immediately as to what it *is* showing.

I think the best example of this is a film shown to some Africans some years ago. The film was set in an African village and was about hygiene, so it portrayed the daily life of a village with people preparing food and repeatedly washing their hands. When members of the indigenous audience were asked what they had seen they talked only about a chicken crossing the road. The mystified makers of the film went back and ran it through very carefully to discover that after about twenty-five minutes a chicken crossed the bottom left-hand corner of the screen. This fleeting appearance had, until then, been invisible to the film-makers but to the African audience the film exemplified a chicken crossing the road in an otherwise boring picture of an African village. In the same way, if we were to have a copy of the initial performance of *Twelfth Night*, what we thought it exemplified would depend on what we found to be its salient features. If called upon to copy it we would copy what we thought was important, and in that very act would adapt the production even if we had agreed to the idea that copying meant producing something indistinguishable. The reproduction of the play would indeed look identical to us but a subsequent generation, twenty-five years later, would wonder why we had picked out various features and not others from the tape.

This is why, when Van Meegeren forged Vermeer, it passed off very successfully at the time when he shared the same sensibility as his audience who saw Vermeer as exemplifying the particular qualities he copied. Now, we notice that it left out what we now believe to be essential in Vermeer. In fact todays forgeries would look different from Van Meegeren's. In short, even if we regard the process of going back to the original as a possibility we have to understand that forgeries are not faithful copies.

The point is that *perception* is determined by the interests, preoccupations and preconceptions of the particular moment. Even if we agreed that the function of the director is to restore as much of the original performance as he can, what he would infer as being important about the original production would not provide a faithful copy of its original but merely tell us what he thought was important in it. He would automatically and unavoidably be introducing an interpretation, and even at his most obedient would introduce preconceptions. I believe that it is better to be conscious of your preconceptions rather than simply to be the victim of them.

To reinforce this, let us just imagine for a moment that by some bizarre magical time warp we were able to duplicate the inaugural production of one of Shakespeare's plays so that a time traveller would be unable to detect the difference. Would it be right to regard these two productions as identical? According to Arthur Danto the fact that the productions are visibly and audibly indiscernible is no justification for thinking of them as such. To illustrate his point, Danto refers to a well-known experiment in aesthetic duplication. Jorge Luis Borges wrote a provocative story about the discovery of a literary fragment that duplicated a passage in Cervantes' *Don Quixote*. Borges points out that the fragment was neither plagiarism nor a transcript of the sixteenth-century prototype but an altogether original work deliberately created by a twentieth-century French poet called Pierre Menard. Borges reports Menard as saying that he was quite capable of imagining the universe without Cervantes' *Quixote* and that, for him, Cervantes' novel was a contingent work and not a necessary one: 'I can premeditate writing it. I can write it without falling in to a tautology.' In Borges' story, Menard imaginatively annihilates the work of his Spanish predecessor and successfully creates a passage of prose indistinguishable from the one that Cervantes wrote four hundred years earlier.

Danto takes Borges to be saying that the indiscernibility of the two passages – one by Cervantes and the other by Menard – does not mean that they are identical, as although visibly indistinguishable, the two passages display a vivid contrast in style. Borges himself points out that, 'The archaic style of Menard – quite foreign after all – suffers from a certain affectation. Not so that of his forerunner who handles with ease the current Spanish of his time.' The point is that the two passages were written at different times by different authors, and although this fact may not be detectable in the printed words it serves to distinguish them as altogether different. As far as Danto is concerned, 'The works are, in part, constituted by their location in the history of literature as well as by their relationships to their authors . . . and so, graphic congruities notwithstanding, they are deeply different works.' Even if you could theoretically avoid those artefacts of interpretation that are built into the process of copying and forging, the hypothetical and unachievable perfect copy would probably strike a contemporary reader as quaint rather than authentic, and even if struck by the work's authenticity, this itself would distance him from the experience of a contemporary reader of the original, as the very idea of authenticity would have been irrelevant. The claim that something is authentic has already pre-empted the possibility of having an authentic experience.

If the notion of theatrical authenticity means anything at all, we might think that the more closely a production duplicates the details of the one supervised and approved by the author the more accurately it conveys his intended meaning. But of course there is no guarantee that any of the contemporary productions expressed everything that Shakespeare had in mind when he conceived and wrote his plays. On the contrary, in the speech that Hamlet delivers to the players, there is evidence to show that the performances were not always what the author hoped they might have been. '*Speak the speech, I pray you, as I pronounced it to you, trippingly on the tongue ... Suit the action to the word, the word to the action...* ' Yet the mere fact that Shakespeare was in a position to administer such criticisms is often understood to mean that the subsequent performance should have come closer to fulfilling his ambitions than any production supervised by a modern director. Even if it could be proved that his advice had not been followed in every detail, the fact that he wrote for a particular type of theatre and for a characteristic form of acting means, according to this view, that a duplicate of the original production would be a more favourable version than any alternative. But would we accept it?

If we were sitting now watching the supposed duplicate of the Elizabethan premiere of *Twelfth Night* we would find much of it impenetrable. Like a work of religious art placed in a modern gallery, we would see many signs and a rhetorical style of acting that would be very hard for us to read. If this preservation was realizable, it may well be that Shakespeare's work would no longer be performed and could well have spent an afterlife in the forlorn library condition to which unperformed plays are consigned. The notion of performance would be altered if we were bound by the one canonical production, and plays would, like pictures, become *autographic* works of art. As a consequence, the theatre would become rather like a museum or a church in which the audiences would be subtly changed into congregations, witnesses of a rite rather than spectators of a play. However interesting this might be from an archival point of view, in that the original would preserve all the idioms of the Elizabethan theatre, the play itself would be imprisoned in its own orthodoxy and prevented from developing that 'emergent' character which is constitutive of great drama. In a paradoxical way, the preservation of the canonical performance, which many people think would express and embody Shakespeare's intentions, is more likely to cut us off from his vital dramatic imagination as we would be distracted by the foreign gestures and style of acting.

It seems to me that it is precisely because subsequent performances of Shakespeare's plays are interpretations, rather than copies, that they *have* survived. The amplitude of Shakespeare's imagination admits so many possible interpretations that his work has enjoyed an extraordinary afterlife unforeseeable by the author at the time of writing. We overvalue the notion of the identity of the work and search fruitlessly for some hypothetical feature that will act as a guarantee or a token of its identity.

There is nothing that satisfies that demand, and we can only recognize the minimum conditions for the performance of a play – that the words that are written must be delivered.

However much we may disagree about what constitutes the identity of a play by Shakespeare, we can agree that it resides at least in his words so that a paraphrase will *not* do.

And yet we are prepared to paraphrase so many other elements, such as the stage-setting and costume, which for Shakespeare would have been an essential rather than, an optional, component of the work.

It was an attempt to restore a far-reaching and, I would argue, unrealizable authenticity that prompted English scholar William Poel to flout recent theatrical convention by re-instating the Elizabethan staging of Shakespeare's plays at the end of the nineteenth century. Poel recognized that the theatre had undergone a peculiar transformation shortly after the dramatist's death and that when his plays were revived after the re-opening of the theatres under the Restoration the staging was recognizably at odds with its original style. In many respects, the subsequent performances of Shakespeare's plays over the next two hundred years was comparable to that of the paintings and sculptures whose afterlives I described earlier. The unfurnished platform was replaced by a proscenium stage and the texts were often mutilated to accommodate the elaborate scene changes that were destined to become the most significant part of the eighteenth and nineteenth-century playgoer's experience. It was to counteract these and other tendencies that Poel undertook his controversial experiments in restoring Shakespearean production to the form in which it was first given to the Elizabethan public. For obvious reasons Poel's experiment differed from the magical duplication that I have already tried to imagine. Two hundred years of theatrical evolution had all but destroyed the memory of the Elizabethan prototype and, until the rediscovery of the famous Swan sketch of the Globe Theatre, little was known about the physical format of the Elizabethan stage.

In the absence of a visible and audible model, Poel had to undertake an imaginative reconstruction.

Although this was helped by the discovery of sixteenth-century prompt copies, Poel's achievement depended on a close study of the written text from which he was able to identify the dramatic genre to which Shakespeare's plays belonged. A close study of the Quartos convinced Poel that the only theatrical format consistent with the text was the one in which the plays had been originally staged. He recognized that Shakespeare's plays were literary creations demanding rapid imaginative transition from one scene to the next and that the uninterrupted thrust was incompatible with the cumbersome changing of illusionistic scenery.

In a series of experimental productions mounted at the turn of the 20th century, Poel abstained from expensive spectacle and substituted a bare format that gave pride of place to the events expressed in, and constituted by, the *spoken* utterances of a play. The experiment was not altogether welcome and audiences, whose taste had been corrupted by the picturesque tradition of the last two hundred years, felt that they had been robbed of the Shakespeare they knew and loved. To a modern eye, however, the photographic records of Poel's productions seem quaintly picturesque in their own way. If such productions were to be accurately duplicated today they would give the same sort of impression as Viollet-le-Duc's nineteenth-century restorations of Romanesque sculpture. As we have seen, the notion of authenticity is an unstable and elusive one, and yet Poel's productions were considerably less *inauthentic* than the ones that had been staged throughout the preceding century. Today it is easy to identify their late nineteenth-century aesthetic characteristics, but these seem trivial by comparison to Poel's success in reproducing the format of the sixteenth-century original.

As long as productions of Shakespeare were occasions for staging colourful historical tableaux comparable to, and in many ways indistinguishable from, the novels of Walter Scott or the romantic canvases of de la Roche, there was no temptation to consider the political or psychological implications of the text. This meant that there was no incentive to stage the plays in terms of some controlling and perhaps reductive metaphor. Ironically, by stripping away the picturesque and releasing the plays into a dramatic rather than a pictorial space, Poel revealed their essentially literary character, making them increasingly susceptible to the sort of 'conceptual' interpretations that critics so often deplore. As soon as the dramatic action was prised away from its literal historical setting, the text acquired an independence that gave subsequent directors a license to re-set them in any period that struck their fancy.

Poel's experiments were conducted in the name of authenticity but their effect upon a twentieth-century audience was more complicated and more disturbing than he recognised at the time. Quite apart from the fact that reproductions of antiquity inevitably strike the modern imagination as affectedly archaic (just as Menard's 'Cervantes' seemed to twentieth-century contemporaries), Poel's departure from recent tradition had the unexpected effect of emphasizing the transferability of the dramatic action. For an audience that had grown accustomed to seeing Shakespeare's plays picturesquely staged in a period that was appropriate to the action, the ease with which Poel transposed it the bare stage of the Elizabethan theatre suggested that there might be no limit to the way in which these plays could be re-staged in the future.

It is true that there has not been a relapse into the pictorial tradition of the Victorian theatre, and it is still possible to identify Poel's influence in the unfurnished starkness of many modern productions, yet the twentieth century has generated more visual variety than ever before. Floridly aberrant though they may have been, the pictorial productions of the nineteenth century were more or less consistent with one another.

Most of them, at least, were painstakingly 'historical'. While the visual representation of the past differed from one production to the next, the amount by which they varied was negligible in comparison to their historicism. Twentieth-century productions, however, have been characterized by a consistent inconsistency and, although 'literal' representation is conspicuous by its absence, they now tend to differ from one another almost as much as a Georgian production differed from a Victorian one. In the last twenty-five years, a regular playgoer could have seen *Julius Caesar* staged in togas, frock coats, jackboots or doublet and hose. Most of these productions were staged in a format that owes much to Poel's 'Elizabethan' experiments, but it would be foolish to pretend that such performances represent a continuation of his original initiative.

The development of the avant-garde in expressionist theatre and constructivist decor of Meyerhold and Mayakovsky, together with the artistic revolutions of the 1900s, had an important effect on the theatre and the role of the director. Cubism, surrealism and Dada, in the 1920s brought with them startling new attitudes to the art of the past. One of modernism's rather paradoxical characteristics was a much more self conscious relationship to the past, which it treated as a plunderable treasure to be re-assembled in new forms, The looting of the past allowed an artist like Picasso to find elements that could be used in new combinations in collage. Many artists took fragments of Oceanic art, for example, and represented them in the art of cubism. In a similar way the director in the theatre began to emerge as someone doing 'assemblage' rather than restoration.

Apart from the transformation that a play inevitably undergoes as its actions, speeches and characters are developed, certain aspects of the afterlife of a dramatic work run parallel to the changes that overtake material artefacts, such as paintings or sculptures. I am referring to the way that a play can alter its appearance, and to some extent its identity, according to how it is staged. Just as a painting changes when it is removed from the Eastern end of a church and placed in an art gallery, so a play by Shakespeare, or an opera by Mozart, changes its character according to the physical format in which it is presented. A play that started its theatrical life on the unfurnished platform of the Globe and then went on to be pictorially represented in the Victorian theatre, with further alterations in physical format when thrust on to the apron stages that developed after the 1950s, has undergone changes that are just as far reaching as the ones that result from reinterpretations of the spoken lines.

These changes are often regarded as incidental transformations in an object that otherwise retains its original identity. I admit that at one level it is true to say that each of these stagings represents an instance of the work in question – *King Lear*, perhaps, the *Ring* or *Mother Courage* – but the differences in visual presentation powerfully influence the way we visualize its identity. Just as Michelangelo altered the aesthetic identity of the statue of Marcus Aurelius by placing it in the grand seigneurial setting of the Campidoglio, so Peter Brook by putting *A Midsummer Night's Dream* into a white gymnasium box altered its status as a dramatic event, and made it altogether different from the sort of object it was when Beerbohm Tree staged it in a realistic midnight forest. The same principle applies to the vicissitudes of Wagner's *Ring*. Pictorially produced at the time of its composition, the *Ring* was stripped of all scenery by Wieland Wagner and transplanted into a ruined industrial setting by Patrice Chereau. While there is an unarguable sense in which each of these subsequent performances was an instance of the opera originally written by Richard Wagner, the work itself developed under the influence of these alterations in theatrical format.

What is it that we are supposed to 'see' when we witness a theatrical spectacle? The whole issue is epitomized in an interesting and provocative remark made by Bernard Williams. It is, he says, reasonable to ask a member of the audience seated in Row F how far he or she was from Laurence Olivier playing Othello. But there is no answer to the question how far he or she was from the Moor, or from Desdemona. The same distinction applies to questions about the distance that separates the audience from the scenery. The spectator may be less than twenty feet from whatever represents the bedroom in Cyprus but no tape measure can tell us how far he or she was from the bedroom itself. By visiting the theatre we are participating in a representational system, and we are reading the play systematically as something that stands for what we suppose it to be. In order to do this we have to recognize the existence of a *frame* within which what is to be seen is taken as representational and beyond which everything to be seen is regarded as part of the real world.

If an outburst of unexpected strangling were to take place beyond the margins of this frame we would summon the manager and ask him to call the police – even if the scuffle was somewhat half-hearted. But when Othello begins to stifle Desdemona – not half-heartedly at all but with every sign of doing the job properly – we would summon the manager only if a member of the *audience* tried to stop him. The frame surrounding the theatrical event enables us to make this useful distinction. In proscenium theatres, inherited from the eighteenth and nineteenth centuries, the frame coincides with the decorative archway separating the stage from the auditorium, and with strong artificial lighting this difference is reinforced by the fact that the audience sits in the dark while the artificial events are brightly illuminated. The raising of a velvet curtain gives additional reassurance of this distinction. Both a thrust stage and a theatre in the round provide the spectator with implicit frames separating the two domains.

It is important to recognize the difference between frames and fences. What prevents the dramatic action from overflowing into real incident is not a mechanical obstacle separating the audience from the cast, as, for example, the spectators watching a lion-taming act at the circus are separated from the action by something that mechanically protects them from undergoing the risks of the courageous *dompteur*. In fact it is because it is a fence and not a frame that the spectators know that the lion-taming spectacle is real – so real indeed that it is only because there *is* a fence that they are happy to sit so close to it. The same distinction applies to the plate-glass window that separates the inquisitive spectator from the poisonous reptiles at the zoo. When we speak of the missing fourth wall of the theatre, however, we are referring to something that has a different logical status altogether, and the events we see through its *notional* transparency require, as Richard Wollheim has pointed out, a type of vision that is altogether peculiar to representational seeing. To understand this form of vision, and what it requires on the part of the spectator, it is essential to realize how representation works as a system, and it presupposes two worlds – the world to be represented, and the world that *does* the representing.

The subtleties of this relationship are all too easily confused by taking illusionistic realism as the paradigm, so that anything less than a convincing illusion is regarded as an impoverished version.

What there is to be seen in a representation largely depends on what we expect it to show us. An Ordnance Survey map of the Barbizon forest is just as much a representation of it as a painting by Corot, and the fact that it tells us nothing about the shimmer of the foliage or the fall of the light does not jeopardize its value as a representation. On the contrary, for the purposes that we consult it, a map of the Barbizon forest represents what we want to know and although Corot's picture represents what is delightful about the forest's appearance it would not help us to find our way out of it. In the map the length of the lines that represent the paths, and the angles at which they meet, do represent the length of the actual paths and the angles of their actual intersections. The fact that the lines are drawn in black or that their width conveys no information about the actual width of the paths is irrelevant. For someone lost in the forest the map provides the useful information he requires, and fulfils its function as a representational system. There are many intermediate examples that may be helpful when thinking about stage scenery in the theatre. An urban developer who had designs on the Barbizon forest might make a scale model of its layout. The model could display many physical properties that resemble those of the actual forest. The metrical width of the paths might now be included, and the trees might be represented by filigreed clumps of plastic whose colour and texture bore some representational relationship to the colour and texture of the trees in the forest. If the budget ran to it the model-maker could even introduce a treatment that gave the paths a physical appearance similar to that of the original, but in terms of cost/benefit this would give more information than was necessary and in all probability the walkways would be colour-coded in brown while the peripheral roads were unambiguously marked in black, because it is useful to make an unambiguous distinction between pedestrian and vehicular traffic. As Nelson Goodman has pointed out, most representational systems are composed in a somewhat hybrid way with analogue components that represent by virtue of resemblance, and digital components that represent by virtue of making unambiguous distinctions.

This analysis makes it possible to understand the different ways in which settings are represented on the theatrical stage. In anything other than the most illusionistic scenery the representation is achieved by an extremely subtle interaction between analogue and digital modes of representation. So-called abstract scenery is not simply scenery that has lost something – or falls bewilderingly short of looking like what it stands for – but like a model or a map it assigns representational significance to some but not all of its physical properties. For the audience to know what is happening on a stage it is necessary for them to read the whole thing as an integrated system and to understand which properties of the representational setting are related to which properties of the represented scene.

Here is an example from my own work in designing a setting for *The Merchant of Venice*. I asked Julia Trevelyan Oman to make the Venetian streets look as real as possible, and not only were the size of the scenery walls metrically related to the size of the walls they represented but also the surface was treated so that it looked like the original. The audience was intended to read both the metrical properties and the textural properties in the analogue mode of representation. When thinking about a production of *The Taming of the Shrew* I decided to take a very different approach. Inspired by Serlio's drawing of an Italian street scene, I asked the scenic artist to represent the architectural proportions so that the shape and size of the scenic colonnades could be taken as an accurate indication of the shape and size of the actual ones although we then assembled the entire set out of untreated timber. I presume, or hope, that the audience did not read into this the assumption that Shakespeare's Padua was actually made from untreated timber.

In the afterlife of every play the manipulation of these representational variables determines the theatrical experience of the audience. It is only when the producer, director and designer understand, even if only implicitly, how these variables are interrelated that the audience can be expected to recognize the visual status of what it sees. The problems of televising plays and operas can be more clearly understood in the light of these considerations. It was only by recognizing the peculiar character of the televisual *frame* that I began to understand some of the difficulties I encountered in deciding on the most appropriate representational idiom for this medium. For plays and operas written for the stage, the frame defining the domain of their distinctive artifice is altogether different from the one that surrounds the television image. Even with stages as different as the Globe and Irving's Lyceum, or the apron stage of Chichester and the sandy arena of Brook's Bouffe du Nord, the representational frame is identical as it marks off two domains within the same physical space. While the dramatic events are prevented by convention from invading the domain of the actual events the spectators sit within a space that includes both domains, and actively experience the fact that the cast abstains from invading their hemisphere. The frame separating the audience from the dramatic action is shared by the spectator and the actor.

In the case of television the space the spectator sits

in does not interact with the one in which the dramatic events occur. The 'transparency' of the screen is quite unlike the notional transparency of the missing fourth wall of a proscenium stage. When the spectator's gaze penetrates the screen its line is not continued into an actual beyond any more than it is when he looks at a picture on the wall of an art gallery. While the spectator seated in the theatre is looking at actual objects that represent notional things, a television viewer is looking at a picture of actual objects representing notional things. This creates awkward problems for the producer or director when choosing the appropriate representational idioms for a stage production on television.

In the theatre the scenery, illusionistic or otherwise, abuts directly on to the non-representational architecture of the auditorium. Even in the absence of visible walls and doors the audience can easily tell when a performer is on or off the scene. In some modern productions where actors about to make their 'entrances' are still visible, the implicit frame makes it quite clear that they are *dramatically* invisible. The imaginative theatre director who takes pleasure in emphasizing the distinctive artificiality of the drama can provocatively exploit this vision of the actor-as-person and the actor-as-character. In television, however, the scenery does not abut with anything and, although it may be cut off by the edges of the domestic screen, the spectator is left with the uneasy sense that the edges of the screen do not coincide with the framework of the dramatic action. There is always the suspicion that if the screen were larger, or the camera angle wider, there would be more of the same to be seen. This suspicion is confirmed when the camera pans right or left to reveal action that was previously out of view. Televising Shakespeare or Mozart forces the director to adopt an illusionistic idiom that he might otherwise resist when staging the same works in the theatre. Abstract scenery only works convincingly when the audience can see the point at which its deliberate artificiality gives way to the non-representational reality of the theatre's auditorium. A television producer who wishes, like William Poel, to revert to the non-pictorial abstraction of the Tudor stage in the effort to honour the artificiality of Shakespeare's dramatic genre has two alternatives, and neither of them is altogether successful. Recognizing that diagrammatic abstraction works only when it is visibly contrasted with the architectural reality of its surroundings he can deliberately shoot off so that the viewer sees the studio where the production has been built, the lights, cameras and even the exit signs. But since this world beyond is not continuous with the room where the viewer sits it creates a puzzling distraction.

The alternative is to build the artificial scenery in the round so that the camera can rotate through 360 degrees without ever shooting off. When this happens the viewer peers in to an artificial world that is completely enclosed but as he does not have the opportunity to contrast the artificiality of *this* world with the actuality of the *real* one the theatricality of the experience is mysteriously diminished.

The only successful televisual counterpart to the Empty Space sponsored by Peter Brook that I remember was Trevor Nunn's version of *Macbeth*, originally staged at the Other Place, Stratford. The characters loomed in and out of a non-committal blackness and as there were no visual representations of place the television audience was left with the reassuring conviction that the drama was located between the faces that came and went on the screen. The success of this enterprise was largely due to the fact that *Macbeth's* dramatic action is contained in the encounters between its characters, and where they come from or where they happen to be is unimportant. In that production, the television screen was like a devotional icon in which the representation was unambiguously confined to the surface of the screen and there was no requirement to read any depth into it. In any play where doors, walls or even natural horizons are essential to the action all this breaks down. The domestic comedies of Shakespeare are inconceivable in this kind of iconic limbo. In *The Taming of the Shrew* Petruchio must penetrate a visible household, and even in *Othello* the jealous suspicions of the play can be incubated only within the chambered privacy of rooms whose doors can be closed. In spite of its mythical placelessness, *King Lear* cannot be televised without visibly representing the contrast between the boundless heath and the walled enclosures of the various palaces. A featureless blackness would make nonsense out of the scene in which Edgar as Poor Tom persuades his blind father to jump over the edge of a non-existent cliff since its non-existence has to be visible to everyone except the blind victim.

Representationalism enforces itself upon the television producer however reluctant he maybe to make use of it. In the television productions of Shakespeare for which I was responsible I am embarrassed to admit that the most successful were those in which the scenery was more real and more pictorial than the nineteenth-century stage versions I have reacted violently against when directing in the *theatre*. For reasons that I cannot explain this realism did not strike me as offensive when confined to interiors, and in my production of *Othello* where the set was carefully based on the rooms in the palace at Urbino, the drama seemed all the more convincing because of its scenic realism. But such realism seems quite absurd when the action calls for an outdoor setting. In the BBC production of *As You Like It,* filmed in the gardens of Glamis castle, the realistic foliage clashed distractingly with the artificiality of the pastoral verse. In both film and television I suspect that the afterlife of plays and operas is undergoing an uneasy passage, and that eventually we will see this interlude as a somewhat anomalous episode in the subsequent life of theatrical works written for audiences who were expected to breathe the same air as the performers.

When appearing on the *screen*, plays and operas undergo yet another change that transforms them into something recognizably different from their previous incarnation on the stage. In the theatre, the audience witnesses a physical event, and although the view is determined by the seating, the spectator sees the action in its entirety. With the invention of cutting, a television or film director could segment the action into separate parts. While the audience can synthesize these sequences, and imagine the total space in which everything occurs, each shot momentarily precludes the possibility of seeing anything else that is happening at the same time, and this transforms the work into something quite different from the one imagined by its original author or composer. If the editor is successful the spectator sees the drama without ever being aware of the abrupt succession of shots from which it is made. Yet if you stand in a darkened road and look at a television through the window of a house on the opposite side of the street all that you can see is the staccato alternation of brightness as one shot gives way to the next. Without the momentum of an intelligible story the only visible property of the programme is the abrupt succession of its component shots.

After years of trial and error, film editors have evolved practical rules of assembly so that when the eye is directed unaccountably towards one group of characters, excluding all the others, the viewer's sense of narrative continuity is left undisturbed. It is the very success of this surreptitious technique that irreversibly changes the dramatic identity of the stage work. Some critics have suggested that this action is no different from that of the spectator in the theatre when he shifts his gaze from one part of the spectacle to another, but this parallel does not work. Physiologists can demonstrate that shifts of gaze are accomplished with a rapidity comparable to the cuts in a film from one shot to the next, but in the theatre the unattended part of the vista is still visible to the spectator so that peripheral events on the stage subliminally modify the experience of the salient ones. When a work is written for the stage – a format in which everything that happens is intended to be seen simultaneously – and is then submitted to this type of segmentation in film it is misleading to suppose that the audience is seeing the same dramatic spectacle in a somewhat different way. In order to see the drama in this *segmented* way and to experience it as a *continuous* narrative demands cognitive efforts that are altogether different from those needed to interpret events happening on a stage. In fact, although the television viewer is unaware of it, when watching the screen he undergoes an experience similar to reading narrative prose. Like sentences, which automatically exclude whatever they do *not* refer to, movie shots eliminate what they do not show. The reader of a written narrative is just as unaware of the succession of separate sentences as the television viewer is of the alternation of discontinuous shots. In both cases what gives the artwork its coherent textuality is the way that the reader of one and the spectator of the other can identify referential implications that cross the boundaries between consecutive but discontinuous sentences and shots.

It would be tempting to assume from this argument that while film or television are inappropriate media for the production of plays they are ideally suited for the dramatization of novels. But this does not follow at all. On the contrary, most novels are irreversibly damaged by being dramatized, since they were written without any sort of performance in mind at all, whereas in plays visible performance is a constitutive part of their identity and translation from stage to screen changes their identity without actually destroying it.

In discussing the influence of film and television upon the afterlife of plays I have deliberately concentrated on the way that these media affect the look of the works and alter their narrative structure. But there is another aspect – the repeatability of a play that has been filmed or televised. In an otherwise interesting essay on *The Future of Art in an Age of Mechanical Reproduction*, Walter Benjamin unaccountably fails to consider what happens to the identity of a play when one of its productions can be replayed as long as it survives physical storage. Until the end of the nineteenth century each production of a play disappeared with its final performance so that its afterlife depended on revival and reproduction. But as soon as any performance is committed to film or tape there is at least one production of the play with an afterlife of its own that parallels that of the play itself if it undergoes revival from one generation to the next.

It is interesting to speculate what Helen Gardner would have thought of the productions of Shakespeare she fondly remembered if they had been recorded and she had watched them again after a lapse of forty years. As Sir Frederick Bartlett demonstrated in 1932 memory is not, as was once supposed, a mechanical record of a previous experience differing from the original merely by virtue of fading or decay. To remember something is to reconstruct it in accordance with current interests; recalling is not simply a question of replaying a neurological record.

We have all had the bewildering experience of disliking a film that once overwhelmed us and we remembered as brilliant. There is the even more bewildering experience of discovering ten years further on that the very same film is paradoxically brilliant once again albeit in a different way from the remembered brilliance of the original showing. This is why when the BBC set out to televise the whole of Shakespeare and hoped by excluding fashionably imaginative productions that they would guarantee the programmes an undatable permanence they began a self-defeating enterprise.

As the story of Van Meegeren's Vermeers proves there is no such thing as a permanently self-evident style. And it is one of the cruel paradoxes of theatrical art in an age of mechanical reproduction that the permanence of the record is the very thing that brings the pretentiousness of these claims to immortality to light. With the passage of time such productions run the risk of looking permanently quaint without ever having enjoyed the privilege of being briefly brilliant.

Film and television have exerted far-reaching influences on the character of dramatic works originally written for the stage but these are, in many respects, incidental to an afterlife that will, in all probability, continue to depend on active revival as opposed to mechanical repetition. Precisely because of their permanence, mechanically reproduced productions will never replace staged revivals, since (as with living organisms) it is only by undergoing the consecutive processes of death and reproduction that plays can enjoy the self-renewal without which an afterlife is inconceivable.

The relationship between scripts and performances is strikingly similar to that between genetic instructions and the biological individuals to which they give rise. At the end of the nineteenth century August Weissmann argued that there was a distinction to be made between the characteristics that a living individual owed to its genetic inheritance, and the features that it acquired under the influence of environmental factors during its early growth and development. A similar distinction can be recognized in the continuing life of a play or an opera. Each performance is constrained by the script but in the process of being brought to life as a living production it acquires characteristics that are due to the interpretive efforts of the performers and producers, not to mention those brought about by staging it in different formats. Once the production has died with its final performance it sheds its acquired characteristics and theoretically reverts to the condition of the script or score from which a new production can be revived. But this is where the comparison between plays and living organisms breaks down. Weissmann insisted that characteristics acquired during the lifetime of an organism could not be inherited since the genetic text remained unaltered by the environmental influences – the children of blacksmiths are not born with brawny muscles developed by the exertion of their fathers. With plays, however, acquired characteristics are often to be found in subsequent productions. This is not because the text has been altered but because human culture is influenced by imitation. The revival or reproduction of a play could never take place in complete ignorance of its previous incarnations, so that although the text has remained unchanged by the vicissitudes of various productions, the memory of previous performances exerts a powerful influence on the shape of subsequent ones.

The influence of precedent, for which there is no counterpart in biology, extends from slavish imitation to radical innovation. But even when the effect of imitation is at its strongest, the mere fact that revival is a reproductive process guarantees the appearance of novelty. During conservative or so called classical periods in the theatre there is still a natural tendency for the production of plays and operas to depart from the inaugural prototype. For complicated reasons the tempo of this natural evolution can change unexpectedly, and Helen Gardner has vividly chronicled the sometimes abrupt alteration in the evolution of Shakespeare upon the stage. But even if we take these rapid changes into consideration, there is a striking difference between the ones that overtook the theatre during its classical period and those introduced in the last fifty years, and Helen Gardner rightly identified the intervention of something altogether new.

In the productions leading up to the ones she enjoyed in the 1940s and 1950s, the appearance of Shakespeare's plays changed, as unsolicited novelties imperceptibly infiltrated themselves into each revival. Each production was realized according to the fashion of the day and, although performers and managers presumably took pride in adding something of their own, originality was painlessly constrained by the influence of precedent. With the emergence of the director, however, plays and operas began to be reproduced with an explicit interest in originality and for the first time in theatrical history it is both legitimate and useful to apply the argument of Paley's watch.

During the high tide of natural theology at the beginning of the nineteenth century, Bishop Paley developed a famous analogy to explain the functional design of living organisms, According to him, if someone who knew nothing about timekeeping were to find a watch lying on the seashore he would find it impossible to account for its efficient mechanism without stipulating the existence of someone who had deliberately designed it. And for this reason he thought it necessary to postulate a supernatural craftsman whose skill guaranteed the efficiency of living things. With Darwin's discovery of the cooperation between unsolicited variation and natural selection this analogy became defunct. It is, however, applicable to the structure and function of modern theatrical productions.

In contrast to a pre-war revival of a Shakespearean play, different though it may have been from its Georgian or Victorian predecessor, productions after 1960 are recognizably produced and in some cases the evidence of explicit design is so prominent that the work in question seems to have been quoted rather than revived. To some extent this is the commendable result of recognizing that the revival of a dramatic work from the distant past is a conceptual *problem* and not simply a theatrical *task*. It is as if these theatrical bequests were now visualized as alien artefacts, and it is understood that they cannot be reproduced without making a conscious effort to reconcile what is foreign and incomprehensible with what is permanent and readily intelligible.

We are witnessing, in our own time, something comparable to what happened during the fifteenth century when the artefacts of classical antiquity were repossessed by the culture of early modern Europe. As Erwin Panofsky has pointed out, the success of the Renaissance presupposed the recognition of a fundamental discontinuity between the culture of the present and that of the distant past. One of the reasons why the proto-renaissances of the ninth, tenth and twelfth centuries were so tentative and short-lived was that this historical discontinuity was still somewhat blurred. It was only when the artefacts of the classical past were seen to be recognizably different that they could be confidently approached and re-incorporated. Panofsky's idea can be usefully applied to the enthusiastic renovations that classical plays and operas have undergone in the last half of the twentieth century.

Until dramatic works from the past were judged to have come from a world that was recognizably different from the one in which they were to be revived, variations in performance appeared by default rather than by design.

Of course, a Hanoverian production of *King Lear* looked and sounded different from a Tudor one, but the distinction cannot be explained by someone having consciously faced the problem of what the play meant or what was meant by trying to put it on in the first place.

But in the last part of the twentieth century even the comparatively recent past is visualized as "a foreign country where people do things differently". Taking care of the *words* in the performance of a play no longer guarantees that the *sense* will take care of itself. In fact the very notion that the sense of a play is unambiguously readable in its text is both problematic and controversial.

It is difficult to explain why all this should have happened now and not before. After all, the interval between a Victorian production of *King Lear* and the first time it was staged is much longer than the period separating the Victorian production from one staged last year. The recognizable discontinuity is not simply a question of the amount of time that has elapsed; the staging of a play written by Chekhov as recently as 1904 is also recognized as a problem.

To explain this in terms of the unwelcome arrival of the director is to put the cart before the horse. Why did the director emerge when he did? Why has his influence now become so strong? The obvious answer is that *cultural* change has accelerated so much in the last fifty years that the differences between 'now' and even a quite recent 'then' are much more noticeable, and the bequests of the past arouse our interpretive energies as never before. Besides, as Clifford Geertz argues, the life of the mind has now taken a distinctively 'interpretive turn', and with the development of self-consciously hermeneutic interests the problem of meaning assumes a paramount importance. Nowadays almost any institution, action, image, utterance or ritual is seen as requiring interpretation.

In its ordinary use, the word 'interpretation' is usually taken to imply the existence of a determinable meaning and one might suppose that the development of the 'interpretive turn' would have led by now to a large yield of commonly agreed readings. But the very opposite has happened. In the study of law, scripture and literature, the emergence of interpretation as a distinct enterprise has coincided with the growth of conflict rather than a consensus. In fact, the very notion of interpretation has itself become a subject of controversy, and although some critics continue to uphold the idea of determinable meanings, there are just as many who claim that this is an unrealistic aim, and that the text – literary, dramatic or whatever – sustains an almost unlimited range of possible readings.

As E. D. Hirsch points out, 'it became fashionable to talk about a critic's "reading" of a text . . . [and] the word seems to imply that if the author had been banished, the critic still remained and his new, original, urbane, ingenious or relevant "reading" carried its own interest.' According to Hirsch, the disadvantage of this particular twist of the 'interpretive turn' is that there are no reliable criteria for distinguishing frivolous readings from ones which 'really' make sense. The only way of quieting the Babel of interpretation is to restore the author as the determiner of the text's meaning since this is 'the only compelling normative principle which could lend validity to an interpretation'. Hirsch then goes on to counter the arguments which have been developed against the author as the final authority.

With texts that come from the more or less distant past, it is often claimed that their meaning inevitably changes with the passage of time, and that it is only profitable to read them for contemporary meanings or for meanings which are interestingly relevant to the modern imagination. Hirsch points out that if this attitude is taken to its logical conclusion the reader encounters no one but himself each time he engages with a text, or an utterance, from the distant past. In any case, it is not the meaning of the text that changes with the passage of time but its significance. The mere fact that a modern reader can recognize implications which would have been unrecognizable to the original author does not imply that its meaning has altered. It is sometimes argued that the author himself can re-identify the meaning of his own work, and that on a subsequent reading he can recognize meanings that were not apparent to him at the time of his writing.

But the fact that an author can revise his opinion, cannot be counted as evidence for or against the identity of his original meaning. He has simply had second thoughts about the meanings which he originally conceived.

The authority of the writer has also been threatened by the development and popularization of psychoanalytic theory according to which the poet or playwright, like anyone else, is under the influence of urges and impulses that he is in no position to recognize or even control. Any conscious meanings that might be expressed in his text are small by comparison to the unconscious ones which lurk beneath its easily readable surface. The problem is that, as with psychoanalytic theory itself there is no reliable criterion for judging whether a given meaning belongs to the mind to which it has been attributed. In the absence of such a criterion, there is virtually no limit to the intentions that are perceivable in any particular work. And although the author is nominally credited with them, thereby apparently restoring him to his rightful role of the determiner of the text's meaning, the authorship is now uneasily distributed between two imaginations and it is impossible to make a reliable judgment with regard to intellectual royalties.

As this hermeneutic curiosity intensifies, cultures that might once have been thought of as almost indistinguishable from our own are increasingly seen to be different and therefore in need of interpretation. The paradox is that at the very moment when one group of critics is laying claim to Shakespeare as our contemporary, there are just as many who recognize his enigmatic difference.

Another factor complicates the issue. Apart from the fact that each play from the past is now seen to be the legitimate subject of interpretation, the director's importance is also emphasized by the unprecedented development of a theoretical attitude to the significance of theatre itself. Many of the transformations that we have witnessed in the last fifty years have been the direct result of conflicting theories about the nature of drama as such; the role of make-believe; the meaning of artificiality and the legitimacy of various forms of representation.

Workers in the theatre now confront the question of what sort of event a play or an opera is, and what sort of staging best realizes the identity assigned to it. While texts have been penetrated by theories that bear upon their meaning, the aesthetic identity of the theatrical experience is now in a state of permanent reappraisal. When Peter Brook restaged *A Midsummer Night's Dream*, the result was determined not only by his substantive theories about the meaning of the text and about the motives of the characters but also by his resolution to change the identity of plays in general. The Empty Space was not simply a new way of staging old plays but, much more radically, a coercive device designed to give the audience a self-conscious awareness of the peculiarity of their predicament as witnesses of a dramatic spectacle.

Subsequent Performances, Viking, 1986

Doing things

My interest in the nature of action was undeniably affected by witnessing the variety of disabilities displayed by patients suffering from neurological disorders, but I can now see that the way in which I visualized these clinical abnormalities was influenced, before I came in contact with patients, by my tutorial discussions with Norwood Russell Hanson who introduced me to the History and Philosophy of Science at Cambridge. In the course of these amiable discussions Hanson directed my attention to the provocative speculations of Ludwig Wittgenstein on the nature of voluntary action.

Amongst the various events and processes which attract our interest and curiosity in the world around us we can distinguish two types. There are the ones which we recognise as the unmotivated effects of equally unmotivated *causes*. And on the other hand there are events to which we give the name of *action* and they are peculiar to a class of entities which we identify as living organisms which distinguish themselves as such by certain characteristics. They can be sorted into recognisable classes within which the individual members resemble one another, albeit with variations. They replicate themselves from one generation to the next with remarkable fidelity. With certain exceptions they display characteristic forms of mobility. And perhaps most significantly they show an apparently spontaneous tendency to *do* things to their own advantage. Something which is conspicuous by its absence from the behaviour of inanimate objects which have, by definition, no interests in their continued existence.

When we see a billiard ball move immediately it has been struck by another one, we visualise the event as a mechanical ricochet and we have no inclination to regard the movement of the first ball as one of escape, or the approach of the second ball as one of threat or aggression, on the contrary we regard it as the unmotivated expression of cause and effect.

The distinction I am trying to make is exemplified in the poem by Robert Frost which I quoted above in *Visualising Action* (p. 206) entitled *A Considerable Speck*

The behaviour he observed, in what he had at first thought to be an inanimate speck of dust blown by his breath, led him to believe that this was after all a living organism with interests in its own survival. It was apparently fending for itself and the poet was observing self-interested *actions* as opposed to mechanical *events*.

However, the extent to which this 'Speck' was conscious of its predicament, and that it actually *wanted* not to die is somewhat questionable. As far as I am concerned Frost was mistaken when he suggested that he was witnessing a 'display of mind' analogous to his own.

Serviceable though its behaviour seemed to be, sufficient to justify its status as an action, it would be wrong to assume that the creature harboured what we would regard as conscious intentions. On the contrary we now know that organisms which are as primitive as this are hard-wired to behave as expediently as this 'considerable speck' did. In other words purposeful though its retreats and advances might have seemed it would be wrong to suppose that it was prompted by conscious purposes or intentions.

The same principle applies to the much more complicated sequence of actions by means of which a spider builds its web. Useful though the artefact is, there's nothing to indicate that the spider has it in mind when it sets out on the task, for the simple reason that an organism as simple as that doesn't have a mind capable of entertaining the relationship between ends and means. The springs of its action are genetically determined and the profitable outcome of its efforts, in other words the completed web, are an example of what Richard Dawkins refers to as an *extended phenotype*. Although the web undoubtedly serves the spider's vital interests the favourable outcome is not foreseen as such by its maker. On the contrary it is no more intended than the genetically determined processes which make the creature's eyes and limbs.

As they ascend the tree of life organisms become increasingly versatile in their ability to serve their own interests, and the repertoire of their opportunistic actions becomes richer and more variable. But the extent to which they are conscious of the risks and opportunities involved is impossible to determine, and although as the American philosopher Thomas Nagel once said there must be something it is like to be a bat, we have no way of knowing whether there is or not, or whether the self-serving versatility of the higher vertebrates is prompted by what we would regard as conscious intentions.

The situation is completely different when we come to consider human actions for the almost self-evident reason that most of the things that we do, that is to say what we regard as our *actions*, are prompted by what we call *intentions*. In fact one of the most distinctive aspects of what we regard as our own actions is that we can be asked to do them or for that matter refrain from doing them, and more often than not we can explain what our intention was.

There are however, important exceptions to this generalisation since not everything that we do is prompted by the conscious urge to bring about a foreseeable result. But even when we act idly, without any conscious intentions, we can recognise our own movements as *actions* of ours. Even if I lift my arm for no apparent reason, I can, as Wittgenstein pointed out, distinguish between my choosing to do it and its mysteriously going up of its own accord. What distinguishes these two events is that I would have had to *observe* the levitation of my arm, whereas when I *lift* my arm, idly or otherwise, I am acquainted with what I do without having to see it happen. In other words even when I do it for no particular purpose I am in no doubt that I am the author of what happens.

This doesn't mean that the exercise of what we call *actions* rules out the occurrence of physical causes. On the contrary, I know as a matter of physiological fact that when I deliberately clench my fist the action was physically caused by the firing of the motor neurones which terminate in the muscles of my hand and that this in turn was immediately preceded by another sequence of physiological events higher up in my nervous system. Am I to regard these antecedent events as *actions* of mine or are they brought about by the activation of nerves further upstream in the nervous system? Am I to assume that because all this is an action of mine that there is something at the upper end of this chain of neurological events which is distinguishable as a conscious personal initiative? If it's nerves all the way up, where, if at all, do I get into the act? In other words even if we accept the undeniable fact that actions such as clenching the fist are activated by a consecutive sequence of mechanical events of which we are completely unaware it is difficult to identify the point at which the conscious exercise of intention occurs.

According to Descartes the bodily events which we regard as actions of ours are inaugurated by something which is fundamentally different from the nervous transmission which terminates in the muscles of my clenching hand. As far as he was concerned the sequence of material events is initiated by an *immaterial* Soul lodged, he insisted, in the pineal gland.

It's difficult to understand how anyone could have visualized this arrangement as a plausible hypothesis. How could an *immaterial* entity activate a succession of physical events culminating in the mechanical contraction of muscles?

Perhaps we have misconceived the causal role of intention and that it is not, as is commonly supposed, something which inaugurates the action in question. Recent experiments have shown that intention is not as we once supposed the *trigger* for actions. I am referring to the somewhat disconcerting results of Benjamin Libet's research in which subjects were asked to press a button in response to a visual stimulus. Libet was surprised to discover that trans-cranial recordings revealed the activity of a so called *readiness potential* in the brain, occurring a few milliseconds before they were actually aware of having made the decision to perform the action. So perhaps we are wrong to suppose that *intention* inaugurates *action*.

I'd like to consider the issue in the light of some interesting facts to which the American philosopher John Searle draws our attention. He invites us to distinguish intentions which are formed prior to actions and those which are not and I quote:

'Many of the actions one performs, one performs quite spontaneously, without forming, consciously or unconsciously, any prior intention to do those things. For example, suppose I am sitting in a chair reflecting on a philosophical problem, and I suddenly get up and start pacing around the room. My getting up and pacing about are clearly intentional actions, but in order to do them I do not need to form an intention to do them prior to doing them. I don't in any sense have to have a plan to get up and pace about.'

According to Searle the intention is somehow incorporated *in* the action as opposed to occurring immediately before it, but he goes on to remind us that we can intend to do something some time before we actually do it and that we can fail to do what we previously intended to do. There can be many different reasons for failing to do what I intend. I can forget what I meant to do, or I can remind myself of previously unconsidered reasons for not doing it. It would be a mistake to regard such unrealised intentions as some sort of mechanical failure.

When one announces the intention to do something or other, one often accompanies the forecast, or it may be a promise, with certain conditional qualifications. The varieties of such qualifications, as the English philosopher J.L Austin pointed out, almost defy description. The inventory of examples which he cites in his remarkable essay entitled 'Ifs and cans' is too lengthy to go through in any detail, so I will make do with this example. When I say 'I'll do it if I can,' the clause which follows the word 'if' can have several different meanings. It can express doubts about my physical capability but it can also make an allowance for unforeseen circumstances. So, for example, I might say I will do it if I can, with the implication that I may not be physically up to it. Or 'I'll do it if I can' could imply that there could be unforeseen difficulties of a social nature.

Although we are unremittingly engaged in actions as long as we are awake, the extent to which we are consciously aware of the intentions which distinguish them as actions is extremely variable. Indeed one may, as Searle points out, be engaged in several actions at the same time – idly pacing round the room, absent-mindedly jingling coins in one's trouser pocket and at the same time trying to think about the meaning of meaning. Even when they are as idle, unnoticed and unproductive as pacing and jingling are, the fact that we can be asked to abstain from them confirms their status as actions and distinguishes them as something fundamentally different from, for instance, the anarchic hand syndrome described by Professor della Sala in which one of the patient's arms assumes a life of its own. And although the patient in such cases unavoidably observes these movements he does not regard them as *actions* of his. In fact he denies all responsibility for them.

Such peculiar events are comparable to what we refer to as automatisms. In certain well-known examples of this, the subject insists that his bodily behaviour is dictated by someone other than himself and that his limbs are at the disposal of an invisible agency. The most notorious examples of this type of attribution occurred during the 19th century when spiritualism was fashionable. During a Séance the participant would manipulate objects such as letters on a Ouija board insisting that this was not an action that he was initiating but that his movements were compulsively dictated by a departed spirit.

Most of the movements we regard as actions of ours are intelligibly related to something we are trying to achieve, although these purposeful procedures are sometimes accompanied by actions of which we are scarcely aware, which make no intelligible contribution to what we are *trying* to do.

Consider the hand movements which so often accompany the intentional act of speaking. Although such movements can be eliminated without any significant loss of understanding on the part of the listener, they are undoubtedly related to what the speaker is expressing with his voice. Recent studies have yielded an interesting classification of these movements. In his book entitled *Hand and Mind* Professor David McNeil has described the way in which hand movements are related to speech. For example, the rhythm of the utterance is consistently underlined as it were with manual gestures which coincide with the vocal stresses. It's as if they beat time to the rhythm of the vocal performance and follow the contours of acoustic intensity. In contrast to this purely phonetic tracking there are movements which are legibly related to the meaning of the discourse. They are in a sense *iconic* representations or illustrations. A somewhat more ambiguous set of movements falls halfway between the beats and the icons and they somehow convey the mood or attitude of the speaker. For example when someone is trying to express an equivocal attitude to something he is discussing he may represent the fact that he is in two minds on the subject by wobbling his hand.

Some of the hand movements I have just referred to bear a striking resemblance to the ones employed by an orchestral conductor. With one hand he may beat time while with the other he may represent the phrasing he requires. The actions of the conductor are much more deliberate than the gestures which accompany speech. And although it would be an exaggeration to say that the orchestra would be at a loss without these movements they are unarguably one of the factors which make a significant difference between one performance and another. At the same time it has to be said that the movements by which the conductor determines the performance of his orchestra may be accompanied by facial movements which have a much more questionable relationship to the musical outcome.

The fact that we can understand what someone is saying without having to look at them indicates that there is a fundamental difference between the hand movements which *accompany* speech and the ones without which the deaf would be unable to communicate with one another. Until the middle of the twentieth century it was generally supposed that the gestures which the deaf employed to communicate with one another were little more than a crude form of pantomime and that it was inconceivable that such silently performed actions could be compared with what could be expressed by spoken language. It's only in the last 50 years or so that it has become increasingly apparent that what we now refer to as 'Sign' is as subtly eloquent as spoken language, with a vocabulary and a syntax which is as complex as that of speech. Intimations of this began to make themselves apparent in France during the Age of Enlightenment when Charles Michel de L'Epée dedicated his life to providing education for deaf children he developed an entirely new approach to the subject. He acquainted himself with the signs which the children in his charge were using to converse with one another and later his successor in the National Institute for Deaf-Mutes in Paris, the Abbé Sicard, began to make the principles more explicit.

In 1815 an American theology student, Thomas Gallaudet went to France in order to acquaint himself with the French techniques for teaching the deaf and after studying with Sicard for a year he returned to the United States and introduced what he had learned in France at the American Asylum for the Deaf and Dumb in

Hartford, Connecticut. By the middle of the 20th century the fundamental principles of American Sign Language (ASL) had become a major subject of enquiry and as the result of detailed research conducted by people such as W.C. Stokoe, Ursula Bellugi and many others it became apparent that the hand movements employed by the deaf were fundamentally different from the incidental gestures which may accompany spoken speech.

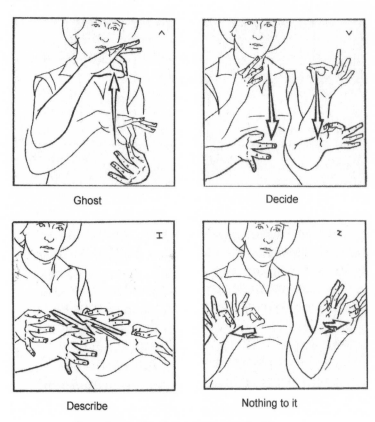

Ghost

Decide

Describe

Nothing to it

American sign language symbols

Taken from The Signs of Language,
by Edward Klima and Ursula Bellugi

Far from being a crude pantomime Deaf Sign is a language as communicative as the ones employing the human voice. So, in contrast to the hand movements which accompany speech, which can after all be ignored by the listener, Deaf Sign is a language in its own right, by means of which the deaf community can express themselves with an eloquence equivalent to that of spoken language. Unlike the movements which so frequently accompany speech which have no explicit intention and have neither grammar nor vocabulary deaf sign is performed with the conscious purpose of communicating meaning according to an organised discipline. In other words unlike the optional gestures which may or may not accompany speech signing is an intentional action deliberately undertaken.

I turn now to what the philosopher Brian O'Shaughnessy has referred to as *sub-intentional* actions. These frequently occur when the subject is doing nothing in particular. At the simplest and most primitive end of the scale they scarcely merit the title of actions at all, since there is no conceivable description of them that would make their purpose intelligible. O'Shaughnessy for example refers to the idle movements of the tongue inside the silent mouth of someone gazing vacantly through the window. Although the subject is unconscious of it, his attention can be drawn to it and he might then refrain from it. In that sense it is distinguishable from bodily events such as sweating, shivering and blushing from which the subject is unable to refrain deliberately. Here is another example. I am told that when I am thinking about something I am trying to write I repetitively rub my thumb and forefinger together. But although I am disconcerted to discover that it is a mannerism of mine I cannot deny that it is an action of mine as opposed to something which uncontrollably happens to me. Whereas in a patient suffering from early

Parkinson's disease, an almost identical movement, the so-called pill rolling tremor, is undeniably something that *happens* to him and he does not regard it as something that he *does* or that he can *not* do when requested to stop.

Breathing is a more puzzling example. Although it is obviously purposeful to the extent that my life depends on it, it is sub-intentional in the sense that I don't have to remind myself to do it and I can do it in my sleep or to be more accurate, something does it on my behalf. On the other hand I can deliberately hold my breath, although there is a limit to how long I can do it for, and I can pant, gasp, and ventilate my lungs at will. The point is that the muscles which are involved are under dual control. Under normal circumstances they function automatically but unlike the muscles of the heart they are accessible to the will. So how about sneezing? Although the muscles which achieve a sneeze are identical to the ones I use when I am breathing, I can't sneeze deliberately. I can make myself sneeze but only by doing something which I know will trigger it, just as I can speed my heart up by vigorous exercise. But in contrast to my breathing which I can consciously suspend for a minute or two, there is no way in which I can decide to suspend my heart beat.

Blinking is another example of a somewhat ambiguous action. I can blink deliberately and wink with one eye if I choose. But as with breathing, the repetitive blinking which lubricates and launders my eyeball goes on as long as I am awake without my having to make any conscious effort. So in spite of the fact that I can intervene and briefly suspend these two functions I am reluctant to regard breathing or blinking as actions of mine, intentional or sub-intentional.

The actions that I have considered so far, intentional or sub-intentional, involve noticeable behaviour. Productive or unproductive, they involve the visible exercise of voluntary muscles. But as O'Shaughnessy points out it would be a mistake to assume that action was confined to physical movements. There are several ways in which the individual can intentionally exercise his or her mind and although these mental actions are frequently accompanied by concomitant movements of the face and the hands which make no contribution to the outcome, the most significant effort is mental rather than physical. The problem is that it is disconcertingly difficult to say what the effort consists of.

I can address myself to a mathematical problem, and as experts in this field often admit the effort involved can be as strenuous as the one which accompanies the performance of physical tasks. But in contrast to a physical task in which the objects and materials involved are both visible and palpable, it's often difficult to describe the entities with which one's ingenuity is engaged in the act of calculation.

The situation I have just described is comparable to the sometimes equally strenuous task of manipulating images in the *mind's* eye. For example in 1971 Roger Shepard and Jacqueline Metzler in a privately circulated short paper entitled 'On turning something over in one's mind.' described an experiment in which subjects were asked to judge whether a pair of three dimensional figures were identical or not. The subjects, it seemed, mentally rotated the perceived images until they were in a position that allowed them to make a reliable comparison of the two shapes. The time taken to decide whether they were identical or not was proportional to the extent by which the two figures were out of register with each other.

In other words the mental act of judging the difference or similarity between imagined shapes is comparable to the physical procedures by which one chooses or excludes the possible fit between two pieces of a jigsaw puzzle.

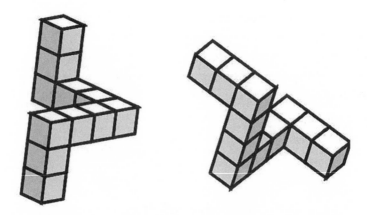

The difference is of course that in the case of the jigsaw puzzle one can pick up the two candidates and rotate them with ones *hands* whereas in the experiments quoted by Shepard and Metzler it's hard to imagine how the subjects achieved the mental action of rotation.

Another group of experiments was conducted by Stephen Kosslyn and his colleagues at MIT. The subjects were required to memorise a picture of a motor launch seen from one side. He asked them whether there was an anchor or a flag on the prow. Having thereby fixed their attention to the remembered image of the prow he then asked them about the furnishings on the bridge and on the stern respectively and found that the speed of their answers was proportional to the distance between the prow and the particular target about which he quizzed them. It seemed as if the minds eyes of the subject was scanning a mental image of the boat from left to right and that it took longer to go from prow to stern than it did from prow to bridge. In another experiment he invited his subjects to conjure up a visual image of an animal from close up and then as seen from far away and he then asked them to report the presence or absence of certain features such as whiskers, claws or split upper lips. The reports were recognisably and repeatedly more detailed when the subject was asked to report the features of the closer image as opposed to those of the distant one. It has been shown several times that when subjects are scanning such *virtual* images with their mind's eye, their real eyes move in the same direction as they would if they had been actually scanning something with their real eyes.

Intriguing though Kosslyn's results are it's difficult to understand exactly what's going on. It's not a question of looking at pictures although that's the way it's often described. As Gilbert Ryle points out when someone says he is visualising something we are tempted to construe his remark to mean that he is contemplating a visible object comparable to a physical picture. 'Some counterpart to a photograph only one made of a different sort of stuff.' Now the reason why we think of it like this is as follows. The verb '*to see*' is transitive, which is another way of saying we cannot see without seeing *something*, and as long as it is out there, in reality, or in the form of a picture there is no conceptual difficulty. But when we *visualise* something there is nothing out there to intercept our gaze. But since we carelessly assume that visualising has the same transitive requirements as seeing, we find ourselves stipulating the existence of an immaterial substitute which somehow resembles what it represents without actually being it.

As Ryle goes on to point out the mere fact that the cognate concepts of picturing, visualising or imagining are both useful and intelligible does not imply the existence of mental images which we scan with the mind's eye. Which means that the action of *visualising* something is logically different from that of *looking* at it.

At the risk of labouring this point let me say this. Although mental images and pictures are undeniably like one another in that they both afford us the experience of seeing things that are not literally there, they differ fundamentally. What we see in a picture, i.e. what it is a picture *of*, is there in front of our real eyes. That is to say it is a physical object with all sorts of objective properties of its own. The properties are such that they can, and often do, afford mutually exclusive visual experiences. Three intersecting lines drawn on a flat piece of paper can host the image of the inside corner of a room or the outside corner of an opaque cube. A symmetrical pattern of black and white patches can yield the impression of a white vase seen against a black background or of two black human profiles facing one another against a white background. What makes these visual experiences so striking is the fact that the alternation between apparent faces and an equally apparent vase is afforded by something that is neither. But when it comes to seeing things with the mind's eye there is nothing objectively there to afford such illusory alternatives. In fact optical illusions are conspicuous by their absence from whatever one visualises.

The point I am trying to make is this, that although the conjuring up of mental images is undoubtedly an action of some sort, it's logically different from the work that is involved in seeing something in front of ones real eyes.

Consider the difference between physical pictures and mental ones. The images which one sees with the mind's eye are not made out of anything. Whereas real pictures are recognisably composed in a medium. As Richard Wollheim pointed out in his *Art and Its Objects,* when I look at a picture – painted, drawn or photographed – my attention must be distributed between the medium out of which the representation is made and whatever it is that it is a representation *of*. And according to Gombrich, the seeing of one, precludes the experience of the other. To reinforce his claim he draws an analogy with the well-known duck-rabbit drawing in which the seeing of one precludes the alternative and vice-versa.

Duck-rabbit

Wollheim insists that this is a misleading analogy and that the proper appreciation of a painting requires the two aspects to interpenetrate rather than alternate. According to him the painterly virtues of an artist such as Manet would be unrecognisable if we had to alternate, duck/rabbit-wise between the masterly paintwork and whatever it represents.

Perhaps it is unreasonable to compare mental images with paintings in which the brush work is such a conspicuous part of the experience. After all we would hardly expect mental pictures to betray any visible signs of handy work. A more reasonable comparison might be made with paintings in which the artist has systematically effaced all signs of his handy work and by means of liquid glazes for instance provided the viewer with an apparently unmediated view of the object or scene itself. Nevertheless, close examination of any picture invariably reveals the physical properties of the medium. And even when the representation is vanishingly diaphanous, as it is in the case of a faithful colour photograph, one can always detect what the picture is made of – something which is inconceivable in the case of mental images in which a physical medium is conspicuous by its absence.

Another difference between mental images and pictures is that it is impossible to imagine what an unfinished mental image would look like. Consider what happens when we visualise something – a scene or a person – in response to a literary description. Although descriptions, as Lessing pointed out, take time to develop as one sentence follows another, the reader does not get the impression of assembling the image piece by piece. In fact it is difficult to imagine what an uncompleted visual image would look like. In the action of conjuring up the image of a described scene the reader may fail to include certain details but he will not be aware of a gap in the picture. Whereas in certain unfinished paintings such as Michelangelo's *Madonna and Child with the infant Baptist and Angels* the spectator cannot fail to see that the representation of the two angels on the left hand side of the picture is conspicuously incomplete. There's nothing like this in the case of mental images.

It's interesting in this respect to interrogate someone who claims to have conjured up a vivid mental picture of a character described in a novel. Mr. Darcy for example. When you ask what colour his waist coat is it's surprising to discover that there is often no answer to such a question. But it is not as if there was a noticeable gap in this allegedly vivid picture. Or that the mental picture was represented in black and white. So it is an odd sort of picture in which the missing parts are inconspicuous by their absence.

The difficulties which I have summarised have led some psychologists to reconsider the status of mental images.

As far as they are concerned there must be an alternative explanation which avoids the unacceptable implications of a mind's eye. They insist that if they have to accept that there *is* a mind's eye there must be a mind's brain which receives what the mind's eye transmits to it, and so on in an infinite regress. What they offer as an alternative explanation is a theory which claims that any information expressed in a pictorial format can be represented much more productively in a propositional form. Unlike pictures or images which represent objects by *resembling* them, propositions or descriptions make assertions about objects and the relations between them. And the opponents of imagery insist that propositional representations can do everything a pictorial one does.

However one wishes to describe it there is no doubt that visualising something is an action of some sort in the sense that it is something which you can ask the individual to do. But it differs unquestionably from seeing things in the ordinary sense of the word. But seeing also requires an action on the part of the individual. It's not, as the English philosopher John Locke suggested, a question of *letting in* a faithful resemblance of things without. The fact that someone has his eyes open doesn't necessarily mean that he is seeing anything in particular. On the contrary, as we all know from personal experience, when the mind is otherwise engaged, in thinking for example, listening or visualising something, the eyes are left unattended. And in spite of the fact that they are undeniably letting in a pictorial image of whatever happens to be in view, the experience of vision is reticent and nondescript during such interludes. And it's not as if the individual is conscious of *failing* to see as he would be if he were blindfolded or in the dark. And it's not as if he's seeing things vaguely as if through a mist. He is, if anything, vaguely seeing. And it isn't until he undertakes the action of *looking* that the normal experience of vision is restored.

So what does the action of looking consist of? Before I go on to consider this problem I must point out that what we see as the result of looking is preceded by a constructive process over which we exercise no conscious control at all, which is not therefore an action. I am referring of course to the process by which the two dimensional image on the retina is transformed into a three dimensional representation of the world at large. Instead of seeing an array of tinted patches on the curved surface at the back of the eye, we see solid objects distributed behind and in front of one another in a three dimensional space out there *beyond*. It's not as if we consciously undertake to see things in this way. It is achieved automatically by a process which was first appreciated by the 19th century German psychologist Hermann von Helmholtz who described the process as one of 'unconscious inference'. The mechanism by which this elaborate process of construction is achieved is the subject of intensive research. And although computational theory has made a significant contribution to our understanding, the achievement remains a mystery.

So how does the action of looking superimpose itself upon what the mind has already achieved without any subjective effort? It is not, as one might suppose, a clear cut transformation from vaguely seeing to one of seeing in detail whatever happens to be in view. In fact it is difficult to imagine what it would be like to see everything that was in view at the same time. As with listening, the experience which looking affords us is inescapably selective. And it's not simply a question of seeing one part of what's in view to the exclusion of all the rest, although that is unarguably part of the process. One of the most significant results of looking is the way in which it introduces us to various *aspects* of what there is to be seen, so that even when we are looking at one particular part of what's in view we can experience it, as the philosophers would say, under several alternative descriptions. For example, let's say that my gaze is directed at a bird on the lawn. If I am interested in identifying the creature, I am visually preoccupied by its shape and by the colour of its plumage. But if I am interested in the peculiarities of its gait, the distinctive hopping for example which differs so recognisably from the characteristic walking of another species, I scarcely notice the colour of the creature's plumage. Here is another example. When someone is playing chess, although their gaze is unarguably directed at the pieces on the board, it's unlikely that they could describe the peculiarities of the design of the pieces. What they are looking at is a relatively abstract thing which we call the state of play. That is to say, the state of affairs which represents the threats and opportunities of future moves. And as long as the participants can distinguish between bishops and queens, pawns and rooks, the detailed appearance of the pieces is a matter of complete indifference.

An even better example is that of reading. Although the reader's gaze is directed at the text – how else could he be reading it? – the extent to which he is looking at the *print* is rather ambiguous. What he is aware of is what the text means and unless he is engaged in proof reading he disregards the appearance of the print.

Finally, consider the relationship between eye and hand. There must be some explanation for the frequency and care with which we look at what we are doing. It's not as if we are spectators, acquainting ourselves with an event which would otherwise pass unnoticed. On the contrary, the knowledge of our own physical activity is not something we acquire by taking the trouble to look. It's an immediate experience for which no visual evidence is required. Or as Elizabeth Anscombe once said, 'it's knowledge without observation.' The reason why we look so often and so carefully at what we are doing is that with certain important exceptions, our physical actions would be hesitant, inefficient, and in many cases quite inconceivable without the aid of vision. Although I can touch my nose, grip my knee and scratch my ankle in the dark, when it comes to handling something beyond the frontiers of my own body it's often difficult, and sometimes impossible, to initiate and then control the necessary movements without using my eyes. Because vision discloses, as none of my other senses do, not only the otherwise unsuspected existence of things in my vicinity but their size, their distance and their physical arrangement. In addition to determining the direction and speed of its approach, the action of looking plays a significant part in preparing the hand for what it's about to manipulate. Using high-speed film the French experimental psychologist Marc Jeannerod became aware of the hitherto neglected fact that before the hand reaches its goal, the fingers and thumb have already parted to accommodate the size and shape of what they are about to grasp. And that at the same time the forearm starts to rotate at the elbow turning the hand so that the grip is already assuming what would be its most efficient alignment. Although we are largely unaware of these subtly orchestrated preparations, they depend entirely on the aid of vision.

The extent to which looking is employed once I have taken hold of the object in question depends on what it is and what I intend to do with it. If it's a glass of water from which I am about to drink I can usually guide it to my mouth without having to look at my now loaded hand on its return journey. But if I want to fill the glass from a jug of water on the other side of the table unless I can estimate the distance by which they are separated, there's no way I can bring the jug to the glass let alone tilt it so that it pours without spilling or overflowing.

Admittedly there are certain mechanical tasks which one can perform quite efficiently without having to look at what one is doing, but that's because vision once played a significant, if now forgotten, part in acquiring such apparently sightless skills. The reason I can now tie my shoe laces with my eyes closed is that I once learned to do so by looking at what I was doing, and having familiarised myself with the tactile and muscular sensations associated with the visual experience of doing it successfully, I eventually liberated myself from the need to see myself in action. Comparable principles apply to musical skills. The novice recognisably uses her eyes to guide her hands to the as yet unfamiliar position of the notes on the keyboard. Whereas the professional performer has graduated from her once hesitant apprenticeship, and having memorised the layout of the keyboard she can direct her gaze to the score, confident that her visually rehearsed hands will automatically find their way to the unseen notes.

The ability to perform such actions, sight unseen, depends on the fact that the layout of the notes is standardised so that the previously memorised map is a reliable guide to all future performances. But such standardised formats are few and far between, and in the normal course of events, confronted as we usually are by variable arrangements we have had no opportunity to memorise, we have to operate 'on-line', improvising the movements of our limbs on the basis of what's currently in view. Even so, the extent to which looking exercises control over doing varies considerably. When the task requires forceful, swiftly delivered movements, the influence of vision is limited to the relatively brief moment of taking aim, because the muscular action which immediately ensues is too rapid to allow visual feedback to influence the outcome. Actions of this sort are sometimes described as *ballistic*, for the simple reason that the sequence of events is comparable to the ones involved in using a projectile.

In contrast to such deliberately explosive performances, most of our skillful actions depend on unremitting visual control. In other words we have to use our eyes to steer the action right through to its conclusion. In the last twenty years it has become increasingly apparent that the part of the brain in which looking interacts with doing is quite separate from the part in which the individual identifies and names what he is looking at.

Acknowledgments

I was undoubtedly fortunate to have the parents I inherited though I didn't always appreciate this during their lifetimes. I look back now with pride at my father's many achievements, both as a founder of English child psychiatry and as a thinker and talented amateur artist. My mother taught me a most valuable lesson which has had a profound effect on my approach to direction. This was that I should make every effort to make the negligible considerable.

After a series of schools around England which I attended during the war my parents sent me to St Paul's in London where I had the good fortune to be taught by a brilliantly inspiring biology teacher called Sid Pask. With me in his class were future lifelong friends, Oliver Sacks and Eric Korn.

At Cambridge, my interest in neurology, animal behaviour and philosophy of mind was stimulated by teachers such as Norwood Russell Hanson, Horace Barlow, Jack Goody and Robert Hinde. My future brother-in-law Karl Miller introduced me to the Apostles, which was at that time a secret society meeting weekly in the rooms in Kings belonging to E.M. Forster. The people I met in the Apostles –

Francis Haskell, Michael Jaffé, Noel Annan, Ronald Bryden, Neil Ascherson, Gary Runciman, Nick Monck, historians, economists, sociologists, and art historians – none of them scientists – were to have a profound effect on the scope of my future interests.

While I was in London completing my medical training I learned a lot from William Goody, the consultant neurologist at UCH, and became friends with philosophers A.J. Ayer, Richard Wollheim and Stuart Hampshire through attending lectures across the road in University College.

Someone who had a great influence on my visual imagination was Germano Facetti who was at that time art editor of Penguin books. He introduced me to pictures and illustrations with which I had been previously unacquainted.

I met Richard Gregory across the road from our house at the home of Colin Haycraft who was the owner of the publishing company Duckworths. In the years that followed I had many conversations with Richard, who directed my attention to his life-long interest in visual illusions. One further philosopher who has had a profound influence on my thought was Brian O'Shaughnessy who introduced me to the notion of sub-intentional actions.

During my time in New York I met people who seemed much more open to cross the boundaries of different fields of interest than anyone I had ever encountered in England. I was there at the moment when the *New York Review of Books* came into existence as a result of a strike at the *New York Times*. Most of my friends were connected with the NYRB – Robert Silvers who has been its editor since that time, Jason and Barbara Epstein, Susan Sontag, Alfred Kazin, Robert Lowell and his then wife Elisabeth Hardwick, Philip Roth, Nelson Aldrich.

During my frequent subsequent visits to the United States I became profitably acquainted with philosophers such as Ronald Dworkin and Colin McGinn.

During my two residences in Berkeley when we stayed in a house once owned by one of my greatest heroes and influences, Erving Goffman, I struck up a profitable friendship with the philosopher John Searle who introduced me to the distinguishable peculiarities of Speech Acts.

Around 1970 I was invited by Jonathan James Moore and Stephen Wright to direct *Twelfth Night* for the Oxford and Cambridge Shakespeare Company which they had founded. This was both successful and enjoyable. I went on to do several further productions for them, among them *Hamlet* in which my Ghost was Andrew Hilton who went on to run the Tobacco Factory in Bristol and many years later invited me there to do a new production of Hamlet in which he repeated his original role.

I would probably never have gone into opera if I had not been invited by Roger Norrington's wife, Sue, to direct a children's production of Benjamin Britten's *Noye's Fludde* in the Round House in Camden Town. In the years that followed I had an enormously enjoyable collaboration with Roger Norrington and Kent Opera. When I told him that I couldn't read music he had said it was OK as he could. And so it turned out.

It was George Harewood, then the artistic director of the English National Opera, who unexpectedly allowed me to update *Rigoletto*. I had the greatest respect for him and it was under his aegis that I went on to do several successful productions including another unexpected interpretation, this time of the *Mikado*.

I can't finish this list without mentioning some of the people whom I have so enjoyed performing with, and others who have so generously allowed me to direct them. I spent two years appearing on stage in *Beyond the Fringe* with Peter Cook, Alan Bennett and Dudley Moore, and we managed to remain good friends. There are some actors with whom I have worked many times over the years always with renewed pleasure – Penelope Wilton, Peter Eyre, John Bird and John Fortune and, of course, the remarkable Michael Hordern. Three singers among many others who have given me outstanding performances have been Thomas Allen, who was in the original production and several revivals of my *Cosi Fan Tutte* at Covent Garden, and John Tomlinson who was my first Sparofucile at ENO and later a wonderful Baron Ochs in *Rosenkavalier*. Ruggiero Raimondi was a most beguiling Figaro in my production of the *Marriage of Figaro* in Vienna.

Although I have designed several of my own productions none of them compared to what I was able to achieve when I collaborated with such talented designers as Bernard Culshaw, Julia Trevelyan-Oman, Pat and Rosemary Vercoe, Richard Hudson, Peter Davison and, lastly, Isabella Bywater with whom I have had a long and affectionate working relationship for the last 16 years.

I also owe a great deal to Karl Sabbagh and Patrick Uden who produced and directed the Body in Question.

Karl Sabbagh encouraged me compile this collection and has worked tirelessly to unearth the writings which we have included.

Last, but not least in this list of friends and influences, I can't even begin to express my gratitude for the assistance and affectionate tolerance of my wife Rachel.

Some of the pieces in this book have appeared in the following works, identified by title after each relevant piece:

Nowhere in Particular, published by Mitchell Beazley, 1999

The Body in Question, published by Jonathan Cape, 1978

Camouflage, published by Thames and Hudson, 2007

States of Mind, published by BBC Publications, 1983 and included with the permission of the Literary Estate of E. H. Gombrich

Subsequent Performances, published by Viking, 1986

In republishing the pieces in this book, I have made occasional small changes or deletions. I am grateful to the following, who first published them and who, where appropriate, have given permission for them to be reprinted:

The Spectator

The New Statesman

The New Yorker

New York Review of Books

Random House, first chapter of *The Body in Question*

Leonie Gombrich, interview with Sir Ernst Gombrich, *States of Mind*

Thames and Hudson, *Camouflage*

The Estorick Collection, catalogue for exhibition, *On the Move: Visualising Action*

Henry Holt and Company, *A Considerable Speck,* by Robert Frost

Index